Name ____________________

What's This?

Underline the meaning that best matches the word in bold print. You may use a dictionary.

1. Steven overheard Mary denouncing her math partner.
   In this sentence **denouncing** means . . .

   a. calling b. calculating c. criticizing d. growing

2. Moles and anteaters are fossorial animals.
   In this sentence **fossorial** means . . .

   a. humane b. dead c. winged d. digging

3. With her keen dagger, Lady Marguerite sliced the pear atwain.
   In this sentence **atwain** means . . .

   a. quickly b. into the woods c. in two d. in a bold manner

4. After the soccer match, a horrid fracas arose between the hot-tempered teams.
   In this sentence **fracas** means . . .

   a. protrusion b. fight c. loud noise d. monstrous sight

5. My uncle was indubitably at fault when his truck slammed into the telephone pole.
   In this sentence **indubitably** means . . .

   a. mightily b. yesterday c. expansively d. unquestionably

6. The sailors hoisted their ship to grave its bottom.
   In this sentence **grave** means . . .

   a. clean b. examine c. destroy d. weep

7. The Greek youth held high the lampad to steal away from her Persian captors.
   In this sentence **lampad** means . . .

   a. flowers b. onions c. insignia d. candlestick

8. While hiking through the wilderness, Fiona lost her boots in the slough.
   In this sentence **slough** means . . .

   a. bog b. station c. backpack d. forest floor

9. To his horror Ronald discovered that his meat patties were not vendible.
   In this sentence **vendible** means . . .

   a. fresh b. odorous c. marketable d. visible

10. Ol' Tex dug his rowel into the mare's flank, speeding her into action.
    In this sentence **rowel** means . . .

    a. treasure b. revolver c. shovel d. spur

11. Tony sat uncomfortably in her grandma's parlor listening to the grownups prate about nothing in particular. In this sentence **prate** means . . .

    a. chew b. sleep c. chatter d. expand

Challenge: Create your own sentence challenges using the words **maraca** and **fetter**.

Name ______________________

Set the Limits

These groups of attributes set limits on what is described. Read the attributes and identify the noun they describe.

Noun	Attributes		
____________	tourism horseshoe world-famous New York	international hydroelectric Ontario	1,000 cubic feet of water per second
____________	118 islands gondola Adriatic	two letter **E**s city architecture St. Mark's Square	canals Italy
____________	slim black-footed scent glands	polecat endangered mammalian	masked six letters
____________	history period before 500 B.C. smelting	coin use stronger than bronze two words	Asia Minor vowels **a**, **e**, **i**, **o**
____________	whirling eye Gulf of Mexico	strong wind counterclockwise alphabetical names	over 75 MPH two **R**s
____________	legendary arrow rebel	sheriff for poor medieval	people's hero Sherwood Forest
____________	wind paper Franklin	box string also bird	aircraft bowed hover
____________	four chambers rhythm two pumps	fist-sized oxygen carrier 2,000 gallons per day	pear-shaped aorta
____________	chosen one Indian by 1649	architecture 20,000 workmen Yamuna River	three letter **A**s mausoleum marble

Name ______________________

Mexico Match-Up

Fill in the blanks with words from the list below.

When U.S. and Canadian Americans ________________ of Mexico, they may imagine hot desert ____________ and cacti. You will find these places if you ______________, but Mexico is much more! Many spectacular animals, like the ________________ and gray whale are found in and __________________ Mexico. Mexico's __________________ are also noteworthy. The *ahuehuete* is a ______________ tree with a gigantic _________________. A ________________ Christmas plant, the ____________________, is native to Mexico.

Many ________________ people live much as other Americans. Differences in ______________ may be found, however, especially in rural ____________. Rural women may be seen wearing ______________ called *rebozos* to _______________ their heads. In many regions the large ______________, called the *la comida*, is served in the early _______________________. After this meal many _____________________ and schools close down for ______________ and reopen when the ____________ has cooled. Many markets can be found in the cities and __________________. *El supermercado* is a large __________________ with higher ________________ but more variety of ___________ than the smaller stores. Mexico has many poor. In some homes, straw mats called *petates* may serve as ____________.

Mexico's history reaches back __________________ of years. It includes its ____________ past as well as the arrival of ________________. Mexico's October 12__________, *Dia de lat Raza,* ____________ the mixing of cultures. Many of Mexico's festivals come from the Christian _______________. In the *Posada* the people re-enact Mary and Joseph's _______________ for lodging in Bethlehem. Yet, like our Halloween, some celebrations ____________ a more distant, pagan past. The Mexican people have a festival in which they await the _____________ of the dead, eating sweets shaped as such things as coffins and ________________.

The ___________ popular sport in Mexico is neither the bullfight nor _____________. Rather, *futbol*, or _______________, claims the most spectators. Also popular attractions are the *charriadas*, or _______________, whose excellent riders are _____________ *charros*. If you _____________ Mexico, don't miss the *los voladores*, or flying _________. In this ancient ceremonial ____________, one man plays an ____________ while dancing on a pole's platform and four others, dressed like birds, tie ropes around their legs and jump into the air, falling in wide circles around the __________. The rope is let out ______________ as they sail downward.

Word List

afternoon	called	goods	meal	popular	siestas	thousands
ancient	celebration	honors	men	prices	skeletons	tradition
areas	cover	huge	Mexican	recall	slowly	trunk
around	dance	instrument	most	rodeos	soccer	villages
baseball	day	jaguar	plants	sands	souls	visit
beds	dress	look	poinsettia	search	think	
businesses	Europeans	market	pole	shawls		

Name ______________________________

Replacement Parts

Replace the words in bold print with suitable words from the list at the bottom of page 5. Then write a great title for this story.

Title: ____________________________________

One Tuesday morning Phil Abbot and his **friends** ____________ Tanya and Adam **decided** ____________ to scuba dive off the **finger of land** ____________ jutting into Blakeston Bay. They **prepared** ____________ a **big** ____________ lunch since they planned to be gone all day. Because none of them **had** ____________ a boat, they **rented the services of** ____________ Captain "Mad Dog" O'Keeley, a **respectable** ____________ **sailor** ____________ and ship captain.

The day began well. The water was **calm** ____________, and the **small** ____________ boat **quickly moved** ____________ over the waters to a **place** ____________ **known as** ____________ Bad Carl's Caverns because of the **dramatic** ____________ underwater hollows. Adam had never **before** ____________ explored underwater, but Tanya and Phil were both **extremely experienced** ____________. They entered the water about 10:00 a.m. The **warm** ____________ water was **filled** ____________ with fish of many colors and **sizes** ____________. Each diver went his or her own way. Phil **followed** ____________ a **group** ____________ of fish into a cave but **stopped** ____________ when his light grew **dim** ____________ and the cave **grew smaller** ____________. Tanya **looked at** ____________ the growths of coral along the ocean **shelf** ____________. The ocean floor was rugged with **cliffs** ____________ and **canyons** ____________ like a moonscape. Tanya **took** ____________ pictures of the many coral formations and the **splendid collection** ____________ of colors they **showed** ____________.

Neither Tanya nor Phil **paid attention to** ____________ where Adam had gone. They assumed he was carefully following them since he was a **newcomer** ____________ to the world **under the ocean** ____________. Only when they returned to the **boat** ____________ did they realize that Adam was missing. When they **asked** ____________ Captain Mad Dog, he **just** ____________ shrugged his shoulders. "You jumped in so fast, I noticed nothing," he **said indistinctly** ____________ as he **pulled out** ____________ a **bag** ____________ of tobacco for his curve-stemmed **pipe** ____________. He continued, "Maybe you should look for him. He must be below still."

So, **putting on** ____________ fresh air tanks, Tanya and Phil **went back** ____________ to the **green** ____________ waters. Swimming **as partners** ____________, they covered a large territory. They **beamed** ____________ Tanya's **light** ____________ in many of the **caves** ____________. Just as they were beginning to **lose hope** ____________, Phil saw a light's **flash** ____________ emitting from a small

Name ______________________

Replacement Parts (Continued)

opening ______________ they had **missed** ______________ . They **swam into** __________ the cave.

Deep within the cave's shadows was Adam. His left leg was **caught** ______________ between two **rocks** __________________ , but **other than** ______________ that he seemed all right. Tanya **used hand motions** ________________ asking him what had **happened** __________________ , but Adam's movements suddenly became so **jerky** __________________ , neither could **make out** __________________ his meaning. Then Phil noticed his air gauge. Adam was **out of air** ______________ ! Tanya **ripped out** __________________ her mouthpiece and shared her air with Adam while Phil **struggled** ________________ with the rocks gripping Adam's leg. He worked **slowly** ____________________ , careful to avoid hurting Adam's leg until **at last** ________________ Phil was able to **move** ____________ the smaller rock and **free** ______________ him.

The three cautiously **made their way** ________________ to the surface. Both Phil and Tanya helped Adam who **seemed** _________________ **slow** _________________ . When they reached the boat, Phil **hopped on** __________________ first. Then he and Tanya pulled and pushed Adam up and into the craft.

Tanya asked, "Where is Captain O'Keeley? Why didn't he **help** _________ us?"

Phil **looked around** _______________ the vessel quickly. The captain and their **food** ____________________ had both **disappeared** __________________ . Adam lay **still** _____________________ on the **floor** ________________ . . .

Word List

advanced	despair	hired	peninsula	spasmatic
aid	dimensions	holes	pinned	striking
appeared	diminutive	ledge	pouch	substantial
array of	dinner	lethargic	previously	suffocating
attaching	elected	liberate	questioned	teeming
beyond	emerald	mariner	removed	tepid
boarded	entered	meerschaum	reputable	together
boulders	examined	merely	returned	torch
called	exhibited	motionless	scanned	trailed
cavity	experts	muttered	school	transpired
chasms	extracted	narrowed	shift	undersea
craft	faint	novice	shone	understand
crags	finally	observed	site	undisturbed
cronies	gestured	omitted	skimmed	vanished
deck	gleam	owned	snapped	wrestled
deliberately	halted	packed		

Challenge: Write an ending to the story.

Fish Facts

Name ______________________________

Fill in each blank with the word that best fits.

1. The oldest fish fossils discovered, those dating back about 500 ______________ years ago, are from fish having _____ jaws. Today the ______________ fish without jaws are lampreys and hagfishes.

2. With their gills, fish are able to ________________ in water. As water ____________ past the gills, oxygen is ______________ from the water and released into the bloodstream.

3. Unlike most animal species, the female sea horse lays her ____________ in the male. Here the eggs _________________ into baby sea horses. As ______________ as 200 newborn may hatch at a time.

4. If you were out in deep water, you might swim to _____________ . But what can a fish do when stuck on land? The blenny has _________________ front fins called pectorals that work like oars to maneuver the creature back to its ______________ home.

5. Have you _____________ of the butterfly fish? This four-inch-long fish will leap out of the water as high as six feet to get its ________________ . The archer fish also leaps but gets its name from its skilled _________________ technique. Don't stand too ____________ to their open aquariums!

6. While all fish have skeletons (after all, they are _________________), some have no _________ . Instead, fish like the ray and shark have ____________________ made of cartilage.

7. Some fish are able to find mates by using ________________ . The drumfish's noise carries well in the water and attracts __________________ mate-seekers who swim close enough to take a __________ at their prospective partners.

8. The European sole lies flat on the ______________ of the ocean. During the first few weeks of its ____________ , one eye "moves" over to the opposite side of the head, ________________ a blind side.

9. Because its mouth lies on the underside of its _____________ , the upside-down catfish has a _____________ up its fin. When it wants to eat _________________ food, it merely turns over for a meal.

Word List

bones	dinner	head	life	only	skeletons	taken
breathe	eggs	heard	many	peek	sound	trick
close	floor	interested	million	powerful	spitting	vertebrates
develop	flows	leaving	no	shore	surface	watery

Name ______________________

Choices

Circle the word that replaces the word in bold print. Use a dictionary only if you must.

1. At the edge of the garden grew a tall **heliotrope** pointing to the sky.
   a. tower b. pole c. flower d. hedge
2. The servant poured water from the **ewer** into a bowl.
   a. pitcher b. pond c. pursued d. receded
3. As the tides **ebbed**, the marine life in the tidal pool caught Jon's eye.
   a. flowed b. washed c. pursued d. receded
4. The **infamy** of the traitor filled our hearts with loathing.
   a. face b. law c. movement d. wickedness
5. The young woman's **mantilla** bordered her face like a frame.
   a. hat b. scarf c. personality d. collar
6. We were unaware of the **reptant** beast until it reached our food supply.
   a. sleeping b. four-legged c. creeping d. repulsive
7. The boy was met with unabashed stares in this **tepid** welcome.
   a. visible b. unenthusiastic c. evil d. strange
8. His face was as **hispid** as the back of a porcupine.
   a. bristled b. sharp c. round d. brown
9. The beautiful child added the candlestick to her **congeries** of knickknacks.
   a. calculation b. superlatives c. pile d. bakery
10. The collector examined the **gerah**.
    a. merchant b. crumb c. steal d. coin
11. Three eggs rested in the **nide** we discovered in the thicket.
    a. dove b. nest c. woodpile d. grass
12. To be sure, the visit by the village's hero caused quite a **shindy**.
    a. commotion b. sadness c. sales d. bit
13. Above our heads was the frightful flapping and shrieking of a **wyvern**.
    a. penguin b. dragon c. infant d. angel
14. Aye, the poor bloke's a most **gormless** fellow.
    a. harmless b. dewormed c. profession d. slow-witted
15. The **dragoons** rushed against the weary enemy with loud cries.
    a. cannons b. mounted cavalry c. wind d. reptiles
16. The **jocular** fellow entertained us with his stories from his childhood.
    a. noisy b. truthful c. humorous d. sporty
17. No one told Ruth just how tasty the **babka** could be.
    a. cake b. root c. salt d. answer
18. No one could match Fern's **acumen** for examining all angles to a problem.
    a. despair b. vision c. shrewdness d. diligence

Name ______________________

Short Tales

After reading each short selection, select the main idea of that paragraph.

1. **Riverboat Ramblers**

One of the river heroes of the 19th-century American frontier was Mike Fink. This legendary boatman showed his mettle early when he left home at the tender age of two days. He returned of course. Later, when his ma's ox died, Mike took its yoke upon his shoulders to clear the land. It is said that Mike could shoot the shell off a hardboiled egg and leave the white intact. Mike Fink conditioned his body by wrestling with live Rocky Mountain grizzlies until he could defeat the best of the lot.

a. Mike Fink wrestled with grizzlies.
b. Mike Fink had extraordinary talents.
c. Mike Fink was an excellent marksman.
d. As a riverman Mike Fink made his mark.

2. **An Iroquois Legend**

According to one story told by the Iroquois people, life on earth began when a "sky woman" dropped through a hole in "sky country." Her children Sapling and Flint completed life's creation in tandem. Gentle Sapling made earth's soil and plants, while Flint made rocks and hard places. Sapling shaped the fish, while Flint designed their small bones to create trouble for hungry earthlings. Sapling created rivers for travel, and Flint added the waterfalls and rapids. When Flint imagined the immovable white man named Snow, Sapling gave him the ability to walk so he could leave and allow Spring to come. For all of life, the children of the sky woman made two sides, the gentle and the challenge.

a. The sky woman began life on earth.
b. Sapling gave a spirit of gentleness.
c. Life has two sides because of Sapling and Flint.
d. We have seasons because of Flint and Sapling.

3. **A Noble Daughter**

In this Japanese tale, Tokoyo, the daughter of a samurai loyal to the emperor, endures many hardships. Her mother has left the earth and her father is banished to the Western Islands because the emperor is afflicted with evil spirits. Tokoyo is left, alone and sad. Desiring to see her father once more, Tokoyo searches for navigators to lead her to the prison islands, but none will go. Tokoyo must buy her own ship and find her way through strange waters. Along the way, she confronts a ghost ship whose haunting passengers greet Tokoyo menacingly.

a. Tokoyo faces many challenges.
b. The samurai is banished.
c. Tokoyo is a Japanese girl.
d. A ghost ship haunts the waters through which Tokoyo travels.

Name ______________________________

Go Ahead

Read the following paragraphs and underline the topic sentence in each.

1. That rat! I'll never trust Kevin again, thinks JoJo. JoJo is upset because Kevin has not shown up at the theater. The movie's about to begin. She has waited 15 minutes for that turkey. A couple of small fry are giving her weird looks. This is strange. Kevin has never done anything like this before.

2. Daryl knew just how to get his mom's permission. He rushed into the house after school. No one else had come home yet. He put his book bag away, straightened out the kitchen, and began to practice the piano. For 15 minutes he practiced—and hard too! He was working on the Chopin nocturne when his mom came through the door with a smile on her face.

3. Behind by a goal with a minute left to play, the Kicks' leading forward, Teo Lew, stole the ball from an opposing Bulldog. Immediately the Kicks surged forward. Teo passed the ball through two defensemen to Rob Jakes, who soon was boxed in by two huge backs. Rob passed it back to Toby Key, who nearly had his jersey ripped off him by an overeager, drooling Dog. The guy was a beast! Toby slicked a liner down left where Teo hopped about shamming a sprain. Teo shirked off the back and kicked a beauty just past the fingertips of the Bulldog goalie. Now this was sweet success.

4. The five-year-old girl at the mall had terror in her eyes. She stared at the clerk arranging clothes on the rack. She hurriedly scanned each aisle up and down. Then she looked through the open door of the changing room. She even peeked under the check-out clerk's counter and dropped her tootsie roll. She had lost her dad three stores ago!

Challenge: Choose one of the paragraphs above. On a separate sheet of paper write two more paragraphs to go with it. Your first paragraph should come before the chosen paragraph and the second should follow it.

Name ____________________

Hey, What's the Big Idea?

Explain what the members of each group have in common.

____________	hallway kitchen	bathroom den	bedroom parlor	utility room attic
____________	face paint wild animals	vendors large rings	cages peanuts	popcorn acrobats
____________	whistle honk	wave rap	shout cry	snap fingers clear throat
____________	diaper rattle	crib teething ring		Barney figure voice monitor
____________	pogo stick roller blades	bicycle glider	bus train	yacht horse
____________	seven 5 3 11	13 seventeen	2 twenty-three	
____________	Bonn Tel Aviv	Tripoli Havana	San Jose Moscow	Seoul Damascus
____________	magenta scarlet	crimson rose	cerise cherry	ruby
____________	pipe wrench soldering gun	plunger pipe dope		snake Drano
____________	bow quarters	brig hold	stern deck	
____________	melon olive	liver blueberry	celery lettuce	cauliflower
____________	Morgan Percheron	Belgian Mustang	Quarter Lippizan	Arabian
____________	chat converse	speak mutter	gab state	
____________	p j g q y			

Name ______________________

Lies My Mother Told Me

Imagine that you are an editor for the *Folklore Newspaper*. Write an appropriate headline for each of the following stories.

Headline: ______________________

1. It was a great shock to me. You know, the story of Rapunzel who was nabbed by an evil witch? Do you remember her long hair? Well, hold your britches. The scoop is that it really wasn't her own hair. No siree! It seems she and the witchy-poo had a wig business going for nigh unto five years. I always wondered how anyone could grow hair as long as that.

Headline: ______________________

2. Don't tell me you believed that story about the wicked wolf blowing down the houses of two of the three little pigs? That's hogwash. I mean, have you ever tried blowing down even a one-foot pile of sticks? Hard to imagine. Now *Folklore Newspaper* has heard from reliable, but anonymous, sources that the wolf purchased seven powerful electric fans. That is the only reasonable solution short of a tornado. Seriously.

Headline: ______________________

3. Ever hear of Mattie Habler? Probably not. People over time have given her the handle Mother Hubbard. Why? Well, we don't know. We can only imagine it's because Hubbard rhymes with cupboard. After all, Mattie was no one's mother. Shoot! She was a mean-spirited, hateful hag, and she was finally kicked out of Gooseberg when she starved that poor dog. No one heard from her since. And there's no truth to her lookin' in her cupboard for dog biscuits or puppy food with the poor pooch pawing at her feet. The dog, a long, thin St. Bernard, was kept chained in a minuscule pen out back. No love lost between those two, let me tell ya.

Headline: ______________________

4. Bob Horner's kid, Jack, was one mischievous little rascal. Ol' Bob never knew quite what to do with that boy. Seems whenever I'd come over for a game of checkers, the boy would either be confined in his room for some transgression or he'd be sittin' in the kitchen corner. That Jack! He had this wonderful grin and the prettiest twinkle in his eyes. Bob could never stay angry with him for long. One time the nervy kid dipped his thumb into a freshly baked cherry pie (no plums at Christmas for him) right in front of his pa. Then he smiled and said, "I'm a good boy, I am, huh, da?" Old Bob just rolled his eyes and shook his head.

Headline: ______________________

5. The poor troll in the Norse tale of the billy goats really gets ripped off in that story. Here he is taking a swim in the river and just as he's pulling himself onto the bridge to dry, that pesky little goat comes prancing over. The troll is so surprised that he falls back in, breaking his brand-new flippers. Then just as he's pulling himself up the second time, the second old goat steps on his hands and back into the river he goes! As you can imagine, the sight of the third goat scared the short, bearded fellow so much he just plain gave up. He dove into the water and swam away downstream. I still have the shoes he left on the bridge. And that's the truth.

Name ______________________

The World of Fashion

Place the following dates in order. Unless noted, dates are A.D.

Date List

1960s mini-skirts
2000 B.C. Egyptian male skirts
mid 1700s powdered wigs
1200s surcoat tunic
1815 men's trousers
1100s wimples
1970s bell-bottoms
late 1500s whalebone-framed underskirts
23000 B.C. needle invented
mid 1800s Singer sewing machine
late 1600s Women's arms are partly bared!
early 1600s shoes with bow trimmings
late 1800s knickers for sports
1910 hobble skirts
late 1400s hennin and long-toed shoes
100 Roman toga
1930s women in slacks
late 1700s pompadours
1100 tailor unions formed

Date	**Fashion Item/Event**
________	________________________
________	________________________
________	________________________
________	________________________
________	________________________
________	________________________
________	________________________
________	________________________
________	________________________
________	________________________
________	________________________
________	________________________
________	________________________
________	________________________
________	________________________
________	________________________
________	________________________
________	________________________
________	________________________

Use your completed time line to finish these sentences. Write **before** or **after**.

1. Tailors unionized ________________ bell-bottoms were popular.
2. The Singer sewing machine came ________________ the tailor unions formed.
3. The surcoat tunic came ________________ the powdered wig.
4. Men wore skirts ________________ women wore trousers.
5. Women wore pompadours ________________ the needle was invented.
6. Whalebone-framed underskirts came ________________ the toga.
7. Bow-trimmed shoes came ________________ the hobble skirt.

Name ______________________

Got the Time, Bud?

Read each sentence below and determine the order of the events. Write each event on the correct line.

1. Cheri could join her friends after she walked her dog.
   first: ______________________
   second: ______________________

2. Even before he joined the Marines, where he later rose to the rank of captain, Tom loved to eat pasta.
   first: ______________________
   second: ______________________
   third: ______________________

3. When the sun rises, the cows will return to the pasture.
   first: ______________________
   second: ______________________

4. Mary remembered that she brushed her teeth and then told Jodi a scary story.
   first: ______________________
   second: ______________________
   third: ______________________

5. The bird fell from its perch because it was weak from hunger.
   first: ______________________
   second: ______________________

6. "I will marry you after I defeat the green aliens," promised Future Man.
   first: ______________________
   second: ______________________
   third: ______________________

7. Before she met with her agent, Gus, Goldy Pawn practiced snapping her bubblegum.
   first: ______________________
   second: ______________________

8. When the snow has fallen and later melts, Clyde will learn to ride his three-wheeler.
   first: ______________________
   second: ______________________
   third: ______________________

Name ______________________

Out of a Dream

Read the article. Then number the events in chronological order.

Martin Luther King, Junior, a black minister and civil rights leader, was born on January 15, 1929. His parents were devout Christians who raised him to respect the law but oppose the injustices around them. After his college training, Martin met Miss Coretta Scott, whom he married June 18, 1953. The following year on the first of September, he began his ministry in Montgomery, Alabama.

1955 was a whirlwind year. In November, the Kings' first child, Yolanda Denise, was born. A few days later on December 1, Rosa Parks, a black worker in Montgomery, refused to give up her bus seat to a white man and was arrested. The following day many of Montgomery's black commuters rallied to boycott the city buses in protest. As a concerned pastor and counselor to his community, Martin spoke out against the injustices done to the people.

Because Martin dared to speak out against the racist policies, his house was bombed on January 30, 1956. Many threats and troubles followed. In September of 1958 he was knifed by a deranged black woman in New York. In October of 1960 King and his companions were arrested at an Atlanta restaurant that refused to serve them. They were charged with trespassing.

Violence continued and on May 14, 1961, a white mob firebombed a bus carrying Freedom Riders. By now many church leaders had joined King to condemn racial discrimination. In April of 1963, King was arrested for protesting in Birmingham, Alabama. It was during this imprisonment that King wrote the famous Letter from Birmingham Jail. In their protest even black children were arrested for marching May 2, 1963. The following month the home of Martin's brother, A. D., was firebombed. Then on August 28, 1963, Martin Luther King, Jr., in the great March on Washington, D.C., gave his "I Have a Dream" speech.

King was pleased to be present when President L. B. Johnson signed the 1964 Civil Rights Act on July 2. Other important events in King's crusade for justice include his acceptance of the Nobel Peace Prize on December 10, 1964, the 54-mile Selma March for voting rights which began on March 6, 1965, and President Johnson's signing of the Voting Rights Act on August 6, 1965. This bill gave all Americans the right to vote.

The threat of death was never far off. On August 5, 1966, King was stoned when he marched with Chicago's blacks to protest their slum conditions. But he could not stop speaking. In protest of the Vietnam War, King spoke at the United Nations building on April 15, 1967. One year later King was assassinated in Tennessee.

_____ Rosa Parks refused to give up her bus seat

_____ he accepted the Nobel Peace Prize

_____ President Johnson signs the Civil Rights Act of 1964

_____ King is born

_____ King gives the "Dream" speech in Washington, D.C.

_____ Yolanda Denise is born

_____ writes Letter from Birmingham Jail

_____ King is killed

_____ the Selma March began

_____ began ministering in Montgomery

_____ Birmingham children arrested

_____ he is attacked by a deranged woman in New York

_____ he spoke against the war in Vietnam

_____ King and others are arrested in an Atlanta restaurant

_____ Martin marries Coretta Scott

_____ he is stoned while marching in a Chicago suburb

_____ King's Montgomery home is bombed

_____ Montgomery's blacks boycott the city buses

_____ President Johnson signed the Voting Rights Act

_____ he is arrested for protesting in Birmingham

Name ______________________________

Now That's Old!

List the events in order from most ancient to most recent. Illustrate four of the events in the boxes.

Dates

525 B.C. Persians rule Egypt
300 B.C. Egyptians first use coins
30 B.C. Cleopatra's army is defeated by Rome
2600 B.C. Great Pyramid is built for Khufu
1085 B.C. Egypt divides and its power wanes
1650 B.C. horse-drawn chariots are used
2650 B.C. Zoser dies; first pyramid is built for him
3100 B.C. Kingdom of Egypt is united
1367 B.C. Akhenaten, who tries changing religion, enthroned
3000 B.C. hieroglyphics first used
332 B.C. Alexander the Great conquers Egypt
1700 B.C. Hyksos invade Egypt
2500 B.C. Ra worship becomes Egypt's official religion
670 B.C. Assyrians defeat Memphis and Thebes
500 B.C. Egyptians start to use camels for travel
1570 B.C. Hyksos are forced from Egypt

Name ______________________

Ten-Hour Madness

On a certain Friday last October, John was assigned to record the events of his amazing day. Now for your assignment. List the events below in the correct order. Then answer the questions.

The Day's Events

9:05	Police arrive. Must prove residence. File report.
7:40	Arrive at school.
3:45	Show mom ankle wound. She sees face. Run to store to buy mom new blades.
6:30	Dress.
8:45	Return home. Keys to locked house on bedroom dresser.
10:35	Rest on bed.
7:00	Change clothes. (Spilled oatmeal.)
8:25	Remember city bus. Find bus token.
8:59	Enter through window. Cut ankle.
3:15	Clean glass from sink and kitchen floor.
6:15	Wake. Take shower.
10:00	Turn on TV. Turn off TV. Stupid junk! Who writes this anyway?
10:15	Shave. Find four whiskers!
8:30	Catch bus.
4:15	Begin yesterday's homework. Good thing no school today!
7:10	Brush teeth.
8:15	Ask school secretary to use phone. (No money for pay phone.)
7:11	Comb hair.
10:05	Clean ankle and apply bandage.
8:20	No answer. Start walking.
10:28	Apply medicating lotion to shaving cuts.
9:50	Change clothes. (Spilled oatmeal again.)
7:25	Take city bus.
3:12	Awaken to hear mom return home.
8:10	Realize no classes due to staff meeting.
6:45	Prepare breakfast.
9:25	Prepare second bowl of oatmeal. Eat.
8:53	Break window over sink.

1. How is your life like John's? Name three ways. ______________________

2. How would you describe John? ______________________

3. If you were John's parent, how would you react to his injury and other problems this Friday? ______________________

Name ______________________

Back to Nature

Oops! Orville's notes for his camping trip are topsy-turvy. Put them in order.

- Air out the sleeping bag the next day.
- Arrive at campground; check in with park ranger.
- Garnish with the condiments of your choice.
- Decide on a hiking trail suitable for you.
- Roll up the sleeping bag again when you finish camping.
- Soak your blistering feet (if you ignored Step C).
- Open a package of hotdogs.
- When you return to site, decide where tent will be set.
- Open the sleeping bag to check it for damage.
- Place the hotdog on a bun.
- Hike at a leisurely pace to enjoy nature with eyes and ears.
- Check a closet, drawer, or shelf to find your sleeping bag.
- Stuff the delicious food into your mouth.
- Clear the camp floor of debris and set up your tent.
- Roll up the sleeping bag, or discard and find a better one.
- Drive around the campground to find a site you like.
- Lay the sleeping bag out on tent floor. Sleep tight!
- Wear shoes and socks that give feet comfort and support.
- Roast or boil a hotdog.
- Return to camp station to register.
- First, check with park rangers for maps of hiking trails.

I. Sleeping Bag Agenda

A. ______________________
B. ______________________
C. ______________________
D. ______________________
E. ______________________
F. ______________________

II. Here's the Camp.

A. ______________________
B. ______________________
C. ______________________
D. ______________________
E. ______________________

III. Hotdog Time!

A. ______________________
B. ______________________
C. ______________________
D. ______________________
E. ______________________

IV. Hiking

A. ______________________
B. ______________________
C. ______________________
D. ______________________
E. ______________________

Name ____________________

Crusade Confusion

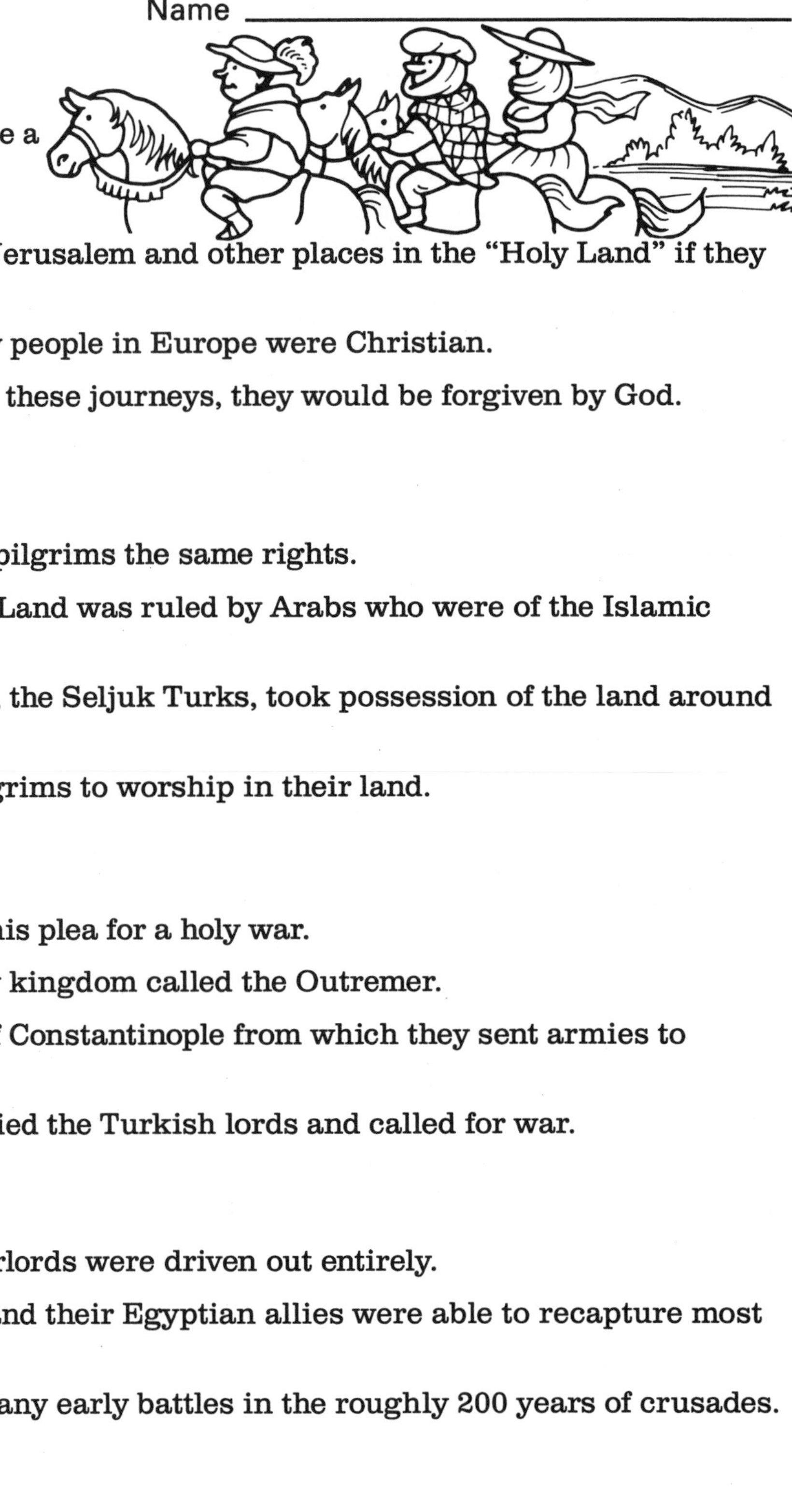

Number the sentences in order to make a paragraph for each sentence group.

_____ They went on pilgrimages to Jerusalem and other places in the "Holy Land" if they could.

_____ About the year A.D. 1000 many people in Europe were Christian.

_____ They believed that by making these journeys, they would be forgiven by God.

_____ These Turks would not allow pilgrims the same rights.

_____ Already in the 600s, the Holy Land was ruled by Arabs who were of the Islamic faith.

_____ In 1071 a less amiable people, the Seljuk Turks, took possession of the land around Jerusalem.

_____ They permitted Christian pilgrims to worship in their land.

_____ Many Europeans listened to his plea for a holy war.

_____ Their success produced a new kingdom called the Outremer.

_____ They met in the capital city of Constantinople from which they sent armies to "recover" the land.

_____ In 1095 the Roman pope decried the Turkish lords and called for war.

_____ Finally, in 1291 Europe's overlords were driven out entirely.

_____ However, the Muslim Turks and their Egyptian allies were able to recapture most of the Holy Land.

_____ The Christian knights won many early battles in the roughly 200 years of crusades.

_____ Each party often wished to get rich and expand its own lands.

_____ The crusades were not merely wars fought so pilgrims could worship freely.

_____ Although battles were fought by people who shared a common faith, crusaders also had different heritages and interests.

_____ One might better think of them as the real estate programs of conflicting cultures.

Name ____________________

Keep Your Eyes Open

The story below has numerous errors. Use the symbols in the key and replace/add the correct words, marks, and letters.

Key

≡	capitalize	¶	new paragraph
∨ ∨	place quotations	~~word~~	delete
⊙	place period	/	make lowercase
∧	add word	⁀‿	close up space
∧	add comma	∨	insert apostrophe
letefrs	reverse letters	!	add exclamation mark

long ago on the iland of cyprus their lived pygmalion, a stone sculptor he was a gifted you man who's talents wer admired through out the land yet he was unhappy and ewe shall lern why he despised wimen. when a female glance his weigh, he mutter and cursed His lips curled his brows joined, and his eyes squinted yet pygmalions prized sculptor was that of a maiden, a beutifol girl, a masterpeace. as time went on pygmalion become Increasingly obsessd with this sculpture each tap of his hammer each scrape of his chesel each rub of his polising cloth was an appeal for effection Pygmalion was smitten by his Creasion

How awkward this woman-hater was in love but the object of his love was stone cold pygmalion brought her boukeys of flowers he ordered bot tles of wine he scrounged for sweets and meets. He kissed her lips and helded her hand from the markets he purchased robes with whom to adorn his lady nightly he tucked her into bed as won might a cherisht treazure this poor Pilgrim came to the temple of venus to sacrifice and pray bitter tears of anquish showered down the crazed artists checks he prayd could not venus, the godess of love, grant me a loving wive like that evoked by my artistree? pygmalion had little Hope that the goddess would here him when he returned home, pygmalian went to the stone as wuz his costume oh, she looked more reel, more lovely, then possible he kissed her the warmth of his lipps softened the stone which returnd his kiss he grasped her Tightly in her arms and to his amazement she embraced him just as tightle She was alive

he named her galatea and there love was blessed buy heven

Name ______________________________

The Never-Ending Story

The story below has numerous errors. Use the symbols in the key and replace/add the correct words, letters, and marks.

Key

Symbol	Meaning	Symbol	Meaning
≡	capitalize	¶	new paragraph
ʼʼ ʼʼ	place quotations	~~word~~	delete
⊙	place period	/	make lowercase
∧	add word	⁀	close up space
∧,	add comma	ʼ	insert apostrophe
∽	reverse letters	!	add exclamation mark

in the land of tartary their once Live a prince who's name was Shah Riyar nowe, as a yuth he had been deceive by his beautiful wife who he beheaded in a furry. his anger was so great thet he hated all woman and trusted the faithfullness of non

however, a prints must have a bride shah riyar order his viziar, or cheif councilor, to search the land four young mai dens daily each maiden he marryed he would behead at sun rise the following day. This way he could be sure that she would not decieve him. as you might expect, after three years the vizier have great dificulty finding new maiden's for his master. Those family's witch still had young girls hide their children Knowing the shahs mad mind

the vizier panicked if he failed to find a young woman for his master his own lives would soon be over. now this loyal consular had two daughters what he loved deerly. The older named Sheherazade was as intelligent. And wise as her father. She new her fathers life was in jeopardy There fore she said father, please send me me to shah riyar that your life may be saved. it may be that allah will be grascious and my lifes will be spared

though he could not bare the though of loosing sheherazade, the reluctant vizier finally agreed to take her to the shahs when the prince saw the beautiful girl, fell in love. Yet, as with the others, he Promised himself she too would die before the night blossomed in to day. For, he thought, he is so lovely she mussed be duplicitous   when the Day's light began to fall sheherazade asked. The prince May I see my sister before i died? To this he gave his permission. When Dunyazad, the younger sister, arrived, she beg sheherazade for a story. This, thought the child may postpone the death of my sibling. shah riyar readly gave his permission. he loved stories and staid to here the tale sheherazade, a marvelous spinner off tales, continued her narrative all night long. when the suns rising brightened the eastern, she retched a Exciting part of the story here she stoped for sunrise was the time of Execution however her story had sew interest the shah he decided to spared her life, til the story was fully tolled After a second nights telling she paused at yet another exciting passage and was gave another day's reprieve from execution And so it continue for a 1,001 nights until finally Shah riyar awaken from his madness and announced an end to his evul ways the prince and. His wife lived happily for many years. The stories sheherazade told are recorded in the *Tales from the 1001 Arabian nights.*

Name ______________________________

Whoomp, There It Is!

Improve each sentence or paragraph by rewriting it in standard English.

1. Please raise your hand up, Charles.

____

2. As usual, I make breakfast every day.

____

3. Carefully to climb the rocky bluff, Patsy trained for weeks.

____

4. Hopefully my hard work will get me to rise in the business world.

____

5. Licking both paws I prepared to feed the fastidious cat.

____

6. The proud artist stood near her statue of a white sturgeon grinning like a monkey.

____

7. The little boy saw his dentist looking very scared and sucking his thumb. Every year the child had his annual check-up.

____

____

8. In my opinion, I feel that you are too noisy. You always are gossiping all the time and you tend to annoyingly talk with food in your mouth.

____

____

9. To well know my dad is to fully enjoy his gift. My dad he is a super cook. His barbecued chicken is loved by us all filling the air with a delicious aroma. His baked potatoes is very excellent too.

____

____

____

10. Marching in our band the stray dog joined our ranks. It's funny how it was able to rhythmically beat its tail to our percussion's cadence. It sure liked Penny too. It was following behind her for three blocks.

____

____

____

Name ____________________________

Merci

Place punctuation marks where they belong in the story below. Draw three lines under letters that should be capitalized.

that daniel is such a chump burbled betsy boisterously as the two girls strolled down the hallway

what do you mean questioned mandy meekly as she prepared herself for an attack on her main man

oh you know gushed betsy hes always talking french with the language teacher miss defleur as if he understood the language

but he does squeaked the defensive mandy hes been to marseilles and lyons

oh mandy chided betsy condescendingly those are places in ohio hes never even been to cleveland

what are you saying gasped mandy are you telling me my daniel the love of my life would lie to me he calls me his mandy candy

yuck girl and you take that from him get a life better still ask him to say something in french when you see him next oh here he comes

hi danny said Mandy

hi mandy candy my sweet thing greeted her velvet-toned daniel

say uh danny tell me how much you like me in french betsy wants to hear you Mandy said

oh said daniel with sudden caution okay um uh mon petite amie je mange un beau coup.

mandy squealed see i told you he could do it daniel youre the best

wow you sure know your stuff chuckled betsy as she sauntered away laughing her head off

uh thanks i guess muttered a red-faced dan with his face hidden in his hands

Name ____________________

Slinging Slang

Fill the crossword with slang terms. Entries of more than one word are followed by __ **wd**. Refer to the choices at the bottom of the page only if you must.

Across

2. clumsy (2 wd)
4. to eat very little (4 wd)
5. stop talking (2 wd)
6. unite (2 wd)
8. keep secret (2 wd)
11. become rambunctious (3 wd)
12. cowardly (2 wd)
13. prevent at the start (4 wd)
15. to delight (2 wd)
17. to make well known (4 wd)
20. scolding
22. wait anxiously (2 wd.)
23. not take seriously (2 wd)
24. the advantage (2 wd)
25. I don't know (2 wd)

Down

1. naughty (5 wd)
3. enthusiastic
7. excess money (3 wd)
9. understand the real meaning (2 wd)
10. obey all the rules (3 wd)
14. immediately (6 wd)
16. to delay (2 wd)
18. a railroad locomotive (2 wd)
19. rapidly (2 wd)
21. nice fellow (2 wd)

Word List

all thumbs	full tilt	join forces	search me	tickle pink
at the drop of a hat	good egg	money to burn	see through	toe the line
clam up	gung-ho	nip in the bud	sneeze at	tongue-lashing
eat like a bird	hush-hush	put off	sweat out	whoop it up
full of the Old Nick	iron horse	put on the map	the edge	yellow-bellied

Name ______________________

The Way We Talk

Use words from the list on page 25 to complete each idiomatic expression.

Now, I'm not one to get my ____________ up, but last Friday my brother Harold really ____________ the cake. It happened out in the barn when Dad was away. Oh, I was ready to ____________ bullets! There was Harry, just a-layin' there in the hay mow as cool as a ________________.

"What'cha think yo're ________ to?" I asked, madder than a __________ hen. Boy, I thought, did that ever stop him dead in his ____________ . Of course, with all that hay there, Harry was as snug as a __________ in a rug.

I guess I had his ____________ , though, 'cuz he got up slow, like there was no ____________ and mumbled, like ____________ thunder, somethin' about knockin' my ____________ off. Harry can be as phony as ____________ .

Yeah, I knew the ____________ . Dad always said to put my thinking __________ on when a problem done come. Lazy Harold had to learn to ____________ a finger and do some work. I decided to make him ____________ in his boots for a spell.

I said, "Harry, you look like the cat that swallowed the ____________ ! Now, you just look me in the __________ and tell me you've been workin' your ____________ to the bone. Did you clean out them stalls like Dad done told you just as ____________ as day?"

Harold hated cat-and-____________ games, so he looked down his __________ at me and said, "Just take a ______________ at the stalls!" I sorta sauntered off like a ________________ inspectin' his troops.

But, sugar in Shiloh! At first ____________ I saw I had my goose ____________ cuz there were the stalls as clean as Ma's good ____________ b'fore Thanksgiving dinner. My twirlin' mind was at sixes and ____________ . This was impossible. Meanwhile Harry was on ____________ nine, smirkin' like he done catched me with my ____________ down.

I cried, "How did you do this, Harry? You couldn't finish this job in a ____________ of

Name ______________________________

The Way We Talk (Continued)

Sundays. This is somethin' else. I figger you must a-worked to set the world on __________ ! I guess you can really put your ____________________ to the wheel when you've got a _______ to hoe."

Ol' Harry just burst out laughing, ___________________ like an old hen. Then to add ____________ to injury, I heard other voices hootin' and hollerin'. I looked up to see a _________________ of Harry's friends pointin' at me like they'd just seen their first picture ______________ or somethin'.

They put me in my ______________ , and I, blushin' like a new ______________ , slowly slunk out of the barn with my ______________ between my legs. The gang, just chock full of ______________ , danced and pranced off to the ballfield, Harry with them. It kinda put my nose out of ______________ .

Harry turned to me thinking, I'm sure, that here was a __________________ two could play. He called, "Hey, Sara! Better put your _________________ to the plow. Dad'll have your ______________ if you don't finish milkin' soon!"

"Get off my ______________ ," I grumbled.

Word List

back	canary	eye	insult	passel	show
baloney	cap	fingers	joint	place	spit
beans	china	fire	lift	plain	tail
block	cloud	game	month	row	tomorrow
blush	cooked	gander	mouse	score	took
bride	cucumber	general	nose	sevens	tracks
bug	dander	hand	number	shake	up
cackling	distant	hide	pants	shoulder	wet

Name ______________________________

I've Heard That Before!

What did Pa and Ma say when they woke us up before sunrise? Find out by completing the expressions and filling in the numbered spaces at the bottom of the page.

1. Absence ___ ___ ___ ___ ___ the heart grow fonder.
2. You ___ ___ ___' ___ take it with you.
3. Little strokes fell great ___ ___ ___ ___.
4. Seeing is ___ ___ ___ ___ ___ ___ ___ ___ ___.
5. To err is ___ ___ ___ ___ ___, to forgive divine.
6. Jack of all trades, ___ ___ ___ ___ ___ ___ of none.
7. The ___ ___ ___ ___ ___ ___ ___ wheel gets the grease.
8. Cold hand, ___ ___ ___ ___ heart.
9. For the want of a nail, a ___ ___ ___ ___ was lost.
10. Brevity is the soul of ___ ___ ___.
11. All work and no play makes Jack a ___ ___ ___ ___ boy.
12. Turn the other ___ ___ ___ ___ ___.
13. Still ___ ___ ___ ___ ___ ___ run deep.
14. Home is where you ___ ___ ___ ___ your hat.
15. There is no place ___ ___ ___ ___ home.
16. Bad ___ ___ ___ ___ travels fast.
17. ___ ___ ___ ___ ___ before breakfast, cry before dinner.
18. It's always darkest before the ___ ___ ___ ___.
19. Monkey ___ ___ ___, monkey do.
20. East, west, ___ ___ ___ ___' ___ best.
21. Easier ___ ___ ___ ___ than done.
22. There is method in his ___ ___ ___ ___ ___ ___ ___.
23. The ___ ___ ___ is mightier than the sword.
24. A ___ ___ ___ ___ is as good as a mile.

___ ___ ___ ___   ___ ___ ___   ___ ___ ___ ___ ___   ___ ___ ___   ___ ___ ___
1 2 3 4   5 6 7   8 9 10 11 12   13 14 15   16 17 18

___ ___ ___ ___ ___ ___.
19 20 21 22 23 24

Name ______________________________

A Good Time Was Had by All

Write the words in order for each cliché below. Then write a letter from the list at the bottom to match each expression with its correct meaning.

____ 1. That's the cookie the crumbles way. ______________________

____ 2. A ton like me hit bricks of it. ______________________

____ 3. Apples do them like how you? ______________________

____ 4. She wrong up bed of the side out of the got. ______________________

____ 5. A need indeed is a friend in friend. ______________________

____ 6. Clock can't the back you turn. ______________________

____ 7. Apron tied he's to the strings. ______________________

____ 8. Throw the bathwater baby out don't the with. ______________________

____ 9. Back give you the he'd shirt his off. ______________________

____ 10. It's as nose as the face on your plain. ______________________

____ 11. Packed were sardines like in we. ______________________

____ 12. Hard habits die old. ______________________

____ 13. Nothing is the sun there under new. ______________________

____ 14. It's off my no nose skin. ______________________

____ 15. The name game of that's the. ______________________

____ 16. Low you're the pole on the totem man. ______________________

____ 17. You clear I hear and loud. ______________________

____ 18. Don't bag the let out of the cat. ______________________

____ 19. Wash come out in the it'll all. ______________________

____ 20. It's worth it not the powder up to blow. ______________________

Meanings

A. I understand.
B. He is dependent on his mother.
C. He is extremely generous.
D. Everything has happened before.
E. She is having a bad day.
F. What happens happens.
G. People don't change easily.
H. True friends help you.
I. We will find out soon.
J. It gave me a shock.
K. It's no concern of mine.
L. Do not discard the essential with the waste.
M. What do you think of that?
N. It is self-evident.
O. Keep it a secret.
P. It is of little value.
Q. That's what it's all about.
R. We were crowded.
S. You cannot return to a past state of affairs.
T. You are the last in line.

Name ______________________

Where the Wild Things Are

Draw a line from each sentence containing an animal metaphor to the metaphor's meaning.

Sentences	Meanings
1. Check out the pool shark.	overeat
2. This car is a real dog.	a young, irritating person
3. Stomp him, Lefty. He's the canary.	complainer
4. Don't be such a crab!	showing off
5. Oooh! He's such a fox!	difficult task
6. Ssh! Here comes that tick again.	skilled person
7. Oh, Harry, don't be such an ox.	worthless thing
8. There's Derek. Watch him pig-out.	afraid
9. It was a bear to lift.	empty talk
10. I wish we could get the bugs out.	informer
11. That is such bull.	play
12. He's putting on the dog.	clumsy fellow
13. You have dragon breath.	greatest
14. My dogs are killing me.	attractive person
15. I bet you're too chicken.	problems
16. What a goose! I think I'd hide if I were him.	silly person
17. We'd never monkey around with your tools, Dad.	foul
18. It's the cat's pajamas.	feet

Write your own creative metaphors using five of these animals. In parentheses explain what your metaphors mean.

List					
goldfish	kitten	anteater	Kodiak bear	tuna	rattlesnake
frog	rabbit	wasp	toucan	eel	mosquito
lizard	aardvark	seal	tarantula	butterfly	koala

1. ______________________
2. ______________________
3. ______________________
4. ______________________
5. ______________________

Name ______________________

Slick Slang

Draw a line through each slang term in the wordsearch below and write it next to its meaning. The first letter of each slang term is given in the First Letter box.

Meaning	Slang Term
1. a dog (five letters)	______________
2. slow (four letters)	______________
3. excellent (seven letters)	______________
4. clumsy person (five letters)	______________
5. dollar bill (nine letters)	______________
6. nothing (six letters)	______________
7. a dwelling (four letters)	______________
8. a large car (four letters)	______________
9. courage (eight letters)	______________
10. left-handed person (eight letters)	______________
11. phonograph record (five letters)	______________
12. an error (six letters)	______________
13. foolishness (ten letters)	______________
14. pimple (three letters)	______________
15. nervous (five letters)	______________
16. convertible car (six letters)	______________
17. an easy task (five letters)	______________
18. hilariously funny (four letters)	______________
19. potato (four letters)	______________
20. a failure (six letters)	______________
21. a blow on the head (four letters)	______________
22. to deceive (three letters)	______________
23. to prowl (five letters)	______________
24. meager (eight letters)	______________
25. money (six letters)	______________
26. to knock to the ground (four letters)	______________
27. a success (three letters)	______________
28. to imitate (three letters)	______________

First Letter

1-p, 2-p, 3-t, 4-k, 5-g, 6-d, 7-d, 8-b, 9-b, 10-s, 11-v, 12-f, 13-t, 14-z, 15-a, 16-r, 17-w, 18-h, 19-s, 20-t, 21-c, 22-c, 23-s, 24-p, 25-m, 26-d, 27-h, 28-a

Wordsearch

E	L	Z	O	O	F	G	Z	T	L	A	W
H	W	G	R	E	E	N	B	A	C	K	K
A	A	T	I	Z	N	I	R	U	B	L	C
L	P	O	K	Y	O	L	A	Q	O	U	E
O	H	M	N	H	B	D	L	S	A	T	D
O	T	F	C	O	K	D	U	Y	T	Z	U
M	U	O	O	G	C	I	B	Y	P	O	P
P	O	O	N	S	A	P	U	L	O	Y	S
P	S	L	K	T	B	P	T	D	T	S	T
C	E	E	T	O	O	H	E	D	G	T	N
T	U	R	K	E	Y	I	H	I	A	N	I
A	L	Y	N	I	V	T	D	D	R	A	T

Name ______________________

Come and Go

In each paragraph, one sentence does not belong. Cross it out. Then choose a closing sentence for each paragraph from the list at the page bottom and write it on the line.

1. I really did not wish to climb that tall oak tree. Sam handed me the saw, though, and gave me a push. Up I climbed, higher and higher. I was afraid to look down for fear that my head would start spinning and I would fall. Seven geese flew above us this afternoon.

   Add: ______________________

2. Last summer Mattie made plans to mow lawns for her neighbors. She hauled out the weed whacker her parents had recently purchased, a rake, and a basket for grass clippings. In the corner of the garage were a brush and roller. After canvassing her block, she had a list of seven weekly customers. Not bad, Mattie thought.

   Add: ______________________

3. Dancing would never come easily for Donald, who sat miserably waiting for today's lesson to begin. Last week he played outdoors with his friends. When Donald had informed his mother that he was too embarrassed to take group lessons, he had thought that would be the end of it. Instead, Mom had signed him up for private lessons . . . with Judy Minelli. Nothing could be worse. Judy was intelligent, athletic, and so beautiful that Don stuttered like a fool whenever she asked him a question.

   Add: ______________________

4. "Bread, milk, and sugar. Bread, milk, and sugar," Jana said under her breath as she sauntered down the aisle of the small grocery. Her mom had sent her to get a few staples to get them through the weekend. Dad was in the city getting the muffler fixed. So here she was at Martel's Market. Jana glanced at the cereal boxes, wishing her mom had purchased Sweet Treateos instead of that horrid Multi-Bland Granolix last week. Then it happened. Jana backed into a tower of towelettes. It was her worst nightmare.

   Add: ______________________

5. Terry groaned as he rolled over on his stomach. He was studying for two tests while lying on his unmade bed. Science was going to be a breeze because he had read up on the stuff. Joel had called to tell him about a new movie. Math, on the other hand, was going to be tough. Who ever heard of "n" to the fourth power?

   Add: ______________________

6. Grandma called to say she was coming over in 15 minutes. Pa was takin' Ma to the hospital 'cuz the baby was coming. Well, the water just broke. And both Pa and Ma were giggling like a couple of eight-year-olds. Yeah, it's about time the little nipper showed his face. Or hers. It was downright stormy outside again. Beth was hoping for a sister.

   Add: ______________________

Final Sentence List

The exercise and money would be great bonuses. Down came 163 packages of super-absorbent Cushy Rolls. He began to wish that he had not protested about the group lessons. Her two brothers were two too many to suit her! Tonight might just be one of those sleepless stretches with which Terry was becoming too familiar. When I reached the branch that Sam wanted cut, I stopped to catch my breath.

Name ______________________

Pigeon Holes

The words below can be divided into five categories. Write them where they belong. Then add a category and list of your own.

Word List

sow bug
levitating body
Ted Danson
bull caribou
Milky Way
garbage removal
poltergeist
meal preparation
comets and meteors
jellyfish
lawn mowing
invisible cloak
quasars
Oprah Winfrey
Barbara Walters
red giants
redwing blackbird
bed making
walking on fire
Tim Allen
black holes
Connie Chung
witch's cauldron
dish washing
marine mollusk

Astronomy Topics	Supernatural Occurrences	TV Personalities
________	________	________
________	________	________
________	________	________
________	________	________
________	________	________

Unusual Pets	Home Chores	________
________	________	________
________	________	________
________	________	________
________	________	________
________	________	________

Challenge: Now write a short story or article in which you include at least one item from each category above.

Name ____________________

Sporting Good Show!

All of these terms can be categorized under the heading of SPORTS. Use the webbing diagram to show how they can be organized.

Terms				
vault	racketball	football	wicket	parallel bars
rink	cricket	badminton	U.S. Open	squash
Wimbledon	bowler	pommel horse	ice hockey	soccer
floor exercise	red card	rugby	rings	puck
penalty kick	tennis	beam	baseball	

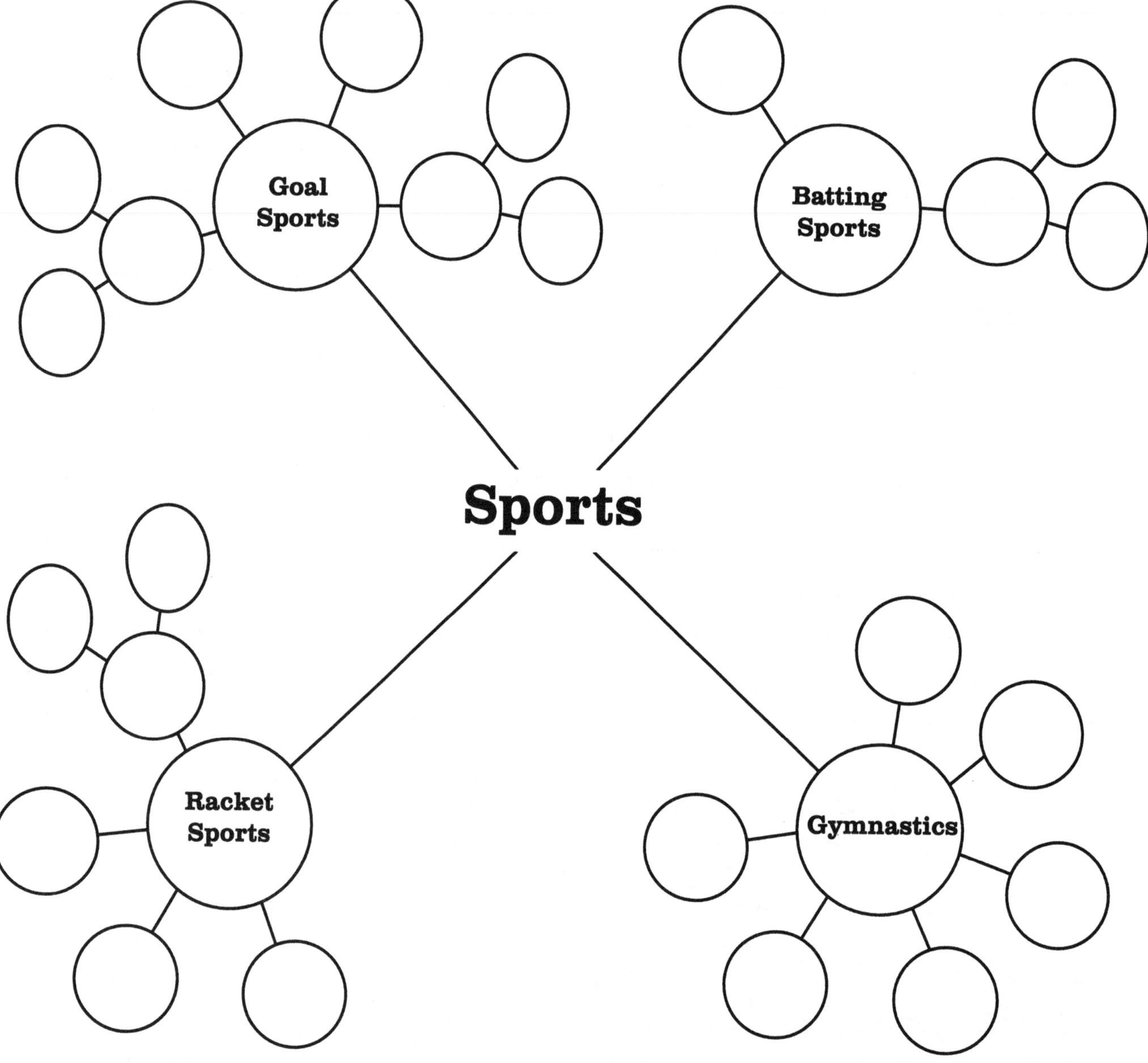

Name ______________________

Shootin' Blanks

Jan Nozdestov studies hard for his school examinations. Help him recall these answers for his history test. Use reference books to answer these questions.

1. In what year did Buddhism come to Japan? ______________________
2. What did the philosopher Diderot compile? ______________________
3. What does *renaissance* mean? ______________________
4. When was the Battle of Britain fought? ______________________
5. What weapons were primarily used in this battle? ______________________
6. What is the Kaaba? ______________________
7. What is Richard Trevithick's claim to fame? ______________________
8. What country did Peter the Great rule? ______________________
9. What was named after him? ______________________
10. For how many years was the Hundred Years War fought? ______________________
11. Who fought against each other in this war? ______________________
12. How did the Tokugawa family influence history? ______________________

    ____
13. Name five European countries that had colonies in South America in the 17th century. ______________________
14. What two families fought the War of the Roses? ______________________
15. Where do the Masai live? ______________________
16. Who was the first person to reach the South Pole? ______________________
17. In what year was the Red Cross Society founded? ______________________
18. Why was Liberia formed? ______________________
19. When did the Concorde begin transatlantic service? ______________________
20. How did the "Red Flag Law" affect the development of automobiles? ______________________

    ____

Name ______________________________

Like Library Lightning

Sugar Sheraton just remembered that he has an assignment due next hour. Help him figure out which of these book titles fit under each category heading. Write each book list in alphabetical order.

Make Way for Sam Houston
Dealing with Dragons
Comparative World Atlas
Columbus and the World Around Him
The Wright Brothers: How They Invented the Airplane
American Heritage First Dictionary
Hatchet
Random House School Dictionary
Howl's Moving Castle
The Summer of the Swans
Penguin Pocket Thesaurus
The Remarkable Journey of Prince Jen
Merit Students Encyclopedia
Jacob Have I Loved
Franklin Delano Roosevelt
Dragonsong
The Runner

Biographies

____
____
____
____

Reference Books

____
____
____
____
____

Fantasy Fiction

____
____
____
____

Realistic Fiction

____
____
____
____

Challenge: What? You have time to spare? Find the names of as many of these books' authors as you are able.

Name ____________________

Parts, Parts, Parts

Anxious Andy went home to review his parts of speech for the final exam. Help him place these words in the outline below.

green	am	young	while	they	threw
because	if	carry	what	which	was
Johanna	mysteriously	me	never	and	hits
tomorrow	raspberry	but	Amy	quickly	those
who	Jordan	this	Islamic	furniture	athlete
tender-hearted	then	breakfast			

Parts of Speech

I. Nouns
   A. Proper Nouns
      1. ____________
      2. ____________
      3. ____________
   B. Common Nouns
      1. ____________
      2. ____________
      3. ____________
      4. ____________

II. Pronouns
   A. Personal Pronouns
      1. ____________
      2. ____________
   B. Relative Pronouns
      1. ____________
      2. ____________
      3. ____________

III. Verbs
   A. Transitive
      1. ____________
      2. ____________
      3. ____________
   B. Linking
      1. ____________
      2. ____________

IV. Adjectives
   A. Which One? adj.
      1. ____________
      2. ____________
   B. What Kind? adj.
      1. ____________
      2. ____________
      3. ____________
      4. ____________

V. Adverbs
   A. When? adv.
      1. ____________
      2. ____________
      3. ____________
   B. How? adv.
      1. ____________
      2. ____________

VI. Conjunctions
   A. Coordinate
      1. ____________
      2. ____________
   B. Subordinate
      1. ____________
      2. ____________
      3. ____________

Name ______________________________

Break Down and Rebuild

A book may be divided into parts by locations or another division of choice. Gary Paulsen's *Hatchet* could be broken down into three sections like the diagram below shows. Take a book you have read and divide it in a similar manner on another sheet of paper.

Example: *Hatchet*

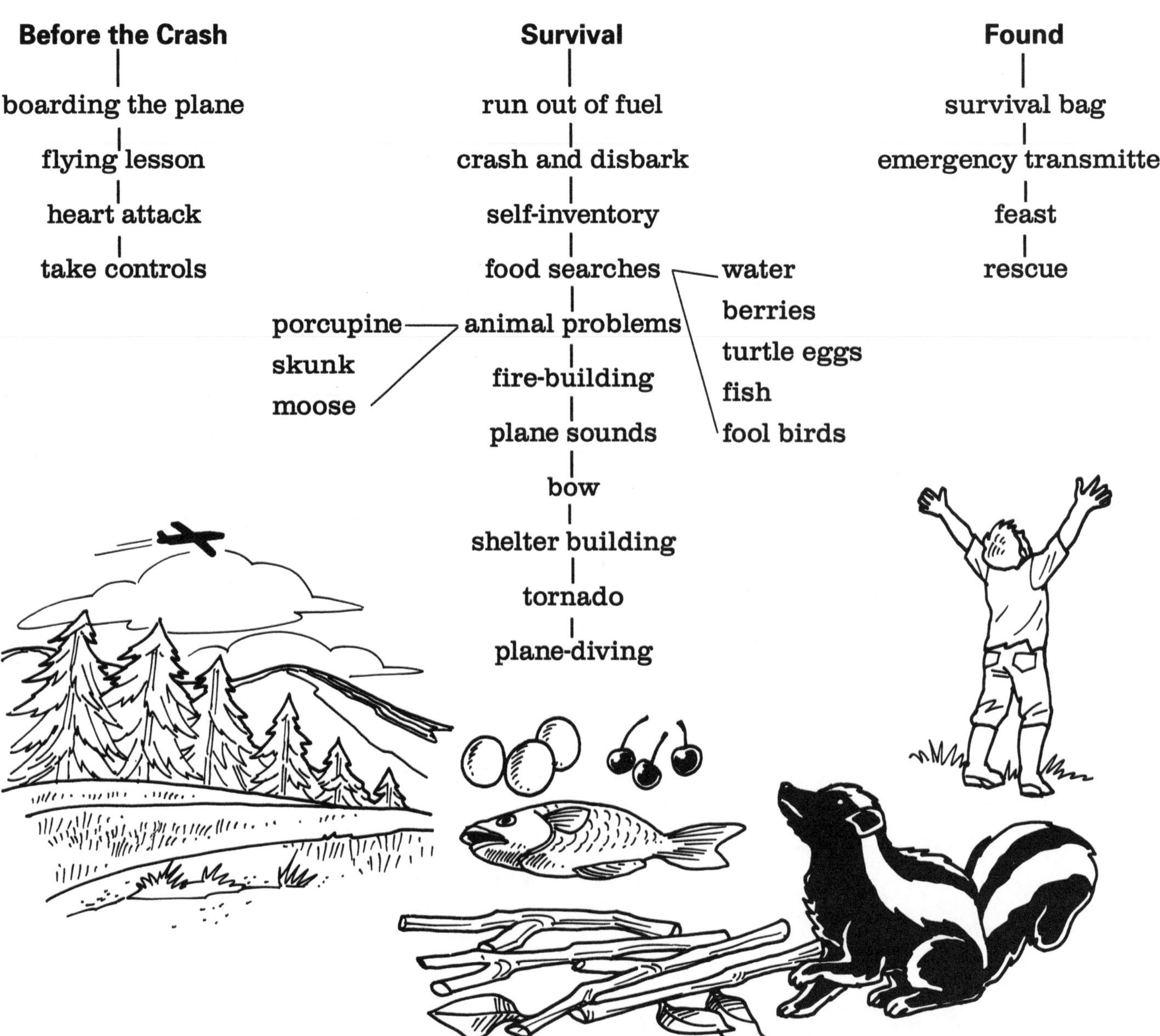

Challenge: Imagine a part of your book from the point of view of an object from it. For example, in *Hatchet* you could imagine the moose's, the plane's, or the hatchet's view. Tell a segment of your tale from the perspective of your choice object.

Name ______________________

Fraternal or Identical?

Heteronyms are words that have the same spellings but different meanings and pronunciations. The word *tear* is an example. When you *tear* the skin off an onion, your eyes might *tear*. Use a dictionary to write the phonetic spelling of each bold-faced word.

1. Please set the platter on the **buffet**. ______________
   The waves **buffet** the beach like a boxer pounds his adversary. ______________
2. Yehudi slid the **bow** across the strings. ______________
   Please set the rope in the ship's **bow**. ______________
3. The planets rotate on their **axes**. ______________
   "I have no **axes** to grind," cried Jack. ______________
4. When he lost his puppy, Snoopy **moped** for days. ______________
   Toby delivers pizza on his **moped**. ______________
5. "Please do not **refuse** my proposal," pleaded Pat. ______________
   Sean carried the **refuse** to the incinerator. ______________
6. The cat destroyed the ball of yarn I had **wound**. ______________
   The dagger delivered an awful **wound**. ______________
7. The **minute** speck was found by our eagle-eyed sergeant. ______________
   "The **minute** I turn my back you disappear!" cried Aunt Polly. ______________
8. May I **present** the king of comedy, Mudley Doore! ______________
   This year Jan's **present** was a box of Cheerios. ______________
9. The large and dirty **sow** chased us across the pen. ______________
   In the yard we watch Mother **sow** grass seed. ______________
10. "We are **putting** this town on the map!" crowed the arrogant clerk. ______________
    Now **putting** on the green is Wom Tatson, the pro. ______________
11. "Your good looks **entrance** me," bubbled Cinderella's suitor. ______________
    "Just see me to the **entrance**," Cindi retorted. ______________
12. Yes, there is Brown Toast in the **lead** by a length! ______________
    "Carrying all those **lead** pencils sure was hard work!" bragged the five-year-old. ______________

Name ______________________________

Dig for It

Use reference materials to identify each statement as either true or false. When you have discovered the 9 false statements, underline the errant word and write above it a word that would make the sentence true. Then discover the name of a mythological warrior band by shading the numbered spaces of the true statements in the puzzle.

_____ 1. An ancient Greek drinking cup was called a kylix.

_____ 2. The most famous city-state in ancient Greece was Selinas.

_____ 3. Josephus was a poet who wrote the *Iliad* and the *Odyssey*.

_____ 4. The Acropolis was the citadel of Athens' kings.

_____ 5. According to legend, a young warrior killed a bull-like creature known as the Theseus.

_____ 6. In mythology, Odysseus and his men escape the cave of the cyclops Polyphemus when they make him drunk and blind him.

_____ 7. Apollo's chariot carried the clouds across the sky each day.

_____ 8. Sophocles and Euripides were two great playwrights of ancient Greece.

_____ 9. An event in the Greek games called the pentathlon consisted of five activities.

_____ 10. In 336 B.C. all of Greece was ruled by a young warrior king named Hercules.

_____ 11. Zeus was known as the father of the gods.

_____ 12. A trireme was a fighting galley ship.

_____ 13. Hippocrates was a famous Greek musician.

_____ 14. Pegasus was tamed by a man who tried to ride him to Hades.

_____ 15. The city-states of Greece combined to thwart an invasion by Persian forces.

_____ 16. In one legend Persian soldiers defeated the defenders of Troy by hiding in a large wooden horse.

_____ 17. The goddess of wisdom and warfare was Hera.

_____ 18. Poseidon was god of the sea.

Name ______________________________

Yea or Nay

Look up the bold-faced words in a dictionary to answer **yes** or **no** to these questions. Write the dictionary page number for each bold-faced word above that word.

_____ 1. Would an **impeccable** driver **double-park**?

_____ 2. Is a London **bobby unkempt** in his appearance?

_____ 3. Could lack of sleep be an **impediment** to your success on a written test?

_____ 4. Is the **omega** related to **fennel**?

_____ 5. Should a court judge be **impartial** during a trial?

_____ 6. Is an **unabridged** dictionary shorter than one that is **abridged**?

_____ 7. Would you expect to see a **spectral** sight on a hot, crowded beach?

_____ 8. Might an **adder** crawl through underbrush?

_____ 9. Would a **lord** pay tribute to his **vassal**?

_____ 10. Might you associate a **pommel** with a horse?

_____ 11. Would a **suffragette** fight for voting rights?

_____ 12. Is the CN Tower in Toronto an **imposing** structure?

_____ 13. Do many pilots release **okra** during flight?

_____ 14. Is a **cosseted** cat likely to get its way?

_____ 15. Should you expect to see a **vestibule** inside a garage?

_____ 16. Are **requiems** frequently heard at weddings?

_____ 17. Is a summertime **bog** a likely place to find a mosquito?

_____ 18. Do raindrops fall **profusely** in a rainstorm?

_____ 19. Is a freshly oiled roller skate at the top of a playground slide likely to remain **immobile**?

_____ 20. Might you expect to hear a **clamor** when a baby awakens?

Name ______________________

Look-See

Use a dictionary and other reference materials to answer these questions.

1. Is the word **jess** a noun, verb, or adjective? ______________________
2. Would you use a **sari** to wash, to wear, or to cut? ______________________
3. How is a **pannier** like a pail? ______________________
4. What does **NOW** stand for? ______________________
5. Where does **Desdemona** appear? ______________________
6. What kind of animal is a **harrier**? ______________________
7. **Southampton** is a coastal town in both Long Island and . . . ______________________
8. If you were **peckish**, would you be angry, sad, or irritable? ______________________
9. Did **Octavia**'s husband treat her well? ______________________
10. Who is Paul John **Flory**? ______________________
11. From what language does **au courant** come? ______________________
12. What is the **AAF**? ______________________
13. Is **chalcedony** a mineral, an animal, or a vegetable? ______________________
14. Does a **roc** fly? ______________________
15. What word is also spelled both **sluff** and **slue**? ______________________
16. What is the mineral **turquoise** made of? ______________________
17. In what state will you find **Walden Pond**? ______________________
18. What does **Rx** mean in medicine? ______________________
19. What is another word for **yelp**? ______________________
20. In what alphabet would one find the letter **resh**? ______________________
21. Who is Yehudi **Menuhin**? ______________________
22. In which two countries is **Patagonia** found? ______________________
23. With what is **Cosa Nostra** associated? ______________________
24. In which school subject is the word **forzando** most likely to be heard? ______________________
25. Is **Onega** a mountain, a lake, a city, or a river? ______________________

Name ______________________

An American Who's Who

Research a famous North American figure and record your findings below. You may choose a name from the following list if you wish.

Canada: Samuel de Champlain, Henry Hudson, Martin Frobisher, Louis Joliet, Jacques Marquette, Alexander Mackenzie, Thomas Douglas Selkirk, John A. Macdonald, Louis Riel, Wilfrid Laurier

U.S.A.: John Smith, William Penn, James Oglethorpe, Thomas Jefferson, Meriwether Lewis, Susan B. Anthony, Robert Fulton, Molly Pitcher, Samuel Morse, Thomas Edison, Martin Luther King, Jr., Roberto Clemente

Mexico: Hernando Cortez, Montezuma, Carlos Fuentes, Maximilian, Frida Kahlo, Antonio López de Santa Anna, Francisco "Pancho" Villa, Emiliano Zapata

Full Name	Date of Birth Date of Death
Where This Person Lived and Worked	Greatest Achievements
Source(s) of Information	
Other Details from This Person's Life	Illustration

Challenge: Make a time line of this person's life, including 6 to 10 items.

Name ______________________

Look It Up

Use a dictionary to answer these questions.

1. Turn to page 47. Name the first city that appears on or after this page. __________
2. Which country is found nearest page 127 in your dictionary? __________
3. Name the first language listed in your dictionary. __________
4. What is the name of the last famous person found in your dictionary? __________

Use an atlas to find the name of the country where each of the following places is found. Include the map page number where you find the city.

City	Country	Page #
Berat		
Cape Town		
Guayaquil		
Henon		
Ipoh		
Keelung		
Göteborg		
Valencia		
Odessa		
Madras		
Walvis Bay		
Tortuga		
Sorocaba		
Resht		
Omdurman		

Find cities that start with each of these letters:

W __________

O __________

R __________

L __________

D __________

Name ____________________

The Date's Right!

In each statement below, the date is right, but one word is wrong. Underline that word and write a replacement to correct the sentence.

1. On December 7, 1989, the Lithuanian parliament abolished the monopoly of power the Republican Party had held since 1940. ____________
2. On February 27, 1844, the Dominican Republic gains independence from Cuba. ____________
3. On March 9, 1943, Bobby Fischer, U.S. soccer player, is born. ____________
4. On April 23, 1910, Mount Etna, on the island of Iceland, erupts. ____________
5. On May 19, 1536, Jane Boleyn, second wife of Henry VIII of England, is beheaded. ____________
6. On November 10, 1775, the Continental Congress established a marine corps to fight in the Civil War. ____________
7. On July 11, 1804, Alexander Hamilton was fatally wounded in a pistol duel with Aaron Spelling. ____________
8. On August 18, 1976, Gerald Ford was nominated as the Democrat Party's presidential candidate. ____________
9. On August 30, 1918, Tito was shot by Dora Kaplan in Moscow. ____________
10. In 1962, U.S. Air Force Major R.M. White made the first shuttle flight into space. ____________
11. Mickey Mouse first appeared in a short cartoon by Walt Disney in 1934. ____________
12. On December 1, 1913, Mary Martin, a U.S. marine, is born. ____________

In the following spaces, write the sentence numbers in order from earliest to latest event.

___ ___ ___ ___ ___ ___ ___ ___ ___ ___ ___ ___

Name ______________________

From Whence Comest Thou?

Use one or more dictionaries to learn from what languages these words come. Follow the word histories as far back as you can. Don't be puzzled if your sources do not always agree! Then match up each word with its source's original meaning.

Abbreviations you may find:

Ar.—Arabic
Heb.—Hebrew
OE—Old English
Chin.—Chinese
Lat. —Latin
OF—Old French
Gk.—Greek
MF—Middle French
ON—Old Norse

Word	Source Language	Original Meaning
1. heresy	______	______
2. sinister	______	______
3. gun	______	______
4. budget	______	______
5. piquant	______	______
6. turquoise	______	______
7. rear	______	______
8. salaam	______	______
9. April	______	______
10. torpedo	______	______
11. tycoon	______	______
12. riffraff	______	______
13. Cheyenne	______	______
14. Satan	______	______
15. average	______	______

Original Meaning List

a. bag
b. to rise
c. peace
d. on the left side
e. adversary
f. goddess of love
g. numbness
h. to speak strangely
i. damaged merchandise
j. to carry off
k. Turk
l. to choose
m. great ruler
n. woman's name
o. to prick

Name ______________________

Hey, Look Me Over

Choose any book of fiction from a local library and read it. As you read, complete this page.

Title: ______________________ Author: ______________________	Time: ______________________ Place: ______________________
One Central Character: ______________________ Name six attributes of this character: 1. ______________________ 2. ______________________ 3. ______________________ 4. ______________________ 5. ______________________ 6. ______________________	How are you like this character? 1. ______________________ 2. ______________________ 3. ______________________ How are you different? 1. ______________________ 2. ______________________

Book Outline: List six main events in this story.

1. ______________________
2. ______________________
3. ______________________
4. ______________________
5. ______________________
6. ______________________

Answer one:

What would you change in the story? Why?

What do you like most about this story? Why?

Which types of readers would like this book most? Why?

____

____

____

Challenge: Build a model environment that will match the story's setting. Label the important items.

Name ____________________

Growth Patterns

Plot the line graph with the statistics given in the box below. Then answer the questions.

1. At what age are boys half their 12-year-old height? ____________
2. Between which two years of life does an average boy grow the most? ____________
3. How much does a boy grow in that time? ____________
4. When is a boy twice the height he was at 1/2 year? ____________
5. According to the chart, how many times do boys' height averages increase 2 inches a year? ________
6. If a boy at birth were 20 inches long and if that boy grew exactly 2 inches each year, how tall would he be at 12 years? ____________
7. If this same boy continued to grow at this rate, when would he be six feet tall (72 inches)? ____________

Statistics

Average Height of Boys

Birth	20 inches
1/2 year	26 inches
1 year	29 inches
2 years	33 inches
3 years	36 inches
4 years	39 inches
5 years	42 inches
6 years	45 inches
7 years	47 inches
8 years	50 inches
9 years	52 inches
10 years	54 inches
11 years	56 inches
12 years	58 inches
13 years	60 inches
14 years	62 inches

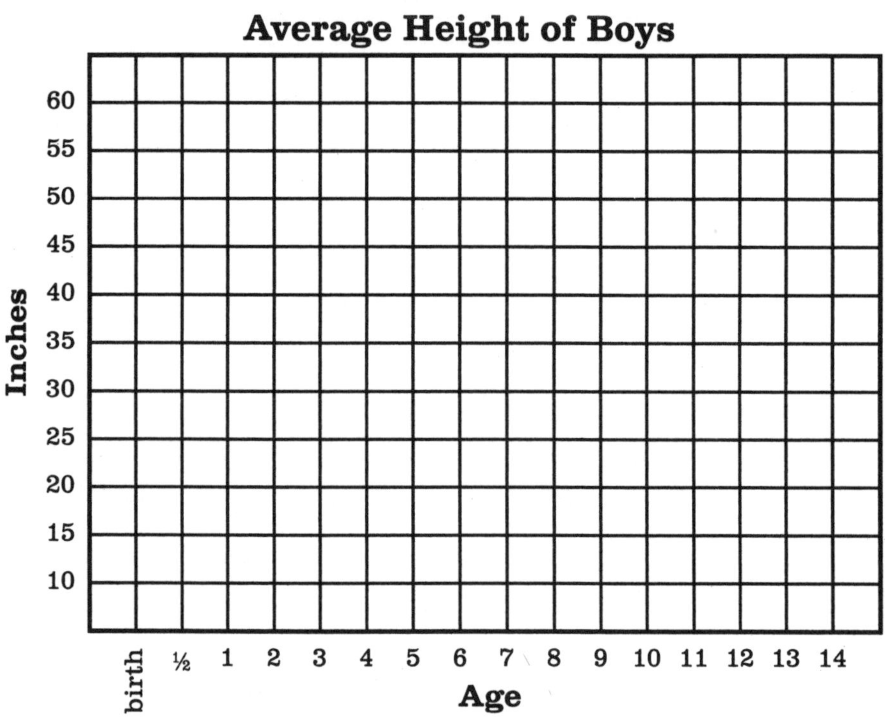

Name ______________________

Just How Long?

Refer to the chart to answer the questions.

Years of Life Expected at Birth		
Year	**Men**	**Women**
1920	53.6	54.6
1930	58.1	61.6
1940	60.8	65.2
1950	65.6	71.1
1960	66.6	73.1
1970	67.1	74.7
1980	70.0	77.5
1990	72.0	78.8

1. In what year was the age discrepancy between men and women greatest? __________
2. By how many years was the age of women greater than that of men that year? __________
3. In what year did men achieve the expected longevity closest to what women expected in 1940? __________
4. In what year was the age discrepancy between men and women least? __________
5. Why do you suppose the discrepancy was minor then? __________

____

____

6. By how many years did men's expected longevity increase in the 70 years shown? _____
7. By how many years did women's expected longevity increase in the 70 years shown? __________
8. If longevity were to increase at a rate of 5% every 10 years, what might the life expectancy be for men and women in the year 2010?
   Men:__________ Women:__________
9. Do you think this increase in life expectancy will continue? Why or why not?

____

____

Name ____________________

English Around the World

Even though many people in the world speak English, they may use words people in other English-speaking countries would find puzzling. Tell from which cultural source these word groups come. Then match each word with its meaning.

Cultural Source: ____________________

kopje	pioneer
veldt	raised plateau
voortrekker	ox-like antelope
gnu	grazing area
mealies	small hill
karoo	corn

Cultural Source: ____________________

ken	a child
bairn	to know
pawky	stern
dour	shrewd

Cultural Source: ____________________

hurling	poet and singer
limerick	field hockey
banshee	dull grayish brown
bard	five-line nonsense poem
dun	a wailing female spirit
brogue	a lake
lough	a heavy shoe

Cultural Source: ____________________

pram	freight car
sweet	elevator
braces	can
truck	gasoline
lift	baby carriage
tin	truck
petrol	radio
wireless	suspenders
lorry	candy

Cultural Source: ____________________

billabong	kingfisher
sundowner	wild dog
kookaburra	pool of water
fossick	a tramp
dingo	to search

Cultural Source: ____________________

cosmos	a test for truth
catastrophe	to obscure or darken
anonymous	a six-sided figure
criterion	universe
hexagon	peculiarity
eclipse	great misfortune
idiosyncrasy	bearing no name

Name ____________________

Flying South

Pilot Penelope Phlite just looked at her flight plans for the next few weeks. The problem is, she has the latitude and longitude markings but no names. Please refer to an atlas and fill in the countries to which she will be flying. She will visit some countries more than once.

	Country	Latitude	Longitude
1.	____________	17.26 S	66.10 W
2.	____________	36.50 S	73.03 W
3.	____________	3.06 S	60.00 W
4.	____________	34.55 S	56.10 W
5.	____________	33.00 S	60.40 W
6.	____________	12.05 S	77.08 W
7.	____________	2.13 S	79.54 W
8.	____________	7.46 N	72.15 W
9.	____________	8.06 S	34.53 W
10.	____________	6.46 N	58.10 W
11.	____________	26.47 S	65.15 W
12.	____________	3.24 N	76.30 W
13.	____________	10.35 N	66.56 W
14.	____________	17.45 S	63.14 W
15.	____________	25.15 S	57.40 W
16.	____________	8.44 S	59.14 W
17.	____________	16.30 S	68.10 W
18.	____________	5.52 N	55.14 W
19.	____________	8.06 N	79.00 W
20.	____________	1.27 S	48.29 W
21.	____________	0.14 S	78.30 W
22.	____________	13.32 S	71.57 W
23.	____________	23.33 S	46.39 W

Over which continent is Penelope flying? ____________________

Name ______________________________

Lost for Time

Find the dates that correspond with these birthdays, holidays, and historical events.

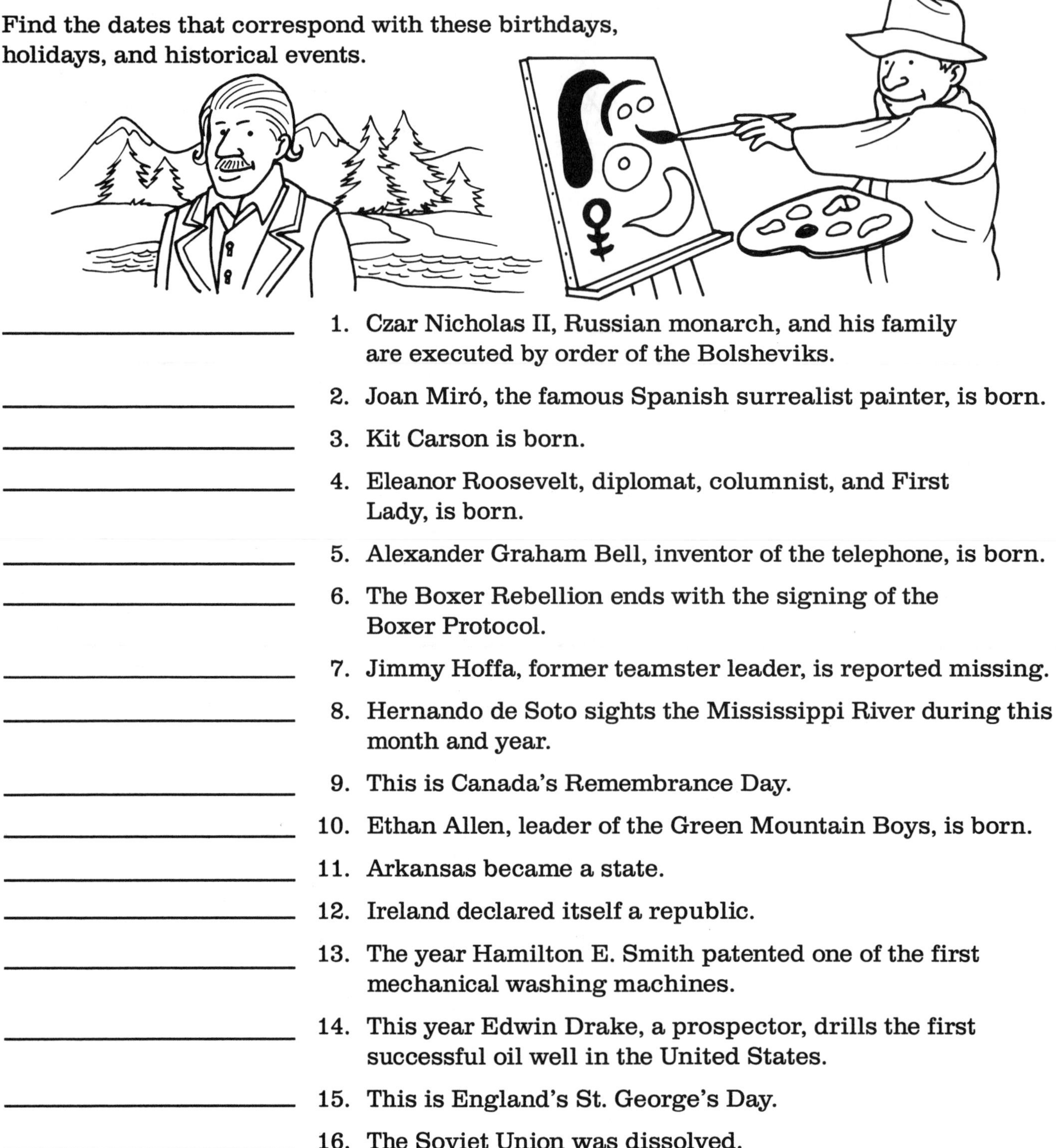

______________ 1. Czar Nicholas II, Russian monarch, and his family are executed by order of the Bolsheviks.

______________ 2. Joan Miró, the famous Spanish surrealist painter, is born.

______________ 3. Kit Carson is born.

______________ 4. Eleanor Roosevelt, diplomat, columnist, and First Lady, is born.

______________ 5. Alexander Graham Bell, inventor of the telephone, is born.

______________ 6. The Boxer Rebellion ends with the signing of the Boxer Protocol.

______________ 7. Jimmy Hoffa, former teamster leader, is reported missing.

______________ 8. Hernando de Soto sights the Mississippi River during this month and year.

______________ 9. This is Canada's Remembrance Day.

______________ 10. Ethan Allen, leader of the Green Mountain Boys, is born.

______________ 11. Arkansas became a state.

______________ 12. Ireland declared itself a republic.

______________ 13. The year Hamilton E. Smith patented one of the first mechanical washing machines.

______________ 14. This year Edwin Drake, a prospector, drills the first successful oil well in the United States.

______________ 15. This is England's St. George's Day.

______________ 16. The Soviet Union was dissolved.

______________ 17. The United States invades Grenada.

Challenge: Make a time line showing what you believe to be the ten most important dates of the 20th century.

Name ______________________

Wide World of Sports

Use your dictionary and your native intelligence to circle the correct answer and the corresponding "Code." Then answer the riddle by putting the code letters in numerical order in the blanks.

Riddle: In what sport do men start play with "the face" and women with "the draw"?

Answer: ___ ___ ___ ___ O ___ ___ ___

		Code	
1. Snooker is played . . .	on a court.	N	18
	on a field.	U	2
	on a table.	R	10
2. A bunker is . . .	a golfing hazard.	A	5
	a skeet shooting penalty.	T	23
	a canoeing goal.	O	11
3. The two events of a biathlon are . . .	fencing and swimming.	E	1
	cross-country running and riding.	G	15
	shooting and cross-country skiing.	S	16
4. A steeplechase is . . .	a car race.	C	4
	a track event.	E	21
	a sledding challenge.	Y	8
5. A scrummage is . . .	a slalom post.	A	7
	a time period in judo.	S	17
	a rugby formation.	L	3
6. A ringer is . . .	a diving judge.	M	14
	a horseshoe term.	C	6
	a handball captain.	E	9
7. Kendo participants use . . .	a bamboo sword.	S	20
	a wooden ball.	F	12
	a glass wand.	W	29

Name ______________________________

What's That You Say?

Unscramble the languages below. The corresponding world regions serve as clues.

Language	Scrambled	World Region
1.	EQUHACU	South America
2.	KVLOSA	Central Europe
3.	LEGAINB	Southern Asia
4.	SNIDAH	Northern Europe
5.	INNAKRAU	Eastern Europe
6.	LESGHIN	North America
7.	NHIPASS	Southern Europe
8.	HECCZ	Central Europe
9.	AFIRS	Southwestern Asia
10.	NUACMH	Northeastern Asia
11.	HASXO	Southern Africa
12.	WIISHAL	Eastern Africa
13.	ABQESU	Western Europe
14.	AGETUL	Southern Asia
15.	BZEKU	Central Asia
16.	RNAADNMI	Eastern Asia
17.	CIBAAR	Northern Africa
18.	IDIHN	Southern Asia
19.	AKRNOE	Eastern Asia
20.	NEAVSEAJ	Southeastern Asia
21.	STUEOPEURG	South America
22.	ELWHS	Northern Europe
23.	NMAAY	Central America

Challenge: Find foreign words in a dictionary that come from five of these languages. Then explain what each word means.

Name ____________________

Back and Forth: A Game

For this game, you need a host and two teams. First cut out the cards below and place them in a cup. The host will pick a word from the cup but will not announce the word. The team to the left of the host begins. A team may guess the word or ask a "yes/no" question. If a question is answered with a "yes," that team continues play. If a question is answered with a "no," the opposing team takes its turn. A team receives a point for each word correctly guessed. The host chooses a new word after each round and the team receiving the last point goes first. **Both teams have access to the master list below.**

Here are the types of questions a team may ask: Does the word have three syllables? Does the word come before "ominous" alphabetically? Does the word name a verb? Does the word have more than five letters?

Master List

assess	clientele	floe	obscure	repress	sleuth
avert	colleague	fume	ominous	restive	stow
boa constrictor	connoisseur	gondola	peer	ricochet	swell
botanist	cranny	mandolin	pensive	sear	talon
cask	exhilarate	meager	plaque	shiftless	trustee
chaos	flawless	monotonous	prig	skeptical	urchin

assess	cranny	obscure	sear
avert	exhilarate	ominous	shiftless
boa constrictor	flawless	peer	skeptical
botanist	floe	pensive	sleuth
cask	fume	plaque	stow
chaos	gondola	prig	swell
clientele	mandolin	repress	talon
colleague	meager	restive	trustee
connoisseur	monotonous	ricochet	urchin

Name ____________________

A Wealth of Words

Fill in the blanks and use the clues to complete the riddle at the bottom.

Word Bank

meager	monotonous	sear	cranny	floe
ominous	exhilarate	ricochet	connoisseur	sleuth
pensive	repress	gondola	mandolin	clientele
flawless	swell	cask	botanist	urchin

		Clues
1. This noun refers to one's customers.	____________	(8th letter)
2. This is a four-syllable verb.	____________	(4th letter)
3. This word means a barrel for holding liquids.	____________	(4th letter)
4. This is a name for a detective.	____________	(1st letter)
5. A three-syllable four-stringed instrument is a . . .	____________	(4th letter)
6. This adjective indicates thoughtfulness.	____________	(1st letter)
7. This adjective suggests dullness.	____________	(6th letter)
8. This verb means to scorch or burn.	____________	(1st letter)
9. A plant scientist is a . . .	____________	(5th letter)
10. A verb that means "bounces off" is . . .	____________	(3rd letter)
11. This is a large, flat mass of ice.	____________	(3rd letter)
12. This word names a mischievous child.	____________	(6th letter)
13. This adjective means threatening.	____________	(3rd letter)
14. A two-syllable word for perfect is . . .	____________	(2nd letter)
15. To expand, as in one's injury, is to . . .	____________	(3rd letter)
16. This word means scant.	____________	(5th letter)
17. An expert, as of fine wine, is a . . .	____________	(6th letter)
18. This noun names a small opening.	____________	(1st letter)
19. A long, narrow boat is a . . .	____________	(2nd letter)
20. This verb means to hold back.	____________	(3rd letter)

Riddle: Pat Donahue ate 91 of these in one minute and eight seconds.

__ __ __ __ __ __ __   __ __ __ __ __ __
6 17 10 3 1 15 5   7 9 2 11 12 4

Name ___________________________

A Hex-A-Mammalian Puzzle

Animals can be named by reading the clues below. Write your answers in a clockwise (CW) or counter-clockwise (CCW) direction around each hexagon. You may consult an encyclopedia if necessary.

A. This tusked sea-loving animal has a thick hide. (CW)
B. This pouched animal will play dead (short form). (CW)
C. This animal is an acrobatic member of the Primate order. (CW)
D. This animal is a wild dog of Asia and Africa. (CW)
E. This tropical cat of the Americas is spotted and begins with same letter as animal D. (CCW)
F. This tropical rodent of the Americas is a bit larger than a rabbit and has three hind toes. (CW)
G. This beaver-like rodent with rear webbed feet is also called the *coypu*. Its 3rd letter is T. (CCW)
H. This large American cat is also called the puma or mountain lion. (CCW)
I. This spotted yellowish or reddish wild cat is known as leopard cat and tiger cat. (CW)
J. This animal is also called the North American prairie wolf. Its 3rd letter is Y. (CW)
K. This small hunter of the weasel family crawls through the tunnel of other creatures to catch its meal. (CW)
L. This is a small member of the weasel family whose 1st and last letter are the same. (CW)
M. This animal is a South American antelope. It has three vowels. (CW)
N. This large, burrowing, American rodent has large cheek pouches. (CW)
O. Animals K and L are this type of animal. (CCW)

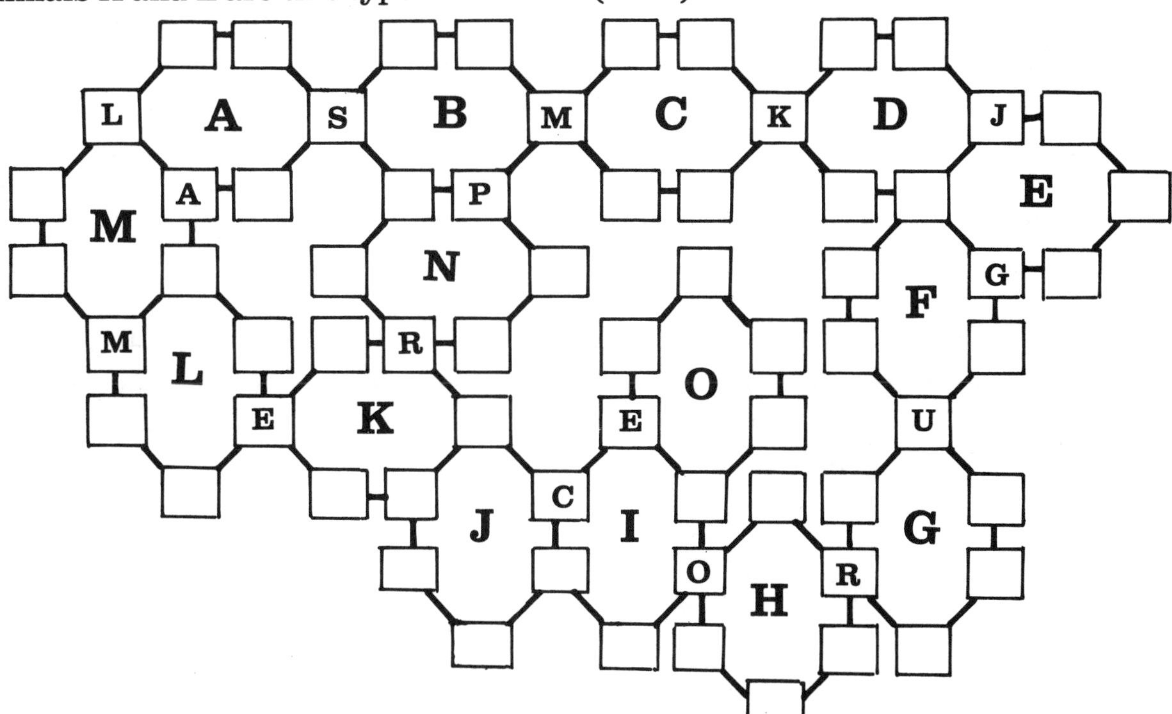

Challenge: Use reference material to find out three additional facts about any one of these creatures.

Name ______________________

The Earth Below

The scrambled words below are missing the letter at the center of their group. Add the center letter and unscramble these geological terms. The first has been done for you. Use an encyclopedia or dictionary if necessary.

A1. *magma* 5. ________
2. ________ 6. ________
3. ________ 7. ________
4. ________ 8. ________

S1. ________ 5. ________
2. ________ 6. ________
3. ________ 7. ________
4. ________ 8. ________

E1. ________ 5. ________
2. ________ 6. ________
3. ________ 7. ________
4. ________ 8. ________

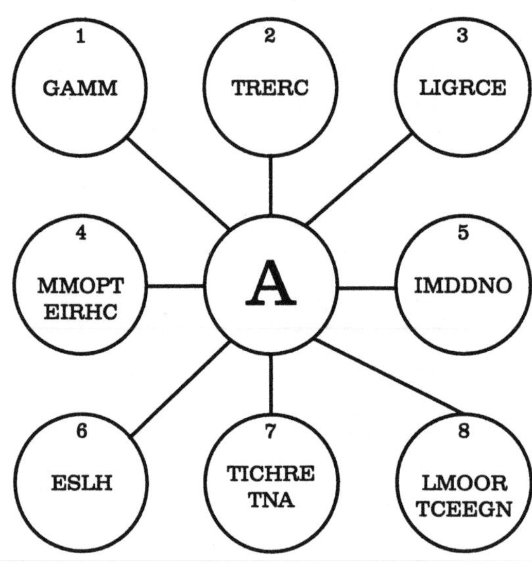

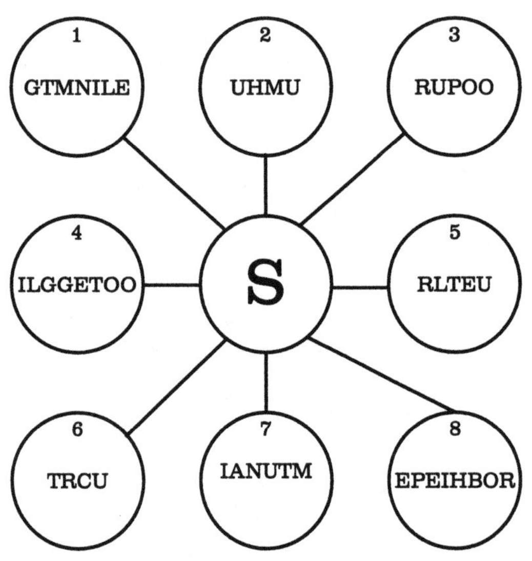

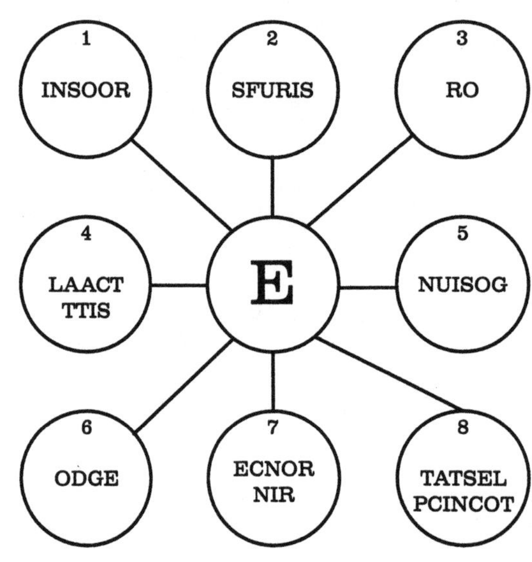

Name ______________________

Can You Hear the Similarity Here?

Homophones are words that sound the same but have different meanings. List the silly homophone pairs that match these descriptions. The first one is done for you.

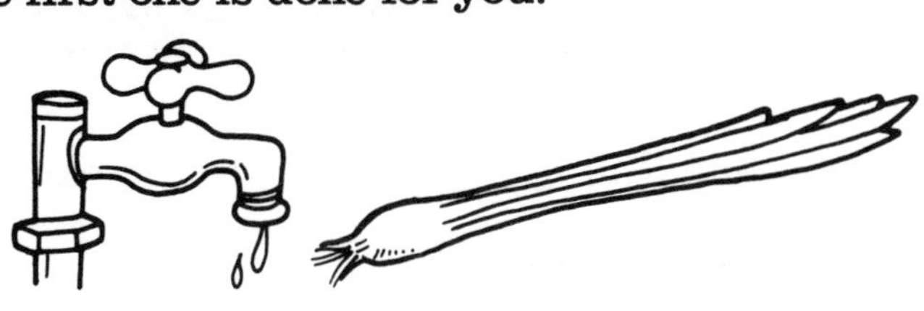

1. The most important shock of horses' neck hair ___*main mane*___
2. The draining of a tubular onion relative ______________
3. Medieval gentleman soldier's evening ______________
4. Many requests for appealing behavior ______________
5. Cut turf marked with Mr. Jenning's name ______________
6. Birds using the business language of Chinese merchants ______________
7. The external appearance of two fellows ______________
8. The inheritance trait determiner's pants ______________
9. Large ape-like irregular soldier ______________
10. A line of pool rods ______________
11. An amphibian pulled by a slowly moving car ______________
12. To squeeze the water out of a circle ______________
13. Small animal pen for a closed two-door auto ______________
14. Steady drizzle throughout a king's rule ______________
15. A resonating hollow metallic device shaped as an attractive woman ______________
16. A weird market place ______________
17. An archer's weapon for a male escort ______________
18. The curved segment of Noah's boat ______________
19. An inheritor's atmosphere ______________
20. A long bladed pole made of a natural mineral ______________

Name ______________________________

Era: Civil War

Fill in the missing words in these crossword puzzle clues. The missing words' first letter and number of letters are given. The first one has been done for you. The puzzle, on page 59, is already complete.

Across

4. new state (f,6) *formed* when part of Virginia remained (l,5) ____________ to the North.
5. (w,6) ____________ ships covered with iron (p,6) ____________
6. (s,6) ____________ in which slavery was (a,7) ____________
8. (a,11) ______________________ novel by Harriet Beecher Stowe
10. one of the (m,4) ____________ notorious (p,6) ____________ camps in the war
11. (f,5) ____________ used in this war to (i,8) ____________ the dead
12. Confederate (g,7) ____________ who (s,11) ____________ his army in April of 1865
13. a system of (e,6) ____________ routes for (r,7) ____________ slaves
15. where John Brown and his (f,9) ____________ attempted a slave (r,9) ____________
18. what (y,6) ____________ troops called Southern (s,8) ____________
19. what Southern leaders (u,5) ____________ the South to do
20. called the (b,9) ____________ day of the Civil War
21. (a,7) ____________ name for the Battle of (m,8) ____________
22. soldiers killed, (m,7) ____________, wounded, or (c,8) ____________

Down

1. a state in which slavery was (p,10) ______________________
2. hard (b,8) ____________ eaten by troops
3. this battle marked the (t,7) ____________ point of the war
4. (a,7) ____________ name for the Civil War
7. (f,7) ____________ from slavery
9. (s,4) ____________ of first Civil War (b,6) ____________
14. the North's (n,5) ____________ suppression of Southern (p,5) ____________
16. U.S. Southerners' (n,4) ____________ for (n,11) ____________
17. those who thought (s,7) ____________ was wrong

Use with page 58.

Name ______________________________

Era: Civil War (Continued)

Name ______________________

Harassing Homophones

Underline the incorrect homophones below. Then on each line at the bottom, write both the incorrect homophone and its matching replacement.

Four two daze Chester could knot Finnish his lickerish Styx. A peace would ketch on his pailet. Than heed cry allowed, whaling that know won paid attention two hymn annie moor and that he kneaded hour love. Chester wood stick out his tung, titan his fist, and grown, "Ewe awl ken jump inn a creak! Eye hope a harry gristly bytes yore knows off."

Of coarse weed never here him. Wee would bee aweigh inn sum gneiss plaice he'd no nothing about.

Name ______________________

Take It Away

Remove one letter from each word on the left to make a new word that fits the definition. Write the letter you removed in the small blank to spell a proverb (written vertically). Write the new word.

Word	Removed Letter	Definitions	New Word
APART	___	to separate	____________
BEEF	___	buzzing creature	____________
OPEN	___	animal yard	____________
CANOE	___	walking stick	____________
LEND	___	extremity	____________
COAT	___	rough bed	____________
RATION	___	proportional relation	____________
TEND	___	X	____________
SHOD	___	turf	____________
RAIN	___	hastened	____________
START	___	sour	____________
MANGER	___	fury	____________
LOOP	___	cut	____________
BAND	___	naughty	____________
HOPE	___	leap	____________
YEARN	___	deserve	____________
STAIRS	___	mixes	____________
SURE	___	bring legal action against	____________
PEAR	___	on average	____________
POSSE	___	model	____________
BOATS	___	baseball clubs	____________
STOOP	___	halt	____________
MEANT	___	carnivore's food	____________
SPOIL	___	earth	____________
BEAST	___	finest	____________
DREAD	___	deceased	____________
MAT	___	mommy	____________
PINE	___	sharp peg	____________
BARD	___	rod	____________

Name ____________________

Precious Stones

Beryl Beckman is a mineral maniac in search of gemstones. Help her find the scattered stones by leading her through this word maze. Begin at **START** with the word "surpass." Connect "surpass" to its synonym in a neighboring pair. Then connect the other word in the pair to its synonym. Continue until Beryl has nowhere to go. She may move up, down, across, or diagonally.

				END			
START surpass	venom lose	shudder brink *emerald*	margin blight	dawdle finish	advise lag	revolt chat	deft mutiny *diamond*
outdo gorge	irritable pleasant	heritage legacy	rude twitch	disease counsel *sapphire*	converse divert	gusto adroit	bide amiable
ravine dominate *moonstone*	control prevent	mode manner	deceitful insolent *topaz*	deflect fraudulent	jolt bounce	abominable loathsome	sanction zest
mislay wait	block haggard *garnet*	begin toxin	signify caution	hole aperture	raw fugitive	step tribe	clan warrant *amethyst*
retreat tumult	careworn shorten	prestige reputation	nurse attend	partisan disciple	obscure tread *ruby*	model example	prosperous peevish
weak constant	abridge annex	attach wind *agate*	crank vapor	husky molder	endow vague	monoton- ous humdrum	unwieldly admonish
yearn crave	independent freedom	orbit circuit	haze tyrant *pearl*	resembling parallel	foster flourishing	believable give	attractive credible *jasper*
decompose originate	commend praise	paltry hotheaded	despot trivial	invent create	overwhelm crush	trickle bulky	hideous fetching
frugal bestow	testy thrifty	uproar indicate	narrative writhe	government regime	runaway hoarse	unanimity ghastly	pitcher jug
data news	award notorious *turquoise*	ill-famed anecdote	miserly cheap	squirm vice	corruption accord	kinfolk relatives	incessant seep

List the stones Beryl found in order: ____________________

Salute to the Past

Name ______________________________

Fill in the blanks to complete each word. Use the small letters and answers to design your own coded saying. Have a friend complete it.

1. DE__N__N__C__HUS
o w e t
the "terrible claw," 9-foot-long dinosaur
2. __ __RAN__OSAU__US __E__
p e l i i r
notoriously vicious predator with small arms
3. __TRU__H__O__IMUS
c p o y
the ostrich dinosaur
4. D__ __OS__U__
o l f i
means "terrible lizard"
5. E__TI__ __T__ON
r l x o
the death of a species of animal or plant
6. __RA__HI__SAU__US
m x w i
this largest of the sauropods stood as tall as a 4-story building
7. __R__C__ __ATO__S
p o v i b
a three-horned, grass-eating creature
8. __IP__O__OC__S
h g h q
a long-necked 80-foot-long beast
9. HA__ROS__U__
h f i
one of the duck-billed dinosaurs
10. ST__ __OSAU__
v a i
creature with double rows of bone plates on its back
11. CO__P__O__NAT__US
y c a t
a small and speedy meat-eater
12. I__UA__O__ON
a l h
a plant eater whose weapon was a large thumb spike
13. __RC__A__ __TER__X
f t v b e
debatably a dinosaur with feathers
14. __TE__ODA__TY__
b i x g
a flying reptile, but not a dinosaur
15. __R__ __ON__LY
h f a k
four-winged insect that lives(ed) now and in the age of dinosaurs
16. __H__S__OSA__R__S
x f y q q
a horned dinosaur with an enormous neck frill
17. __R__N__O__AURUS
m w p c
also called apatosaurus, about 70 feet long

Name ______________________

Telescopic Triumph

Use references and your knowledge of astronomy terms to fill in the boxes below.

Puzzle A

1. a road map of the sky (2 words)
2. a cloud of gas and dust in space
3. an autumnal constellation that is also called the Goat
4. the oval-shaped phase of the moon
5. energy produced when several small particles become one big particle; stars produce energy this way (2 words)
6. a collection of dense matter with such strong gravity that not even light can escape it (2 words)
7. the brightness of a celestial body
8. two dates of the year, about March 21 and September 21
9. a pattern of stars in the night sky
10. this planet was bombarded with comet fragments in July of 1994
11. a star's nuclear explosion that is so powerful and bright it can outshine a galaxy of 100 billion stars
12. a system in which two stars orbit a common center of gravity between them (2 words)
13. large groups of stars often in the shape of spirals
14. the point in the sky directly overhead
15. the summer constellation also known as the Northern Cross

Puzzle B

16. the nearest spiral galaxy to the Milky Way
17. a large orange-colored star 50 times bigger than Sol—it can be found in Taurus the Bull
18. the distance light travels in one year (2 words)
19. rocky bits of asteroids that blaze through the Earth's atmosphere and hit the Earth
20. the space telescope orbiting Earth 400 miles above us
21. stars categorized as the smallest in size

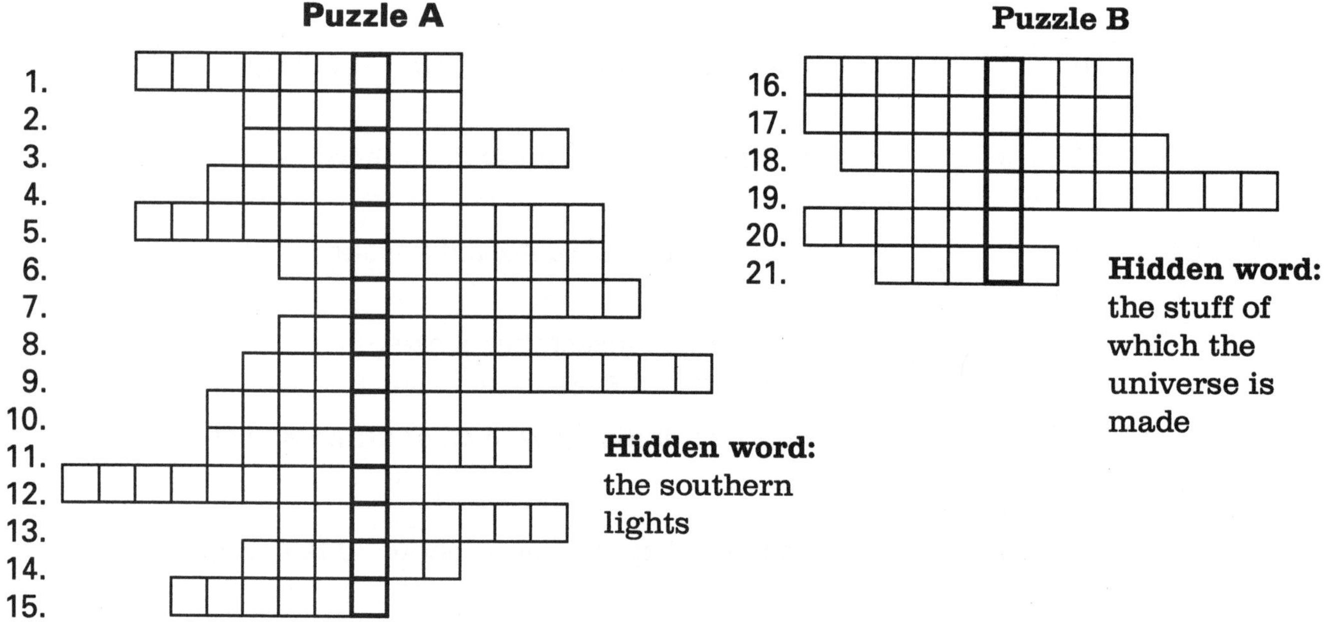

Name ______________________

Double Agents

Our poor Word Chief! She has discovered that enemy agents have infiltrated her bureau. But which words are double agents (have two meanings)? Chief has two clues on each double agent. Circle the double-crossing word after reading the clues to its double meaning.

Your Clues		The Bureau's Agents			
1. squeeze tightly	improvise	ad lib	jam	squish	press
2. urge	newspaper folks	writers	prompt	reporters	press
3. a ridge of earth	home for money	hill	purse	bank	pocket
4. deduct pay	wharf	dock	buoy	pier	harbor
5. sheep flock	bend	enclose	fence	fold	quill
6. burial site	serious	head	grave	primary	tomb
7. spool	sway	reel	dizzy	lean	roller
8. high point	child's toy	yo-yo	crux	zenith	top
9. steal	a weapon	knife	ransack	rifle	sword
10. you stop with it	a fern	brake	reins	thicket	grip
11. special market	equitable	carnival	frank	fair	gentle
12. playing card	military aviator	jack	captain	flyboy	ace
13. keep watch	trails a boat	trace	wake	follow	vigil
14. push	rummage	bonnet	sack	poke	shove
15. to heat and spice	ruminate	line	gingham	ponder	mull
16. an animal's skin	thrash	fur	wallop	pounce	hide
17. mother animal	a wall of sorts	dam	mare	ewe	sheet
18. part of the sea	long, deep bark	yelp	bay	coast	howl
19. chief	architectural structure	column	arch	master	supra
20. toll road	fish	highway	sole	pike	eel
21. record	scratch	stroke	score	check	cut
22. the play's actors	throw	toss	hurl	characters	cast
23. kindness	body organ	kidney	gentleness	heart	arm
24. set against	thin	lean	place	bother	narrow
25. tolerate	a stream	allow	brook	endure	river

Name ____________________

A Blank Look

Fill in the blanks with words from the list. You will not use every word.

1. Trinidad and Tobago seem like ____________ lands to many Northerners.
2. On this ____________ occasion we wish to celebrate with a display of fireworks.
3. The soft belly of a porcupine is most ____________ to attack.
4. Because of Tom's ____________ of broccoli, he starved at supper time.
5. I ____________ you to drive on your own side of the divided highway.
6. The unchallenged worker went about her tasks in a most ____________ manner.
7. We had our dinner on the ____________ overlooking the grounds.
8. Following her punishment, Tony ____________ herself in her room.
9. Jan is ____________ about her bicycle training.
10. The ____________ sniffled with a slight cold, scratched with soon-to-arrive hives, and hobbled with a sprained knee.
11. The ____________ chirped softly while waiting for its parent.
12. The overlord and his steadfast ____________ stalked solemnly into the hall with vengeance in their hearts.
13. The weather signs were ____________ as we prepared for yet another family picnic.
14. The mother sent her kids ____________ outside just to have silence in the house.
15. When Marty and her brother Jules quarrel, their peace-loving sibling Daniel struggles to remain ____________ .
16. The water from the tap was so ____________ we spit it out.
17. Because the caller was ____________ in his storytelling, the deejay at WOOF hung up her phone.
18. We added mustard, barbecue sauce, green pepper, and onion to doctor our ____________ -tasting hamburgers.
19. My great-uncle Morton is so ____________ , people run at the sight of him.
20. A fully-loaded baby stroller is a ____________ to a parent looking for bargains at a six-hour sale.

Word List

auspicious	evaded	foreboding	insipid	nestling	sequestered
boondoggling	exhort	gamut	interminable	neutral	veranda
brackish	exotic	hindrance	lackadaisical	proscribe	visionary
cantankerous	fanatical	hypochondriac	loathing	retinue	vulnerable

Name ____________________

Switched at Mirth

Change the position of the letters in these words to form other words.

1. evil ____________
2. lump ____________
3. lure ____________
4. unite ____________
5. mane ____________
6. clam ____________
7. tome ____________
8. stale ____________
9. stake ____________
10. rate ____________
11. teas ____________
12. phase ____________
13. nave ____________
14. near ____________
15. item ____________
16. dusty ____________
17. cheap ____________
18. save ____________
19. moor ____________
20. stare ____________
21. mate ____________
22. ate ____________
23. tacit ____________
24. heart ____________
25. throw ____________
26. mete ____________
27. tone ____________
28. stoat ____________
29. goat ____________
30. wear ____________
31. post ____________
32. please ____________
33. staple ____________
34. leap ____________
35. ripe ____________
36. mates ____________
37. earl ____________
38. angle ____________
39. raked ____________
40. vein ____________
41. steal ____________
42. bear ____________
43. flesh ____________
44. blame ____________
45. thorn ____________
46. stream ____________
47. citric ____________
48. star ____________
49. lance ____________
50. liver ____________

Challenge: List ten words that can be made into new words by rearranging the letters. List the new word next to the original.

Name ______________________________

Raise Your Hand if You're Sure

Write **O** if the sentence states an opinion. Write **F** if the sentence states a fact. Are you sure?

____ 1. The pen is mightier than the sword.
____ 2. The capital of Colombia is Bogotá.
____ 3. Henry is a better name than Tara.
____ 4. The best book in the world is *To Kill a Mockingbird*.
____ 5. You will never get married.
____ 6. This assignment is a cinch to do.
____ 7. Stacy's temperature is about 98.6 degrees F.
____ 8. Middle school is much easier than kindergarten.
____ 9. There are at least four weeks in a month.
____ 10. That musician is as gifted as Ludwig von Beethoven.
____ 11. In the northern hemisphere, December is generally much colder than June.
____ 12. You've got the right one, baby.
____ 13. My brother is the best baseball player in town.
____ 14. People who own Porsches are popular.
____ 15. That book was really exciting!
____ 16. Tom's bedroom looks like a hurricane struck it.
____ 17. You have the greatest teacher who ever lived.
____ 18. I cannot run the mile in less than four minutes.
____ 19. Melissa's parents were once teenagers.

1. Which of these sentences did you find the hardest to label? ________ Why?__________
____
2. Change one opinion into a fact.
Sentence # ___ ______________________________
3. Change one fact into an opinion.
Sentence # ___ ______________________________
4. Write an opinion you have heard in a television advertisement. (Not listed above.)
____
5. Write a fact you have heard on a television advertisement. (Not listed above.)
____

Name ____________________

Words By Heart

Fill in the blanks with words that complete the associations. The colon (:) stands for "is to."

1.	five : ten	as	three : ________
2.	word : book	as	note : ________
3.	yes : ________	as	large : small
4.	fish : scales	as	bird : ________
5.	water : drink	as	bread : ________
6.	________ : up	as	low : down
7.	hat : head	as	glove :________
8.	snow : toboggan	as	________: skate
9.	fly : kite	as	________: boat
10.	Jack : ________	as	Hansel : Gretel
11.	Yogi : bear	as	Rocky : ________
12.	________ : light	as	speaker : stereo
13.	________ : France	as	Beijing : China
14.	strike : bowling	as	homerun : ________
15.	watch : ________	as	odometer : distance
16.	three : ________	as	five : pentagon
17.	________ : nose	as	hear : ear
18.	cry : weep	as	chuckle : ________
19.	ab : cd	as	______ :qr
20.	tiger : Asia	as	zebra : ________
21.	Baltic : ________	as	Atlantic : ocean
22.	came : come	as	saw : ________
23.	rabbit :________	as	shark : swim
24.	insect : six	as	spider : ________
25.	go : went	as	fly : ________
26.	1, 2, 3 : 3, 4, 5	as	2, 4, 6 : ________
27.	how : adverb	as	which : ________
28.	rustle : verb	as	cattle : ________
29.	________ : 24	as	minute : 60
30.	shiver : cold	as	________ : heat

Name ______________________________

It's Like This

Complete each sentence below.

1. RAKE is to ________________ as SWEEP is to DIRT.
2. HAWK is to SKY as WORM is to ________________ .
3. LAMP is to LIGHT as RADIO is to ________________ .
4. STUDY is to DESK as SLEEP is to ________________ .
5. GREEN is to BLUE/YELLOW as ________________ is to RED/YELLOW.
6. BOOK is to LIBRARY as COAT is to ________________ .
7. TOE is to TOW as ________________ is to MINER.
8. DOG is to DOGHOUSE as COW is to ________________ .
9. HE is to ME as ________________ is to US.
10. 1 is to 3, and 7 is to 9, as ____ is to 14.
11. ELBOW is to BELOW as ________________ is to CLOUD.
12. LEAVE is to EXIT as ARRIVE is to ________________ .
13. JOEY is to PUP as ________________ is to SEAL.
14. HANDS is to PEOPLE as ________________ is to CATS.
15. STAR is to ASTRONOMY as NaCl is to ________________ .
16. LISBON is to PORTUGAL as DAMASCUS is to ________________ .
17. NIAGARA is to FALLS as GOBI is to ________________ .
18. 2 is to 8, and 4 is to 64, as ____ is to 729.
19. TOP is to SPIN as SLED is to ________________ .
20. LIRA is to ITALY as FRANC is to ________________ .
21. DRUM is to M as PICCOLO is to ________________ .
22. OSPREY is to BIRD as NEWT is to ________________ .
23. ROMEO is to ________________ as NAPOLEON is to JOSEPHINE.
24. MINUSCULE is to ________________ as LOATHSOME is to PLEASANT.

Challenge: Write five of your own analogies, leaving a blank for one of the key words. Trade analogies with a partner and see if you can complete each other's.

Name ______________________________

The Mixed-Up World of Sports

Cob Bostas has a terrible time as a sports commentator. He often switches word sounds around into verbal nonsense. Rearrange the letters of the words below and write sensible sentences.

1. Geh Lourig has the grost sland-mams at the age of thwenty-tree.

   ____

2. Heiric Eden won dive findividual mold gedals at the 1980 spolympic skeed cating ompetition.

   ____

   ____

3. Shoeie Willmaker, who fands at stour eet feleven inches tall, is the sost muccessful rorse-jacing hockey.

   ____

   ____

4. The basest gameball long on record thook thrirty-tee pinnings to lay.

   ____

5. Ron ecord the basketest plallball tayer at feight eet was Uleiman Nali Sashnush lor Fibya in 1962.

   ____

   ____

6. The rirst Famerican icycle bace plook tace in Boston on a mee-cile throurse on Tway menty-four, 1878, and cas wompleted in mearly nelve and hone-alf twinutes.

   ____

   ____

7. On Tarch en and meleven Stavid Deed bolance an bis hicycle on a sarpeted curface for fenty-hour sours mix strinutes twaight.

   ____

   ____

8. In 1988 Warles Chalker chayed pleckers against wo hundred and tone sopponents imultaneously and eat bem thall.

   ____

   ____

9. Gesjorie Martring of the Stunited Ates won an Goldympic me oldal in spomen's cringboard dive wompetition at the age of yirteen nears mine thonths.

   ____

   ____

Name ____________________

Squaresville, Blockoslavia

In Squaresville all city blocks, as you can tell from the map, are perfectly square. Recently Joni Rundjik put together a trivia quiz about the city. Answer her questions.

1. Which point is five blocks from point A? __________
2. Which point is seven blocks from point A? __________
3. Which point is five blocks from G and eight blocks from E? __________
4. Which point is 12 blocks from C and 11 blocks from J? __________
5. Which three points are exactly four blocks from each other? __________
6. Which two points are equal distances from point F—G, B, or C? __________
7. Starting at point D how might you visit seven different points in 24 blocks?

   ____

8. What distance is the shortest circuit to get from J to H to A? Give the number of blocks. __________
9. Which four points create the shortest circuit distance? Give the number of blocks.

   ____

10. Which point is four blocks from J, six blocks from F, and seven blocks from C? __________
11. Which point is 11 blocks from H, seven blocks from D, and seven blocks from E? __________
12. Draw this route traveling the number of blocks given to move from point to point, starting from and returning to point I without crossing any lines: 7>4>5>4>11>4>5>4>6>6 **Hint:** Move in a counter-clockwise direction.

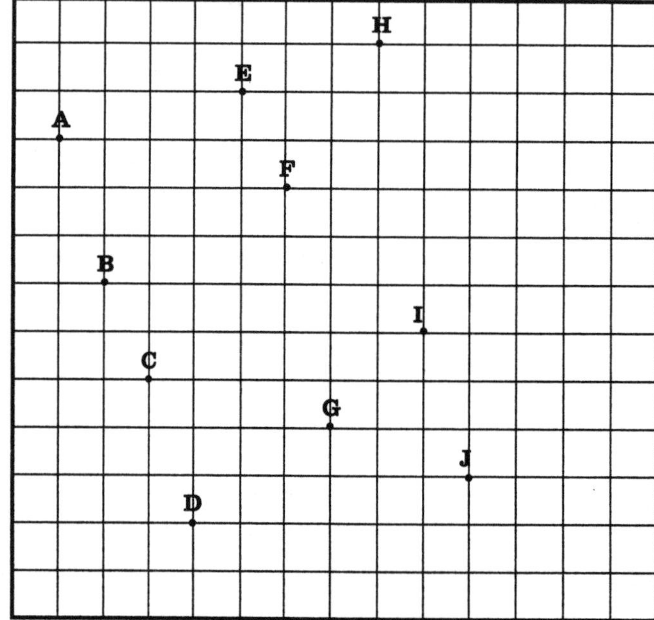

Name ____________________

Answer My Question

Each of these groups of words answers one or two questions. Put checks in the boxes of the questions being answered by each word group.

1. suddenly, after the accident
2. nobody
3. under the ashes
4. Julius Caesar
5. danced frantically
6. over the river
7. at the stroke of 4
8. on Halloween at the party
9. the thunderstorm
10. the young fawn
11. forever with adoration
12. our neighbor's sister, traveling
13. awkwardly falling down
14. in a flash, vanished
15. every other weekend
16. the baby mouse
17. at the mall, stubbornly
18. a toddler
19. two worlds collided
20. 9:30 A.M. noisily
21. Edmonton, Alberta
22. rowboat out to sea
23. now at a theater near you
24. the melancholy troubadour
25. here on tiptoes
26. Goldilocks ran

Where?	When?	How?	What?	Who?

Name ___________________________

Capital Questions

Read each sentence below. Mark the phrases that answer the questions *who*, *what*, *when*, *where*, and *why* as follows:

who—underline once
what—underline twice
when —draw an oval around it
where—draw rectangle around it
why—underline with wavy line

1. Senator Bucky Wholsteen, angered when his roast beef sandwich turned cold, climbed the 150-foot satellite receptor pole above the corner of Constitution Avenue and 20th Street last week Saturday.

2. Embarrassed without his effervescent bow tie, Senator Saul Bimon, on the MLK Memorial Library's second floor, hid behind an opened newspaper on November 4, 1995.

3. On Tuesday her Washington page slipped Hennie Pfennig a personal note under the table so fellow representative Tink O'Kwartles would not be made suspicious.

4. During the first course at the President's dinner Congressman Kenny Teddedy, the champion of the space program, suggested that the Pentagon pay for the next five years' space exploration with its excess Star Wars funds because no legislator wished to raise taxes.

5. Since she was exhausted from her afternoon hearing with the health board, lobbyist Smoky Thins skipped the last hour debate being held in Senator Trublood's office.

6. Standing on the podium above the milling crowd of his angry constituents, Representative Mel O. Mahrs, a first-term legislator, waved his hands frantically to ask for quiet at the beginning of the Sweet Tooth Rebellion.

7. Because of the strength of her stalwart aide's study made last July, Claudine Quickhart was able to introduce the popular Caffeine Bill limiting coffee drinkers to three cups per morning session in the House Chamber.

8. After hosting a seminar with East Asian delegates on the lawn outside the Smithsonian Institution Building, St. Paul's own Senator Slick distributed free musical frisbees to close his conference on a high note.

Name ______________________________

Where's My Freddy?

Help! Jackie lost his Fred Flintstone felt-tipped pen. He let one of his study partners borrow it and now cannot remember who. J. J. didn't (Jackie is sure) and neither did the American literature partner. But who did? Each of Jackie's partners shares one class with him. Each also has a different hair color. Identify each partner by gender, hair color, and the class shared with Jackie to discover who borrowed his pen. To do this, complete the matrix. Mark a **B** or **G** for boy or girl. Place an **X** in a square for each "no." Place an **O** to indicate "yes." Once you record an **O**, place an **X** in all remaining boxes in that row and column.

1. Neither the red-haired person, nor Mic (who is not in algebra) borrowed Jackie's pen, but one of them is a male.
2. The three females include the algebra partner, the brunette, and Terri.
3. The two boys are the ones with either black hair or early civilization studies.
4. The brunette, not Kim, is Jackie's orchestra partner.
5. Either the early civilization partner or the blonde has the pen.
6. A girl borrowed the pen, not the auburn-haired boy.
7. Terri's red hair sometimes bothers her partner Jackie. This wouldn't happen in geology.
8. Both Shawn and the black-haired kid joined the boys' wrestling team.

	boy or girl	black	blonde	brunette	auburn	red	algebra	Amer. lit.	early civ.	geology	orchestra	Has pen?
J. J.												
Kim												
Mic												
Shawn												
Terri												

Name ______________________

Mighty Fine Folk

Fill in the chart on these story characters by writing **X** if an attribute fits the character or story.

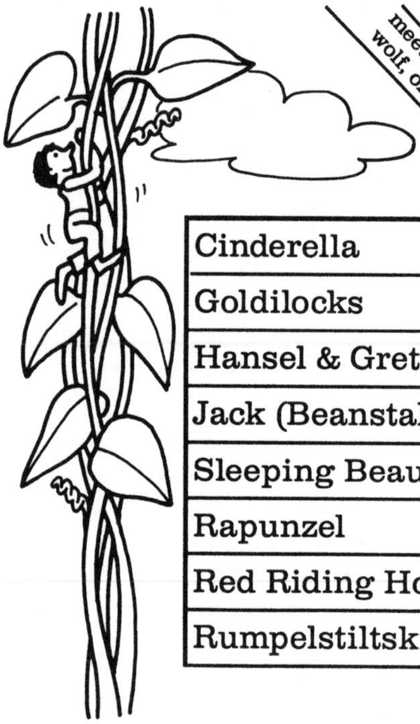

	The main character . . . meets an evil man, wolf, or beast	meets an evil woman	is primarily good	is neutral/bad	marries in story	goes from rags to riches	In the story . . . **3** is important	the antagonist dies	animals act as humans
Cinderella									
Goldilocks									
Hansel & Gretel									
Jack (Beanstalk)									
Sleeping Beauty									
Rapunzel									
Red Riding Hood									
Rumpelstiltskin									

Now re-read two of these stories and give specific examples of the attributes checked.

Choose another folk tale and list eight specific attributes of that story's main character.

1. ______________________
2. ______________________
3. ______________________
4. ______________________
5. ______________________
6. ______________________
7. ______________________
8. ______________________

Brain Power

Name ______________________

Use your head, your paper, pencil . . . whatever you need to figure out these problems.

1. Over the next five years Dan, who is 52" tall, will grow at a rate of 2 inches per year. Meanwhile, his younger brother Dave, standing at a mean 48", will grow at a rate of 5 inches per year and Rick, their 36" tall baby brother, 6 inches per year. Call their current height, their height in year 1, and the next year's height, year 2, and so on.

   a. In what year will Rick be four inches shorter than Dan? ______________

   b. In what year will Dave outgrow Dan? ______________

   c. What will be the height of each boy in year six?

   Dan: ______________ Dave: ______________ Rick: ______________

2. Danielle can divide her Gershey Kisses, a famous chocolate treat, evenly among her friends. She is unable to split the candy 5, 8, or 9 ways, but she could evenly divide the candies. She started with a bag of 40 and ate less than 18 herself.

   a. How many friends does she have? ______________

   b. How many kisses will each friend receive? ______________

3. A dad and his daughter went fishing. While neither caught fewer than three fish or more than seven, together they caught an odd number of each of three fishes: perch, bluegill, and bass. They told us (truthfully) this:

   They caught more bass than bluegill and perch combined.

   They caught four more bluegill than perch.

   So, how many of each fish did they catch?

   a. number of perch: ______________

   b. number of bluegill: ______________

   c. number of bass: ______________

Name ______________________

War of the Networks

Lord Nelson and five other greats from world history were remembered in television specials last week by six television networks including CBS. These famous historical people came from Germany, Mongolia, or four other cultures. Strangely enough, each special ran a different length of time, one as short as 15 minutes.

Using the chart below and the eight clues, learn which historical character representing what culture appeared on which station for what length of time. To use the chart, read each clue. Check a box with an **x** if it is a no. Use an **o** if it is a definite yes. When you enter an **o**, you may place an **x** in all remaining boxes for that category's row and column.

Clues:

1. Joan of Arc, who is not from Egypt, has a longer program than Lord Nelson.
2. Xerxes I, not showing on either CBS or the 45-minute program, is from Persia.
3. Ramses I is not the longest program, but it is 30 minutes longer than Joan's.
4. Rommel, whose program is shorter than Joan's, is not found on HBO. Neither is he from Mongolia.
5. ABC is proud of its Genghis Khan documentary which was 15 minutes shorter than Lord Nelson's but not the shortest program whose historical figure is German.
6. Starting from the very shortest, the programs were FOX, a Mongolian hero, Lord Nelson, and the CBS documentary.
7. The DIS station showed its Egyptian warrior for 90 minutes.
8. The English Nelson program is 15 minutes shorter than the French documentary. Lord Nelson is not on NBC!

TV Specials Chart

	HBO	FOX	NBC	ABC	DIS	CBS	Egypt	England	France	Germany	Mongol	Persia	15	30	45	60	90	120
Joan																		
Khan																		
Nelson																		
Ramses																		
Rommel																		
Xerxes																		

Fill in this chart with the information you discovered.

World History Greats	Culture	Network	Length of Time
Joan of Arc			
Rommel			
Genghis Khan			
Xerxes			
Lord Nelson			
Ramses I			

Name ______________________

Wise Guys Buys

Ted wants to buy his first car, a bright red '67 jeep, which has been advertised in the classifieds for five days. He and his dad checked it out. It was cool. Not a speck of rust showing! Now he must decide where to apply for a loan.

Check out these figures and fill in the chart below to determine the cost of the jeep including finance charges for each institution.

Better Bank and Trust

See Us and Compare

$100 down payment; monthly payments of $25 for 3 years

Honest Folks Loan

Trust Us!

no money down; monthly payments of $65 for 1½ years

Loyalty Loans, Inc.

A flag with every $25 deposit

$99 down payment; monthly payments of $99 for 9 months

Lance's Family Bank

We're like family

$80 down payment; monthly payments of $34.56 for 27 months

Ansel's Banking Corporation

Simple as ABC

$40 down payment; monthly payments of $70 for 14 months

Financial Institution	Monthly Payments	Number of Payments	Down Payment	Total Cost
Better Bank & Trust	$ ________ X	________ +	$ ________ =	$ ________
Loyalty Loans, Inc.	$ ________ X	________ +	$ ________ =	$ ________
Ansel's Banking Corp.	$ ________ X	________ +	$ ________ =	$ ________
Honest Folks Loan	$ ________ X	________ +	$ ________ =	$ ________
Lance's Family Bank	$ ________ X	________ +	$ ________ =	$ ________

Circle the name of the company that offers the best financial plan. Be ready to explain why you think it is the best plan.

Name ______________________

Imagine That!

Write responses to each of these situations.

1. You hear a bird flapping its wings and squawking loudly while a cat fiercely cries. What may you conclude? ______________________
2. You walk into a room to discover glass scattered over the floor and a softball lying on the floor. What may you conclude? ______________________
3. You see an empty cookie bag held by your brother whose mouth is full. What may you conclude? ______________________
4. At a campground you hear a whining dog, smell a horrid smell, and watch a young woman leave to buy several cans of tomato juice. What may you conclude? ______________________
5. At the airport a speaker asks a question, and her listener looks puzzled but makes no reply. The speaker again questions, and the listener still has no response. What may you conclude? ______________________
6. You watched a uniformed man run, stop, wait, run, run, and then slide toward another man. What may you conclude? ______________________
7. You are surprised by a crack of thunder, and all the lights go off. What may you conclude? ______________________
8. A plane smashes into the earth without a sound. No one is hurt. What may you conclude? ______________________
9. A noisy crowd gathers on the playground. Then, as a teacher approaches, all is quiet. You see two red-faced boys glaring at each other. What may you conclude? ______________________
10. All that can be seen down the city block are buzzing insects. No other animals or people are visible. The sun is at its zenith. What may you conclude? ______________________
11. You wake to a humming sound. Two blades are swishing back and forth as liquid hits the windshield. It is not raining. What may you conclude? ______________________
12. As you walk into the lunchroom, you see a red-faced boy holding an empty lunch tray. What may you conclude? ______________________

Name ______________________

What Really Happened in the Black Forest

Fill in the blanks in this Hansel and Gretel story to discover the "truth" behind the tale.

Even before Hansel and Gretel made their ____________ to the ____________ where they eventually lost their ______________ , the children spent much of their time ______________ inventive games such as "Escape from the ______________ Witch" and "What's on the Roof?"

Now Gretel had the ____________ of pushing people. One day Hansel's seven-year-old ____________ pushed him off of a ______________ which caused him to ____________ his finger. Because of her physical and vocal ______________ , Gretel developed both strong ______________ and a colorful vocabulary.

Hansel had a very ____________ imagination. Every tree and rock ____________ a wicked troll or mean-spirited ______________ . He would converse with his ____________ as though it were ____________ . Adamantly, he proclaimed that a dove __________ him its name was Dave. Hansel, an ______________ nine-year-old, had no ______________ convincing his sibling that he could ________ the languages of birds and __________ .

It is no ____________ that the simple-minded Fräulein Trudi, a ______________ , crippled almswoman ______________ near the Rhine, became the children's ______________ witch. Her brightly colored ________ became a __________ gingerbread house and her grain crib was transformed into a ____________ cage by the fanciful Hansel and his ______________ sister.

Fortunately, the children's visit was ______________ when Gerhardt Buchende, a parish deacon, ____________ Trudi from her locked cellar. The two __________ - scolded rascals were required to work for Fräulein Trudi for ________ weeks as punishment. Hence, the children ________________ Gerhardt Buchende as a wicked and ________ stepmother.

Did they live happily ____________ after?

Word List

beasts	vivid	forest	swing	conjurer	sister
habit	lonely	ever	imaginary	Wicked	freed
became	two	prison	way	imagined	hut
living	sprain	speak	playing	kitten	difficulty
visit	boisterous	soundly	shortened	biceps	dominance
perfect	told	human	cruel	wonder	expressive

Challenge: Write two possible titles for this story.

3-Word Title ______________________________

5-Word Title ______________________________

Name ______________________________

Good Advice Is Beyond Price

Match each of these sentences with the American proverb given at the bottom.

____ Elevate the part of your face just below your lower lip.

____ Give a guy good food to eat, and he'll warm up to you very fast.

____ Exclamations of expiration are no-nos.

____ If one fails to get the latest information, so much the better.

____ The deprivation of one's treasure brings lamentations; but to he who requisitions the prize belongs the reward.

____ Solid emulsion of milky fat globules should not be diffused over the opposing faces of a portion of baked goods.

____ The pullet who expends all its energy in vociferous cacophony has little opportunity to consume enough to gain in stoutness.

____ One should not be disconcerted by a minuscule soil portion.

____ Fools spend too much of their energy on the mundane.

____ One's blood pump has vision undiscernable to one's central nervous system.

____ A person is doing something? That's cool. But if you add a noggin, you double your power.

____ If you were to eat a McIntosh on Tuesday and again on Wednesday and Thursday, and if you were to continue this pattern for an infinite length of time, most likely you will not be visited by a medical practitioner.

____ How can it be that this ugly human being eating next to you was once a cute little diapered infant?

____ If you hear the canine's yap, you have no reason to concern yourself with its teeth.

____ The dunce is difficult to discern if he is wise enough to keep the vow of silence.

American Proverbs

1. Never say die.
2. No news is good news.
3. Little things worry little minds.
4. A clucking hen never gets fat.
5. The heart has eyes that the brain knows nothing of.
6. The quickest way to a man's heart is through his stomach.
7. A little dirt never hurt anyone.
8. Two heads are better than one.
9. Nothing can hide a fool like a closed mouth.
10. An apple a day keeps the doctor away.
11. Finders keepers, losers weepers.
12. Don't be afraid of a dog that barks.
13. Pretty in the cradle, homely at the table.
14. Keep your chin up.
15. Don't butter your bread on both sides.

Challenge: From neighbors and friends, make a list of ten additional proverbs or maxims.

Name ______________________

Puzzling Plurals

Some nouns are made plural in peculiar ways. Which actual singular/plural pairs would rhyme with the following made-up pairs? If . . .

1. fan became fen? ______________________
2. moose became meese? ______________________
3. blouse became blice? ______________________
4. booth became beeth? ______________________
5. fox became foxen? ______________________
6. mild became mildren? ______________________
7. wish remained wish? ______________________
8. soot became seet? ______________________
9. practice became practi? ______________________
10. tedium became tedia? ______________________

Plural rules do not always work. Which of the following noun plurals look right? Circle the correctly spelled plural word for each pair.

11.	bills-of-sale	bill-of-sales
12.	radios	radioes
13.	diarys	diaries
14.	tomatos	tomatoes
15.	chiefs	chieves
16.	corps	corpes
17.	loafs	loaves
18.	boxs	boxes
19.	scarves	scarfs
20.	glass's	glasses
21.	ladys	ladies
22.	proves	proofs
23.	halves	halfs
24.	echoes	echos

Name ______________________

Yikes!

What do you think will happen next? For each problem write at least two sentences.

1. You just broke your bed by falling on it too hard. Your mom walks in.

____

____

2. You begin running the 100-meter dash and notice that your left shoe is untied.

____

____

3. You're beginning to ask a girl out to the ball game and then notice the 6'6" upperclassman behind her.

____

____

4. You're holding a crystal bowl filled with punch, and your obnoxious cousin suddenly frightens you.

____

____

5. In the middle of an important science test, one of your contact lenses vanishes.

____

____

6. You faked being sick so you could stay home. Then you remember that it's the day for the field trip to the best theme park in the state.

____

____

7. The jelly sandwich you're eating drips onto the computer keys.

____

____

8. Your dad comes in with the mail, which includes your report card.

____

____

9. You thought the recipe called for 450 degrees instead of 250 degrees.

____

____

Name ____________________

Think Tank

What do people think about at work? Match these folks to their most likely thoughts.

____ 1. botanist
____ 2. ice-cream vendor
____ 3. coffee taste-tester
____ 4. fast-food cook
____ 5. newspaper editor
____ 6. soldier
____ 7. airplane pilot
____ 8. deep-sea explorer
____ 9. toy-store clerk
____ 10. bank teller
____ 11. school teacher
____ 12. building janitor
____ 13. sports announcer
____ 14. horse jockey
____ 15. beauty pageant contestant
____ 16. babysitter
____ 17. UPS delivery person
____ 18. park ranger
____ 19. hospital receptionist
____ 20. baseball coach
____ 21. hair stylist
____ 22. garbage collector
____ 23. clock maker
____ 24. carpenter

a. Where are the stats on the boxer? I read them ten minutes ago.
b. By 4:00? We've got three more stories to print!
c. Is that the same child who came in yesterday with a broken toe?
d. Do you think that dad will buy it for that whining kid?
e. When will the bell ring?
f. What would you like, Marcy? Last week you chose a fudge bar.
g. Another open bag? This stuff stinks!
h. I really don't know how I can cover his bald spot.
i. Hmmm, let me guess. A double-stemmed bluebell.
j. We are ten minutes out of Cleveland.
k. Let's see, he gets 1 ten and 3 fives.
l. Oh, yeah? Well, I can scowl too!
m. Step, step, step, smile. Step, step, step, smile.
n. Time just keeps on ticking.
o. Three strikes? Can that ump count?
p. Go, Fatal Attraction, go! You can catch her.
q. Attention! . . . At ease.
r. Octopi don't frighten me. It's those spooky squid that shoot by.
s. Oh, no! Dropped the hammer again!
t. If I get bit by another dog, I quit!
u. Who's the kid who put gum on all the door handles?
v. Would you like fries with that?
w. Why is there a fire out of the pit? Where's Smoky when you need him?
x. These beans aren't mountain grown!

Name ______________________

A Hungry World

People who live in Canada and the United States are among the wealthiest people in the world, and these countries still have hungry people. In other parts of the world the hunger problem is much worse. Read these facts.

More than 15% of the world's population is malnourished.

Some social scientists believe that as many as 67 % of the world population suffers from poor nutrition.

Every year many millions of people die from diseases caused by malnutrition. Of these people, children suffer the most deaths. UNICEF figures show that 15 million children die each year due to famine or illness.

In some countries, 50% of all children are killed by malnutrition before the age of five.

In these countries, the average life expectancy is between 40 and 45 years.

Four chief causes of famine are drought, flooding, plant disease, and war.

In 1993, 29 nations suffered from malnutrition and excessive food shortages because of war. In these countries hunger was used as a weapon by warring parties.

In the United States 12 million children often do not have enough to eat. More than 2,000 babies are born into poverty every day. Each day 107 babies under a year old die as a result of impoverished conditions.

Western industrialized nations donate four billion dollars a year to alleviate world hunger. These same nations spend more than eight billion dollars on sports shoes.

Use facts from the above list to campaign for world hunger awareness in your school and community. Some questions you should answer are these:

1. What specific goal do you have for your campaign?
2. Who is your audience?
3. What medium will you use to spread your message? (Examples: a dramatic presentation, a video message, a song, poem, or story, a visual display such as a painting, sculpture, poster, or banner)

Write a paragraph for your teacher in which you explain what your plans are for this hunger campaign. ______________________

Name ______________________

The Absolute Truth

Respond to these questions. You may need to write some long answers on another piece of paper.

1. What is your greatest fear? ______
2. What are three of the first words you learned? (guess) ______
3. What would you most hate to touch? ______
4. What was the last food you ate? ______
5. What dream do you remember? ______
6. Where would you feel the safest? ______
7. What do you do in your spare time? ______
8. How would you like to be remembered? ______
9. What is your favorite three-color combination? ______
10. How would you help a friend who broke the law? ______
11. When are you most serious? ______
12. What would you do if you saw an automobile accident? ______
13. What foreign country would you like to visit? ______
14. What one wish do you have to improve your community? ______
15. What impossible pet animal would you wish to own? ______
16. What occupation might you enjoy having? ______
17. What was an unpopular but important thing you once did? ______
18. Would you read your sister's/brother's diary if you were sure you wouldn't get caught? ______
19. What would you say if someone accused you of cheating? ______
20. What would you do if you were required to witness against a friend? ______
21. How would you react if someone spilled ketchup over your shirt? ______
22. What would you do if you knew you were dying soon? ______
23. What is your best memory? ______
24. Who is the funniest person you know? ______
25. What is your least favorite question on this page? ______

Challenge: Write one paragraph answering this question: How would you like to change yourself?

Name ______________________

Pin Point

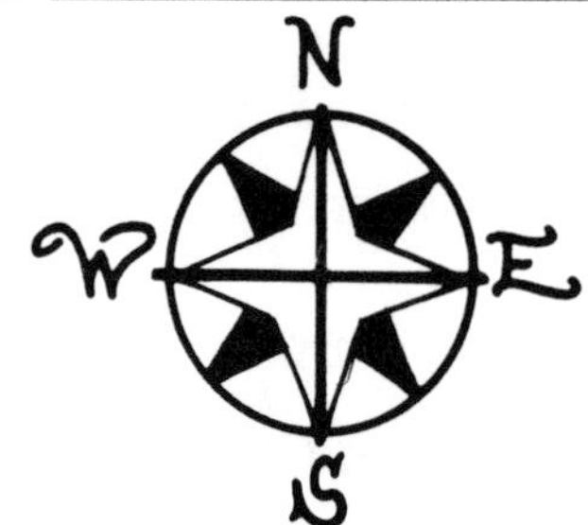

For this activity you must follow the directions and measure precisely. Use the blank map of Africa on the next page, a political map of Africa, a pencil with a sharp point, and a well-marked ruler.

1. Find the point that is 6 inches south of Cairo. Name the country. ______________
2. Find the point that is 3 inches north of Johannesburg. Name the country.

   ____
3. Find the point that is 2 inches north of Lagos. Name the country. ______________
4. Find the country bordered by Algeria and Libya. Name the country. ______________
5. Find the country that is east of Nambia. Name the country. ______________
6. Find the country that is east of Mali. Name the country. ______________
7. Name and label the country in which Cairo is located. ______________
8. Name and label the country in which Lagos is located. ______________
9. Name and label the country in which Johannesburg is located. ______________
10. Name and label the country in which Mogadishu is located. ______________
11. Find the country that is north of Chad. Name the country. ______________
12. Find Madagascar. Label it. Is it east or west of Mozambique? ______________
13. Find the point that is 2 inches east of Lagos. Name the country. ______________
14. Find the point that is ½ inch west of Lagos. Name the country. ______________
15. Find the point that is ½ inch west of Mogadishu. Name the country. ______________
16. Find the country that is south of Kenya. Name the country. ______________
17. Find the point that is 4 ½ inches north of Johannesburg. Name the country.

   ____

Name ________________________________

Pin Point (Continued)

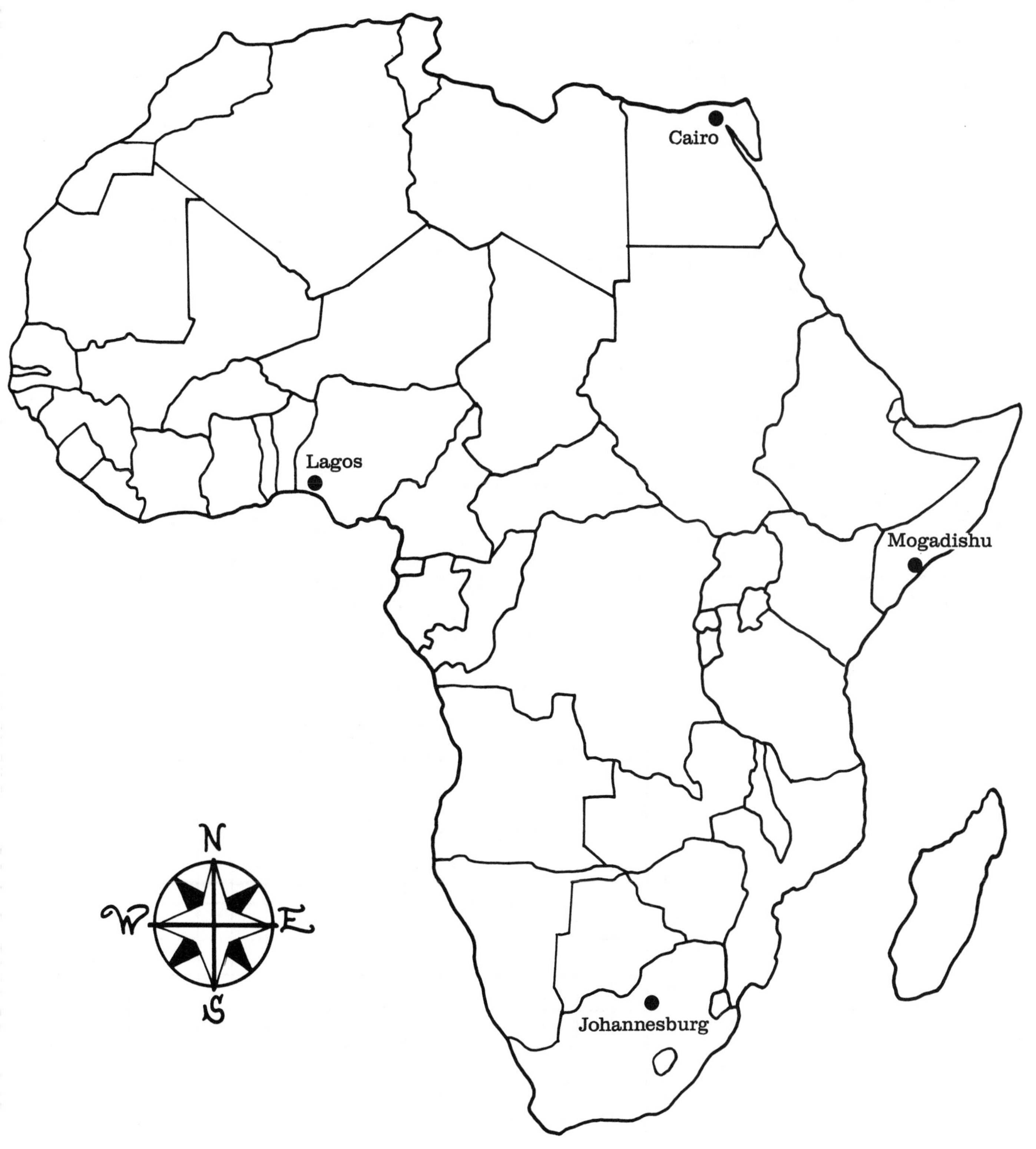

Name ___________________________

Shadow Boxing

Each number/letter combination labels a square on the grid. Fill in each square listed here. Then give a title to each picture.

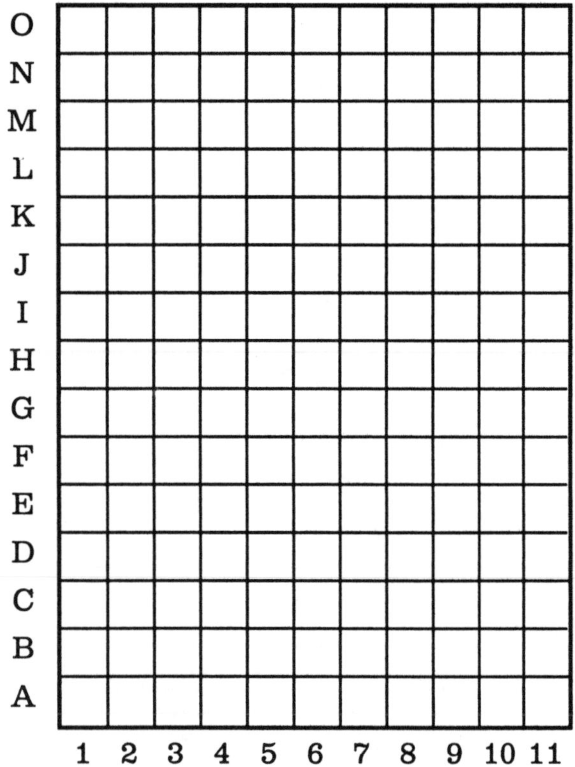

Puzzle A

1D, 2B, 2C, 2D, 3A, 3B, 3C, 3D, 3E, 4A, 4B
4C, 4D, 4E, 5A, 5B, 5C, 5D, 5E, 6B, 6C, 6D
6E, 6F, 7C, 7D, 7E, 7F, 7G, 7H, 7I, 7J, 7K
8B, 8C, 8D, 8E, 8F, 8G, 8H, 8I, 8K, 8L, 8M
8N, 8O, 9A, 9B, 9C, 9D, 9E, 9F, 9G, 9H, 9J
9K, 10B, 10C, 10D, 10E, 10F, 10G, 10H, 10I
10K, 10L, 10M, 10N, 11A, 11E, 11F, 11G
11I, 11J, 11K, 11N

Title: ____________________

Puzzle B

1A, 1B, 2C, 2D, 2H, 2I, 3E, 3F, 3G, 3H, 3I
3J, 3K, 3L, 3M, 4A, 4B, 4C, 4D, 4E, 4F, 4G
4H, 4I, 4J, 4K, 4L, 4M, 5H, 5I, 5J, 6E, 6F
6I, 6L, 6M, 7G, 7H, 7I, 7J, 7K, 14I, 15I, 16I
17H, 17I, 17J, 18I

Title: ____________________

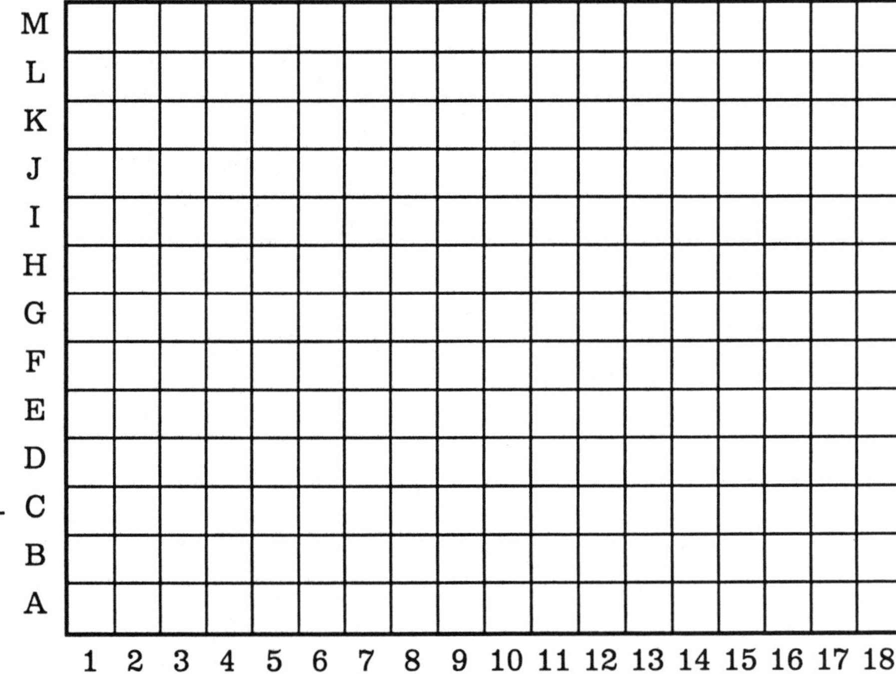

Name ____________________

Lookin' a Bit Dotty

Connect the coordinates in each grouping below. The vertical number comes first.

(1,1),(4,1),(4,4),(4,1),(1,1)
(10,10),(13,10),(13,13),(10,13),(10,10)
(4,4),(6,5),(7,7),(5,6),(4,4)
(10,10),(8,9),(7,7),(9,8)(10,10)
(1,4),(3,7),(5,6)
(13,4),(11,7),(9,6)
(10,13),(7,11),(8,9)
(1,10),(3,7),(5,8)

(10,1),(13,1),(13,4),(10,4),(10,1)
(1,10),(4,10),(4,13),(1,13),(1,10)
(10,4),(9,6),(7,7),(8,5),(10,4)
(4,10),(5,8),(7,7),(6,9),(4,10)
(10,1),(7,3),(8,5)
(13,10),(11,7),(9,8)
(4,13), (7,11), 6,9)
(4,1),(7,3),(6,5)

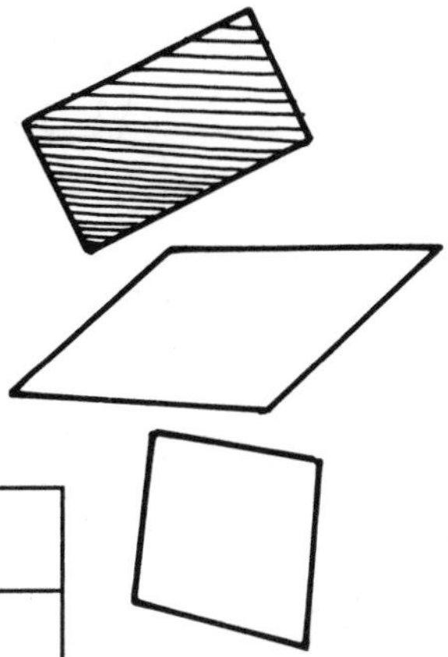

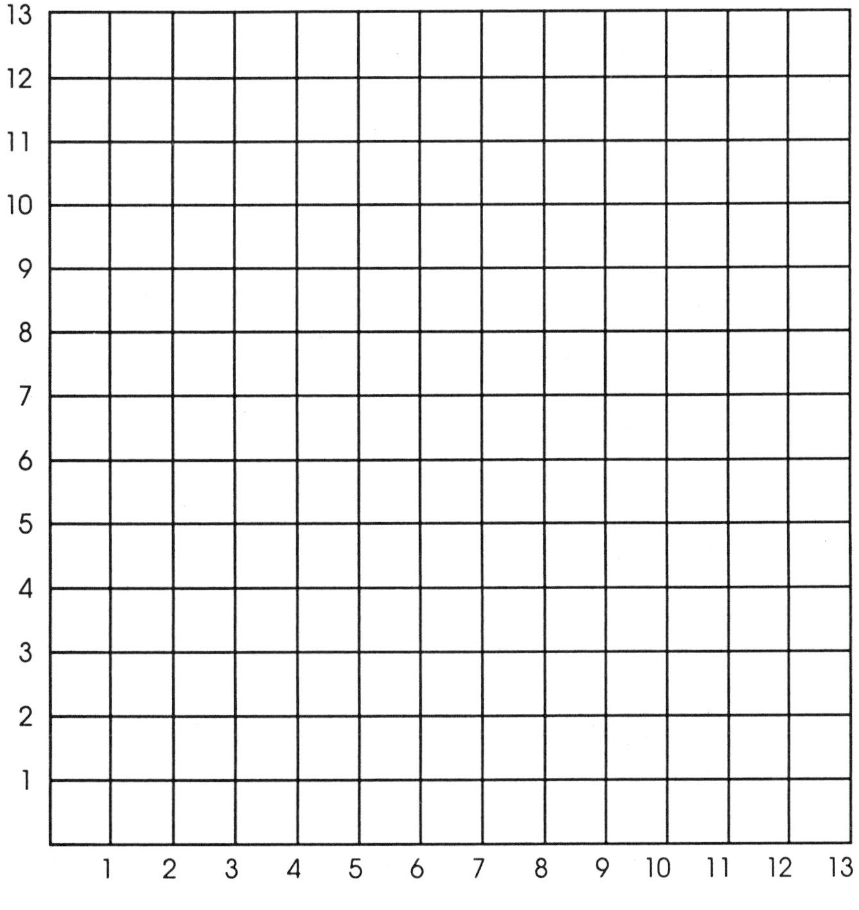

Color each quadrilateral so no two polygons of the same color share a common side. Use only these three colors: red, blue, yellow.

Name ______________________

Dot II Dot

Connect the coordinates in each group below to name an early American author. The horizontal number comes first.

(1,9), (1,10), (2,10), (2,7), (3,7) (16,9),(18,9) (11,9)—dot here
(3,8), (3,7), (4,7), (4,10) (6,7), (6,8), (5,8), (5,7), (8,7)
(11,7), (11,8) (7,7), (7,8), (8,7), (9,8), (9,10) (13,7),(13,8)
(9,7),(9,8),(10,8),(10,7),(12,7),(12,8),(14,8),(14,7),(16,7) (20,7),(20,8)
(15,7),(15,8),(16,8),(16,6),(15,6),(17,8),(17,10) (11,2),(11,3)
(18,7),(18,8),(21,8),(21,7),(22,7) (17,8),(17,7),(19,7),(19,8) (9,4)—dot here
(3,2),(3,4),(3,5),(3,2),(2,2),(2,3) (13,2),(13,3),(14,3),(14,1),(13,1),(15,3)
(4,2),(4,3),(5,3),(5,2),(6,2),(7,3),(7,2),(8,2),(8,3),(9,3),(9,2),(10,2)
(10,2),(10,3),(12,3),(12,2),(14,2)

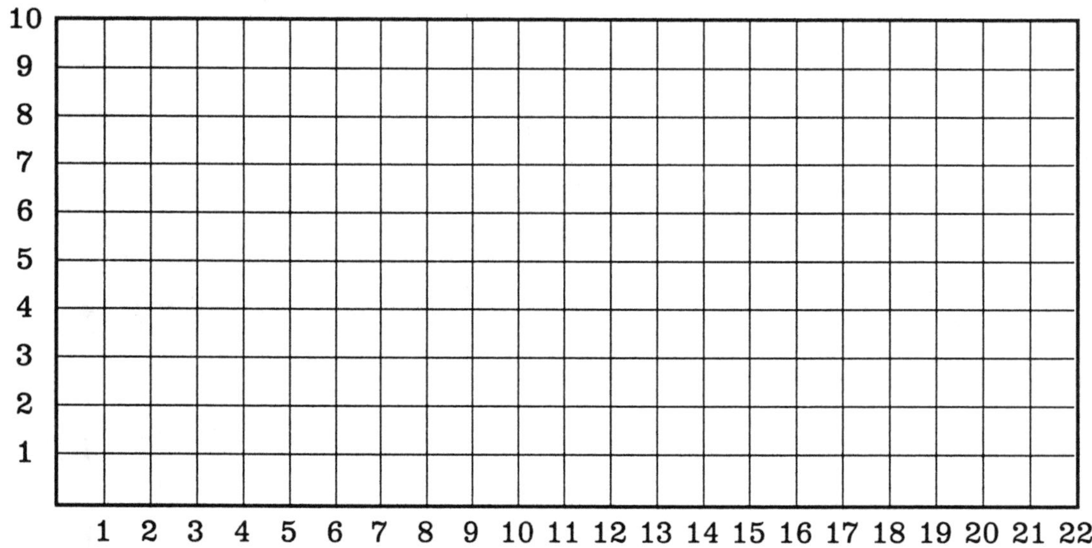

Research to discover the names of three writings by this New York writer.

1. ______________________
2. ______________________
3. ______________________

Name ______________________

Up in the Air

Follow the directions to answer these two questions.

Question #1: Who was the first commander of Skylab? ______________________

1. Write SPACE ______________________
2. Change S to N ______________________
3. Reverse the first and fourth letters ______________________
4. Change the 2nd and 5th letters to their alphabetic precedent ______________________
5. Add O's to the beginning and end ______________________
6. Reverse the D and C. ______________________
7. Add T to the beginning ______________________
8. Place a P in the third position ______________________
9. Change OA to AR ______________________
10. Remove the first O and place the last O before C ______________________
11. Add E's before and after T ______________________
12. Reverse the first 4 letters and reverse the last 6 letters ______________________

Question #2: How much did Skylab cost? ______________

1. Begin with one gross $ __________
2. Subtract 20 $ __________
3. Divide by 4 $ __________
4. Multiply by 5 $ __________
5. Reverse the order of the digits $ __________
6. Add 452 $ __________
7. Reverse the 2nd and 4th digits $ __________
8. Multiply by 2 $ __________
9. Add 6 zeros to the right $ __________

To learn more about one astronaut's life in space read *How Do You Go to the Bathroom in Space?* by William R. Pogue.

Name ____________________________

Pathfinder Test #1

1. Write your full name backwards along the bottom of this page.
2. Count by 3's starting with the number 2. Write the 14th number you reach in the square.

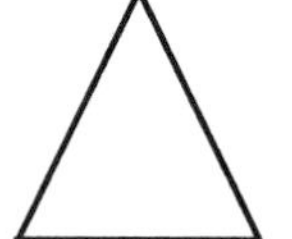 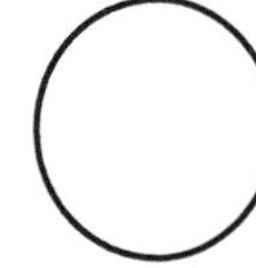 

3. Go directly to direction #8.
4. Write out a nursery rhyme on the back of this page.
5. Draw eight diamonds at the bottom of this page.
6. Underline every second vowel in direction #1.
7. Name three Disney characters to the right of this direction.

   ____

   ____

   ____

8. Do the remaining directions in this order: 10, 18, 14, 11, 9, 7, 5, 12, 6, 15, 4, and 17.
9. Skip the next direction entirely.
10. With your non-writing hand, circle the fifth word in direction #4.
11. Stare at the person directly to your left for three seconds. If there is no one to your left, touch your nose for five seconds.
12. Add these numbers: the month of your birth, your age, the number of people in this room, and 523. Please show your work.
13. Cross out the ninth word in this direction.
14. Fold this sheet into quarters, then unfold it again.
15. Write the name of the last person you spoke to in the triangle under #2.
16. SHAOUKT "I QLOXVEC YOMU, MOARNIGLOLFD!" TIHRUEED TIAMEUS.
17. Either complete direction #13 or give this sheet to your teacher.
18. Cross out every third letter in direction #16.

Name ____________________

Sound the Trumpets

Princess Petronella is off to fight a dragon. Shade in her picture using the directions below.

Shade these squares with this pattern......  H25, I25, K19, L1, L22, L28, M2, M17, P27, R17

Shade these squares with this pattern......  A23, A24, B31, G4, G13, H21, H27, I17, J2, K3, K28, L29, R29, S32

Shade these squares with this pattern......  C22, C23, D21, I19, L21, L27, M13, N20, N29, O19, P28, T29

Shade these squares with this pattern......  A21, B20, C19, G7, G17, H22, J1, K7, K17, M28, N17, N27

Shade these squares with this pattern......  A22, B21, B22, B23, B24, B25, B26, B27, B28, B29, B30, C20, C21, E2, E3, F2, F3, G2, G3, G8, G9, G18, H2, H7, H8, H9, H13, H14, H15, H16, H17, H18, H19, H20, H23, H24, H26, I1, I2, I7, I8, I9, I13, I14, I15, I16, I18, J13, J14, J15, J16, J17, J19, J25, K1, K2, K8, K9, K13, K14, K15, K16, K18, K25, K26, K27, L2, L3, L6, L7, L8, L9, L13, L14, L15, L16, L19, L20, L23, L24, L25, L26, M3, M6, M7, M8, M9, M18, M19, M20, M29, N18, N19, N28, O27, O28, P17, P18, R18, S1, S2, S3, S4, S5, S6, S7, S8, S9, S10, S11, S12, S13, S14, S15, S16, S19, S20, S21, S22, S23, S24, S25, S26, S27, S28, S29, S30, S31

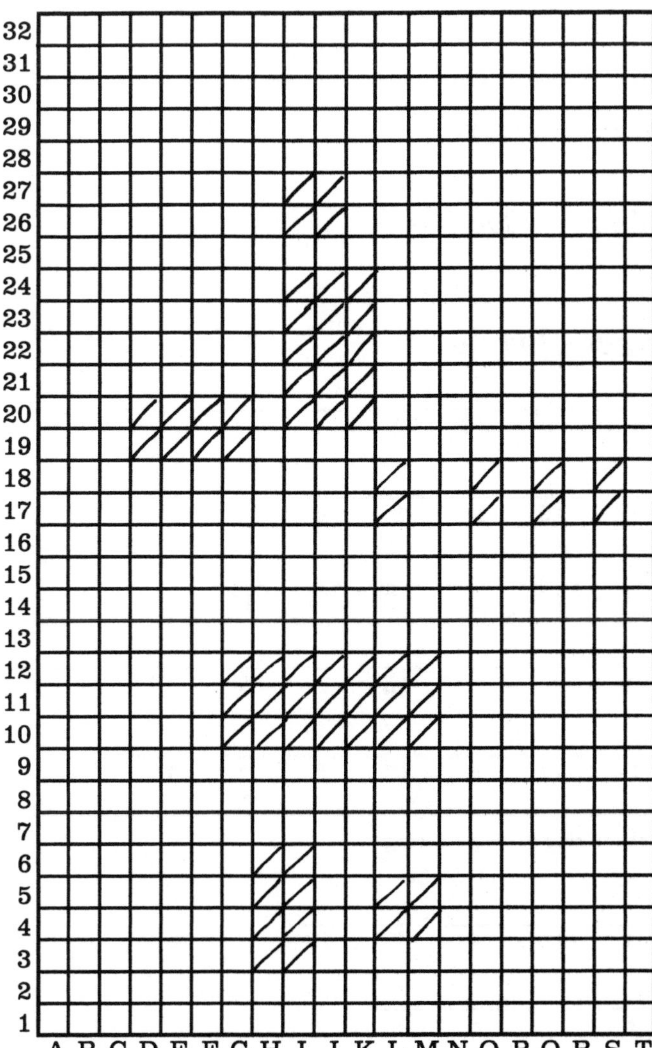

Name ______________________________

Leading Characters in Greek Mythology

Follow the directions below. Use the letters you find to complete the Greco-Puzzle.

_____ 1. Write the fifth letter of *tragedy*.
_____ 2. Use the fourth to the last consonant in *Trojan War*.
_____ 3. Use the second consonant in *Sophocles*.
_____ 4. Use the second syllable's vowel in *Mercury*.
_____ 5. Use the consonant that appears twice in *Apollo*.
_____ 6. Use the vowel of the third syllable in *Iliad*.
_____ 7. Look at the third letter of *Zeus* and count back two letters in the alphabet.
_____ 8. Use the fourth vowel in *Helen of Troy*.
_____ 9. For *Kronos* write the letter that lies between the two vowels.
_____ 10. Look at the seventh letter of *Classical*. Write the letter that follows it in the alphabet.
_____ 11. Use the fifth letter of *labyrinth*.
_____ 12. Take the letter that preceeds the second vowel in *Artemis*.
_____ 13. Use the letter that appears three times in *Ulysses*.
_____ 14. Use the second vowel in *Menelaus*.
_____ 15. Take the second letter of the 2nd syllable of *Orpheus*.
_____ 16. Use the center letter in *Homer*.
_____ 17. Use the second consonant of the first syllable in *Bacchus*.
_____ 18. Use the the last letter of *Medea*.

Greco-Puzzle

the killer of the Minotaur
___ ___ ___ ___ ___ ___ ___
12 15 1 13 1 4 7

the goddess of wisdom, war, and peace
___ ___ ___ ___ ___ ___
18 12 15 14 9 6

the goddess of grain
___ ___ ___ ___ ___ ___ ___
10 1 16 1 12 14 11

the god of craftsmen
___ ___ ___ ___ ___ ___ ___ ___ ___ ___
15 1 3 15 18 14 7 12 4 13

a hero renown for strength
___ ___ ___ ___ ___ ___ ___ ___
15 14 11 6 17 5 1 13

the Titan who holds up the sky
___ ___ ___ ___ ___
18 12 5 6 13

the snake-haired monster
___ ___ ___ ___ ___ ___
16 1 10 4 7 18

the leader of the Argonauts
___ ___ ___ ___ ___
2 6 7 8 9

Name ____________________

Proverb Problem

Decode the proverb at the page bottom by reading the clues and matching the letters to the spaces.

Clues

____ II-3 Write the consonant that is three letters before the fifth vowel in the alphabet.

____ III-4 Write the letter that follows your answer to II-1.

____ III-6 Write the fourth letter from the end of the alphabet.

____ I-4 This letter is the eighth after I.

____ II-5 This consonant is four before the fourth vowel.

____ I-6 Write the vowel you hear in plane.

____ II-2 Write the letter that comes half-way between S and W.

____ I-3 Skipping all vowels, this is the tenth after H.

____ III-5 This is two vowels before X.

____ I-1 If you count every other letter after B, this is the sixth letter.

____ III-2 This is the fifth letter after the fourteenth letter.

____ II-6 If the alphabet were numbered 1 to 26, this letter would be the answer to 98 divided by 14 minus 4.

____ I-5 Write the letter that immediately precedes your answer to III-1.

____ III-3 This letter follows the fourth consonant by 6 letters.

____ I-2 Counting backward from J, this is the sixth consonant.

____ III-1 Skipping letters D through F, this would be the sixth letter.

____ II-1 Write the thirteenth consonant before T.

____ II-4 Write the letter that is half-way between your answers to III-5 and III-1.

Write the correct letter on each line to read the saying.

I-6   I-4 II-2 III-1 II-6 II-5   I-1 III-1 II-6 II-5 III-4 II-4

III-1 III-2   I-2 III-4 I-3 I-3 III-4 II-3   I-3 I-5 I-6 I-1

I-6   III-2 III-3 III-5 III-6   II-1 III-5 III-3 II-4 I-6 II-3

Name ______________________

You're the Eyewitness

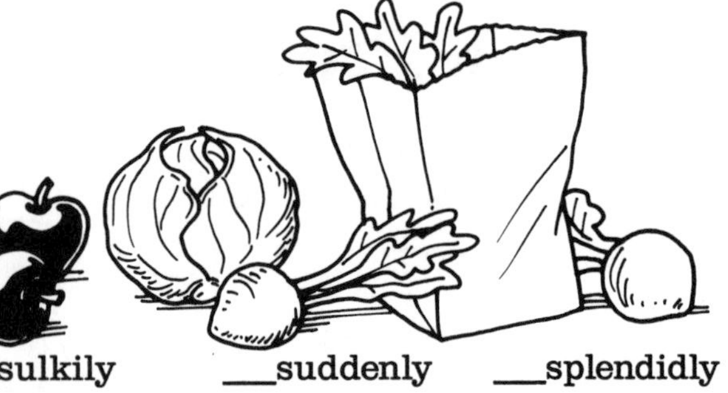

Number 1–6 to alphabetize the words on each line. Then write each fourth alphabetically ordered word on the corresponding lines below.

A.	___swiftly	___softly	___sturdily	___sulkily	___suddenly	___splendidly
B.	___backsaw	___biscuit	___bandit	___babushka	___blow	___babble
C.	___clout	___climb	___cloth	___codfish	___clench	___class
D.	___by	___bus	___buy	___bygone	___byte	___but
E.	___skid	___sound	___soot	___speedy	___sloppy	___soup
F.	___echoes	___eagerly	___east	___eats	___earshot	___edifies
G.	___aisle	___aimlessness	___agouti	___Alaska	___alabaster	___airway
H.	___proceed	___proclaim	___proffer	___program	___prison	___produce
I.	___discovers	___disappoints	___disinfects	___discerns	___directs	___discusses
J.	___shear	___shop	___sieve	___semaphore	___shorten	___sequel
K.	___heat	___hauberk	___hartebeest	___head	___hedgehog	___ham
L.	___rushes	___roosts	___rows	___rustles	___rumbles	___rusts
M.	___tourist	___thirst	___tissue	___terrace	___ticking	___thyme
N.	___oatmeal	___outrigger	___outrageous	___outrank	___occasion	___obscure
O.	___squarely	___stiffly	___stably	___stealthily	___splendidly	___steeply
P.	___rakes	___radishes	___rabbits	___radios	___racks	___rattraps
Q.	___sledge	___slaughter	___slip	___slush	___slack	___sleep
R.	___secretly	___segment	___ security	___seawater	___seignior	___scum

The one-eyed **(B)** ____________ slips through the broken window of the empty **(J)** ______________ . Not a **(E)** ______________ can be heard but the **(M)**____________________ of a grandfather clock. **(O)** ____________________ the villain slithers down **(G)** ____________ seven where the fresh **(H)** ____________________ is displayed. Into a **(C)**______________ bag go four apples, a bag of **(P)** ____________________ , and a **(K)** ______________ of lettuce. **(A)** ________________ an alarm rings out, and **(R)** ____________________ storms in! The thief **(L)** ______________ into the women's bathroom, **(F)** ______________ all the produce, and feigns **(Q)** ________________ in the last stall. When security **(I)** ____________________ her, they are surprised **(D)** ________ the calm on the face of the **(N)** ______________________________ chimpanzee.

Name ______________________________

48 Contiguous States

Use the map and a political map of the United States to answer the following questions. You may use a ruler and lightly pencil marks on the map on this page. Erase as you go.

1. Lightly draw a line segment from the letter D to the letter H. How many states does this segment go through? ____________________
2. Imagine a segment from letter A to letter G. What states beginning with the letters H through N does it go through? ______________________________
3. Letter D is on the border of which states? ______________________________
4. Imagine a line passing through letters C and F. What states does it pass through? ______________________________ ______________________________
5. Imagine a line passing through letters D and B. What states does the line pass through? ______________________________
6. Imagine a quadrilateral bounded by letters D–G–I–C and D. What states ending in a consonant lie partially within this quadrilateral? ______________________________ ______________________________
7. How many states lie entirely outside this same quadrilateral? ____________________

Name ______________________

Sounds of the Game

Follow the directions to make mutations of these words.

Workspace	Directions
UMPIRE YELLS	
______________	add a B after PI and join all letters
______________	change all Es to As. Drop the final S
______________	remove the U and I
______________	drop an L
______________	reverse the RA
______________	move the last three letters to the front
______________	take out the M and R
______________	put a space between P and B
______________	place two Ls at the end
______________	reverse the first four letters
POPCORN	
______________	move the first three letters to the end
______________	reverse the third and fourth letters
______________	change the R to S
______________	drop the final P
______________	add an E before the last two letters
______________	reverse the S and C
______________	change the N to T and the C to U
______________	reverse the letters
______________	add ANO between the adjacent vowels
______________	drop all Os

Challenge: Now create your own drill. It must be five lines or more. End with the name BABE RUTH.

Name ______________________

Money Talks

Solve this rebus to gain wisdom.

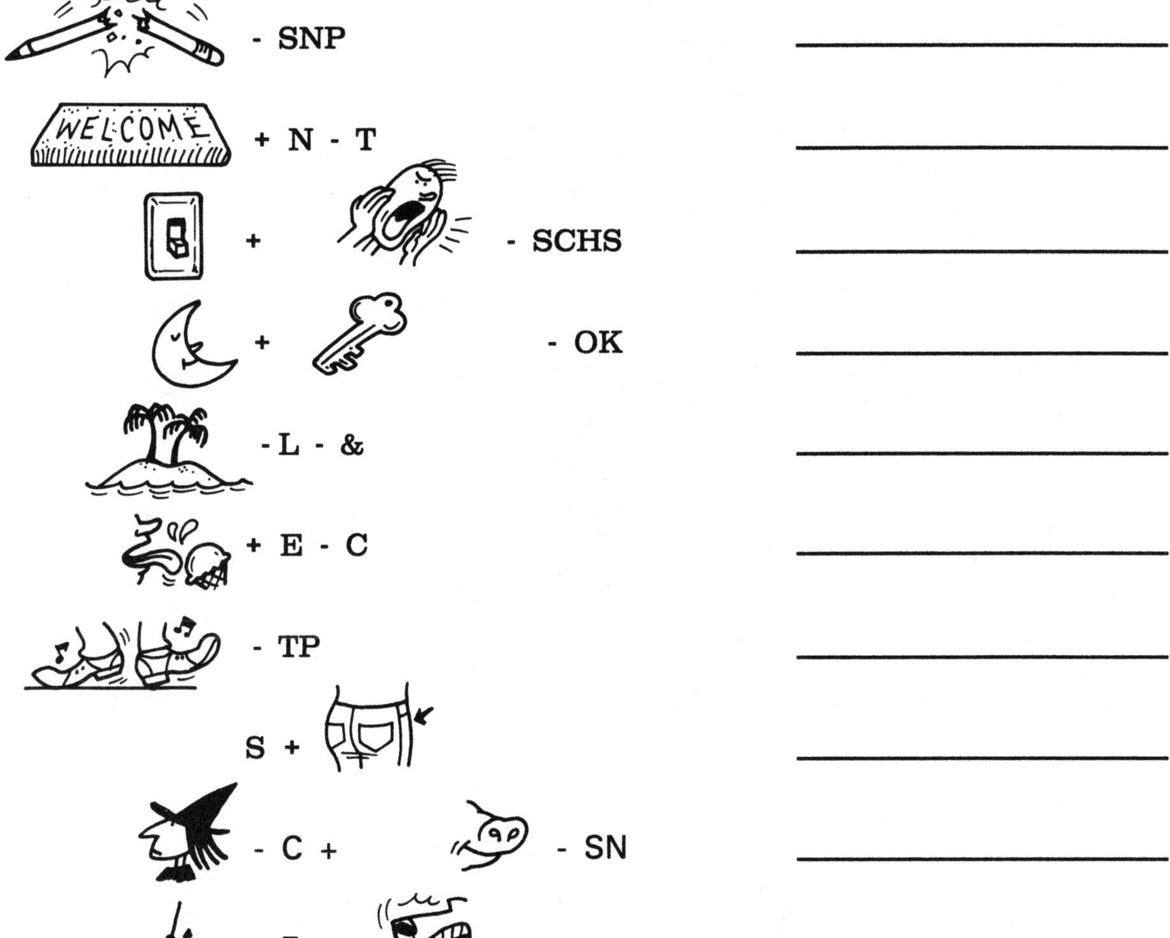

- N

Solve these rebuses. They have something in common.

1. - T + - K + 2000 lbs. ______________
2. - AI + + - EF ______________
3. - IN + ______________
4. L + - K + + 2nd I2L ______________

Name ______________________

Pathfinder Test #2

Read each direction carefully and do exactly what it says.

1. Keep track of how many minutes it takes you to complete this test. Starting Time: __________
2. Starting with the second word, cross out every other word in the following sentence:
   You should never have played hand ball poorly against the Pink Panther's Floyd Randolph.
3. Write your full name across the top of the back of this page.
4. Tear off a one-inch square from the bottom right corner of this page. Save it.
5. Name three country capitals that begin with the letter B. Write these along the left edge of this paper.
6. Write your address backwards under your name.
7. Count backward from 10 to 1 aloud; then stand up and say the name of the Vice President of the U.S. or the Prime Minister of Canada or both.
8. Write your initials on the one-inch square and hand it to your teacher saying, "My! This sure is paper!"
9. Add up the number of fingers and toes, ears, and noses you see in the room. __________
10. Circle all of the vowels in #6.
11. Write the palindrome partner of 1,375,731. ______________________
12. Smile serenely at your classmates until someone smiles at you. Write his or her name here. ______________________
13. On the back of this paper, write a four-line nursery rhyme of your choice, but change the fourth line to something original.
14. Write five prepositions in reverse alphabetical order. ______________________
15. Circle six words taken from different sentences on this page to form a sentence. Write your sentence here. ______________________
16. Now circle all numbers on this page containing the digits 2 and 3.
17. Write how many minutes it took to complete this test. ______________________
18. Place your completed paper on the teacher's desk, return to your seat, and close your eyes for two minutes.

Answer Key

for

Reading Skills

Grades 7 – 8

---

context clues

Name ______________________

What's This?

Underline the meaning that best matches the word in bold print. You may use a dictionary.

1. Steven overheard Mary denouncing her math partner. In this sentence **denouncing** means . . .
   a. calling b. calculating c. criticizing d. growing
2. Moles and anteaters are fossorial animals. In this sentence **fossorial** means . . .
   a. humane b. dead c. winged d. digging
3. With her keen dagger, Lady Marguerite sliced the pear atwain. In this sentence **atwain** means . . .
   a. quickly b. into the woods c. in two d. in a bold manner
4. After the soccer match, a horrid fracas arose between the hot-tempered teams. In this sentence **fracas** means . . .
   a. protrusion b. fight c. loud noise d. monstrous sight
5. My uncle was indubitably at fault when his truck slammed into the telephone pole. In this sentence **indubitably** means . . .
   a. mightily b. yesterday c. expansively d. unquestionably
6. The sailors hoisted their ship to grave its bottom. In this sentence **grave** means . . .
   a. clean b. examine c. destroy d. weep
7. The Greek youth held high the lampad to steal away from her Persian captors. In this sentence **lampad** means . . .
   a. flowers b. onions c. insignia d. candlestick
8. While hiking through the wilderness, Fiona lost her boots in the slough. In this sentence **slough** means . . .
   a. bog b. station c. backpack d. forest floor
9. To his horror Ronald discovered that his meat patties were not vendible. In this sentence **vendible** means . . .
   a. fresh b. odorous c. marketable d. visible
10. Ol' Tex dug his rowel into the mare's flank, speeding her into action. In this sentence **rowel** means . . .
    a. treasure b. revolver c. shovel d. spur
11. Tony sat uncomfortably in her grandma's parlor listening to the grownups prate about nothing in particular. In this sentence **prate** means . . .
    a. chew b. sleep c. chatter d. expand

Challenge: Create your own sentence challenges using the words **maraca** and **fetter**.

Page 1

---

context clues

Name ______________________

Set the Limits

These groups of attributes set limits on what is described. Read the attributes and identify the noun they describe.

Noun	Attributes		
Niagara Falls	tourism horseshoe world-famous New York	international hydroelectric Ontario	1,000 cubic feet of water per second
Venice	118 islands gondola Adriatic	two letter Es city architecture St. Mark's Square	canals Italy
ferret	slim black-footed scent glands	polecat endangered mammalian	masked six letters
Iron Age	history period before 500 B.C. smelting	coin use stronger than bronze two words	Asia Minor vowels a, e, i, o
hurricane	whirling eye Gulf of Mexico	strong wind counterclockwise alphabetical names	over 75 MPH two Rs
Robin Hood	legendary arrow rebel	sheriff for poor medieval	people's hero Sherwood Forest
kite	wind paper Franklin	box string also bird	aircraft bowed hover
heart	four chambers rhythm two pumps	fist-sized oxygen carrier 2,000 gallons per day	pear-shaped aorta
Taj Mahal	chosen one Indian by 1649	architecture 20,000 workmen Yamuna River	three letter As mausoleum marble

Page 2

---

context clues

Name ______________________

Mexico Match-Up

Fill in the blanks with words from the list below.

When U.S. and Canadian Americans think of Mexico, they may imagine hot desert sands and cacti. You will find these places if you look, but Mexico is much more! Many spectacular animals, like the jaguar and gray whale are found in and around Mexico. Mexico's plants are also noteworthy. The *ahuehuete* is a huge tree with a gigantic trunk. A popular Christmas plant, the poinsettia, is native to Mexico.

Many Mexican people live much as other Americans. Differences in dress may be found, however, especially in rural areas. Rural women may be seen wearing shawls called *rebozos* to cover their heads. In many regions the large meal, called the *la comida*, is served in the early afternoon. After this meal many businesses and schools close down for siestas and reopen when the day has cooled. Many markets can be found in the cities and villages. *El supermercado* is a large market with higher prices but more variety of goods than the smaller stores. Mexico has many poor. In some homes, straw mats called *petates* may serve as beds.

Mexico's history reaches back thousands of years. It includes its ancient past as well as the arrival of Europeans. Mexico's October 12 celebration, *Dia de lat Raza*, honors the mixing of cultures. Many of Mexico's festivals come from the Christian tradition. In the *Posada* the people re-enact Mary and Joseph's search for lodging in Bethlehem. Yet, like our Halloween, some celebrations recall a more distant, pagan past. The Mexican people have a festival in which they await the souls of the dead, eating sweets shaped as such things as coffins and skeletons.

The most popular sport in Mexico is neither the bullfight nor baseball. Rather, *futbol*, or soccer, claims the most spectators. Also popular attractions are the *charriadas*, or rodeos, whose excellent riders are called *charros*. If you visit Mexico, don't miss the *los voladores*, or flying men. In this ancient ceremonial dance, one man plays an instrument while dancing on a pole's platform and four others, dressed like birds, tie ropes around their legs and jump into the air, falling in wide circles around the pole. The rope is let out slowly as they sail downward.

Word List

afternoon	called	goods	meal	pole	shawls	think
ancient	celebration	honors	men	popular	siestas	thousands
areas	cover	huge	Mexican	prices	skeletons	tradition
around	dance	instrument	most	recall	slowly	trunk
baseball	day	jaguar		rodeo	soccer	villages
beds	dress	look	plants	sands	souls	visit
businesses	Europeans	market	poinsettia	search		

Page 3

Use with page 5. context clues

Name ____________

Replacement Parts

Replace the words in bold print with suitable words from the list at the bottom of page 5. Then write a great title for this story.

Title: _Titles will vary._

One Tuesday morning Phil Abbot and his **friends** _cronies_ Tanya and Adam **decided** _elected_ to scuba dive off the **finger of land** _peninsula_ jutting into Blakeston Bay. They **prepared** _packed_ a **big** _substantial_ lunch since they planned to be gone all day. Because none of them **had** _owned_ a boat, they **rented the services of** _hired_ Captain "Mad Dog" O'Keeley, a **respectable** _reputable_ **sailor** _mariner_ and ship captain.

The day began well. The water was **calm** _undisturbed_, and the **small** _diminutive_ boat **quickly moved** _skimmed_ over the waters to a **place** _site_ **known as** _called_ Bad Carl's Caverns because of the **dramatic** _striking_ underwater hollows. Adam had never **before** _previously_ explored underwater, but Tanya and Phil were both **extremely experienced** _experts_. They entered the water about 10:00 a.m. The **warm** _tepid_ water was **filled** _teeming_ with fish of many colors and **sizes** _dimensions_. Each diver went his or her own way. Phil **followed** _trailed_ a **group** _school_ of fish into a cave but **stopped** _halted_ when his light grew **dim** _faint_ and the cave **grew smaller** _narrowed_. Tanya **looked at** _examined_ the growths of coral along the ocean **shelf** _ledge_. The ocean floor was rugged with **cliffs** _crags_ and **canyons** _chasms_ like a moonscape. Tanya **took** _snapped_ pictures of the many coral formations and the **splendid collection** _array_ of colors they **showed** _exhibited_.

Neither Tanya nor Phil **paid attention to** _observed_ where Adam had gone. They assumed he was carefully following them since he was a **newcomer** _novice_ to the world **under the ocean** _undersea_. Only when they returned to the **boat** _craft_ did they realize that Adam was missing. When they **asked** _questioned_ Captain Mad Dog, he **just** _merely_ shrugged his shoulders. "You jumped in so fast, I noticed nothing," he **said indistinctly** _muttered_ as he **pulled out** _extracted_ a **bag** _pouch_ of tobacco for his curve-stemmed **pipe** _meerschaum_. He continued, "Maybe you should look for him. He must be below still."

So, **putting on** _attaching_ fresh air tanks, Tanya and Phil **went back** _returned_ to the **green** _emerald_ waters. Swimming **as partners** _together_, they covered a large territory. They **beamed** _shone_ Tanya's **light** _torch_ in many of the **caves** _holes_. Just as they were beginning to **lose hope** _despair_, Phil saw a light's **flash** _gleam_ emitting from a small

Page 4

Use with page 4. context clues

Name ____________

Replacement Parts (Continued)

opening _cavity_ they had **missed** _omitted_. They **swam into** _entered_ the cave.

Deep within the cave's shadows was Adam. His left leg was **caught** _pinned_ between two **rocks** _boulders_, but **other than** _beyond_ that he seemed all right. Tanya **used hand motions** _gestured_ asking him what had **happened** _transpired_, but Adam's movements suddenly became so **jerky** _spasmatic_, neither could **make out** _understand_ his meaning. Then Phil noticed his air gauge. Adam was **out of air** _suffocating_! Tanya **ripped out** _removed_ her mouthpiece and shared her air with Adam while Phil **struggled** _wrestled_ with the rocks gripping Adam's leg. He worked **slowly** _deliberately_, careful to avoid hurting Adam's leg until **at last** _finally_ Phil was able to **move** _shift_ the smaller rock and **free** _liberate_ him.

The three cautiously **made their way** _advanced_ to the surface. Both Phil and Tanya helped Adam who **seemed** _appeared_ **slow** _lethargic_. When they reached the boat, Phil **hopped on** _boarded_ first. Then he and Tanya pulled and pushed Adam up and into the craft.

Tanya asked, "Where is Captain O'Keeley? Why didn't he **help** _aid_ us?"

Phil **looked around** _scanned_ the vessel quickly. The captain and their **food** _dinner_ had both **disappeared** _vanished_. Adam lay **still** _motionless_ on the **floor** _deck_ . . .

Word List

advanced	despair	hired	peninsula	spasmatic
aid	dimensions	holes	pinned	striking
appeared	diminutive	ledge	pouch	substantial
array of	dinner	lethargic	previously	suffocating
attaching	elected	liberate	questioned	teeming
beyond	emerald	mariner	removed	tepid
boarded	entered	meerschaum	reputable	together
boulders	examined	merely	returned	torch
called	exhibited	motionless	scanned	trailed
cavity	experts	muttered	school	transpired
chasms	extracted	narrowed	shift	undersea
craft	faint	novice	shone	understand
crags	finally	observed	site	undisturbed
cronies	gestured	omitted	skimmed	vanished
deck	gleam	owned	snapped	wrestled
deliberately	halted	packed		

Challenge: Write an ending to the story.

Page 5

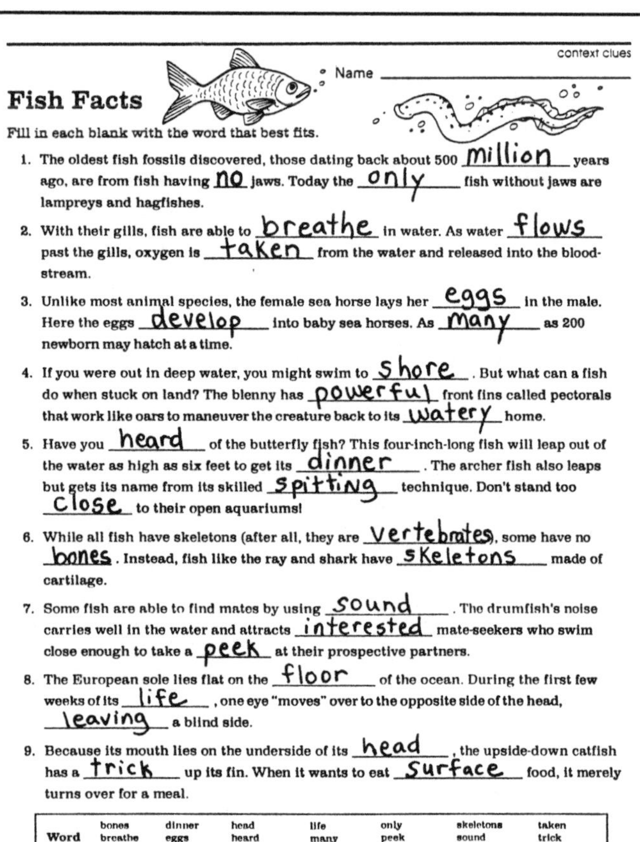

context clues

Name ____________

Fish Facts

Fill in each blank with the word that best fits.

1. The oldest fish fossils discovered, those dating back about 500 _million_ years ago, are from fish having _no_ jaws. Today the _only_ fish without jaws are lampreys and hagfishes.
2. With their gills, fish are able to _breathe_ in water. As water _flows_ past the gills, oxygen is _taken_ from the water and released into the bloodstream.
3. Unlike most animal species, the female sea horse lays her _eggs_ in the male. Here the eggs _develop_ into baby sea horses. As _many_ as 200 newborn may hatch at a time.
4. If you were out in deep water, you might swim to _shore_. But what can a fish do when stuck on land? The blenny has _powerful_ front fins called pectorals that work like oars to maneuver the creature back to its _watery_ home.
5. Have you _heard_ of the butterfly fish? This four-inch-long fish will leap out of the water as high as six feet to get its _dinner_. The archer fish also leaps but gets its name from its skilled _spitting_ technique. Don't stand too _close_ to their open aquariums!
6. While all fish have skeletons (after all, they are _vertebrates_), some have no _bones_. Instead, fish like the ray and shark have _skeletons_ made of cartilage.
7. Some fish are able to find mates by using _sound_. The drumfish's noise carries well in the water and attracts _interested_ mate-seekers who swim close enough to take a _peek_ at their prospective partners.
8. The European sole lies flat on the _floor_ of the ocean. During the first few weeks of its _life_, one eye "moves" over to the opposite side of the head, _leaving_ a blind side.
9. Because its mouth lies on the underside of its _head_, the upside-down catfish has a _trick_ up its fin. When it wants to eat _surface_ food, it merely turns over for a meal.

Word List						
bones	dinner	head	life	only	skeletons	taken
breathe	eggs	heard	many	peek	sound	trick
close	floor	interested	million	powerful	spitting	vertebrates
develop	flows	leaving	no	shore	surface	watery

Page 6

context clues

Name ____________

Choices

Circle the word that replaces the word in bold print. Use a dictionary only if you must.

1. At the edge of the garden grew a tall **heliotrope** pointing to the sky.
   a. tower b. pole **(c. flower)** d. hedge
2. The servant poured water from the **ewer** into a bowl.
   (a. pitcher) b. pond c. pursued d. receded
3. As the tides **ebbed**, the marine life in the tidal pool caught Jon's eye.
   a. flowed b. washed c. pursued **(d. receded)**
4. The **infamy** of the traitor filled our hearts with loathing.
   a. face b. law c. movement **(d. wickedness)**
5. The young woman's **mantilla** bordered her face like a frame.
   a. hat **(b. scarf)** c. personality d. collar
6. We were unaware of the **reptant** beast until it reached our food supply.
   a. sleeping b. four-legged **(c. creeping)** d. repulsive
7. The boy was met with unabashed stares in this **tepid** welcome.
   a. visible **(b. unenthusiastic)** c. evil d. strange
8. His face was as **hispid** as the back of a porcupine.
   (a. bristled) b. sharp c. round d. brown
9. The beautiful child added the candlestick to her **congeries** of knickknacks.
   a. calculation b. superlatives **(c. pile)** d. bakery
10. The collector examined the **gerah**.
    a. merchant b. crumb c. steal **(d. coin)**
11. Three eggs rested in the **nide** we discovered in the thicket.
    a. dove **(b. nest)** c. woodpile d. grass
12. To be sure, the visit by the village's hero caused quite a **shindy**.
    (a. commotion) b. sadness c. sales d. bit
13. Above our heads was the frightful flapping and shrieking of a **wyvern**.
    a. penguin **(b. dragon)** c. infant d. angel
14. Aye, the poor bloke's a most **gormless** fellow.
    a. harmless b. dewormed c. profession **(d. slow-witted)**
15. The **dragoons** rushed against the weary enemy with loud cries.
    a. cannons **(b. mounted cavalry)** c. wind d. reptiles
16. The **jocular** fellow entertained us with his stories from his childhood.
    a. noisy b. truthful **(c. humorous)** d. sporty
17. No one told Ruth just how tasty the **babka** could be.
    (a. cake) b. root c. salt d. answer
18. No one could match Fern's **acumen** for examining all angles to a problem.
    a. despair b. vision **(c. shrewdness)** d. diligence

Page 7

main idea

Name

Short Tales

After reading each short selection, select the main idea of that paragraph.

1. **Riverboat Ramblers**

One of the river heroes of the 19th-century American frontier was Mike Fink. This legendary boatman showed his mettle early when he left home at the tender age of two days. He returned of course. Later, when his ma's ox died, Mike took its yoke upon his shoulders to clear the land. It is said that Mike could shoot the shell off a hardboiled egg and leave the white intact. Mike Fink conditioned his body by wrestling with live Rocky Mountain grizzlies until he could defeat the best of the lot.

a. Mike Fink wrestled with grizzlies.
b. Mike Fink had extraordinary talents.
c. Mike Fink was an excellent marksman.
d. As a riverman Mike Fink made his mark.

2. **An Iroquois Legend**

According to one story told by the Iroquois people, life on earth began when a "sky woman" dropped through a hole in "sky country." Her children Sapling and Flint completed life's creation in tandem. Gentle Sapling made earth's soil and plants, while Flint made rocks and hard places. Sapling shaped the fish, while Flint designed their small bones to create trouble for hungry earthlings. Sapling created rivers for travel, and Flint added the waterfalls and rapids. When Flint imagined the immovable white man named Snow, Sapling gave him the ability to walk so he could leave and allow Spring to come. For all of life, the children of the sky woman made two sides, the gentle and the challenge.

a. The sky woman began life on earth.
b. Sapling gave a spirit of gentleness.
c. Life has two sides because of Sapling and Flint.
d. We have seasons because of Flint and Sapling.

3. **A Noble Daughter**

In this Japanese tale, Tokoyo, the daughter of a samurai loyal to the emperor, endures many hardships. Her mother has left the earth and her father is banished to the Western Islands because the emperor is afflicted with evil spirits. Tokoyo is left, alone and sad. Desiring to see her father once more, Tokoyo searches for navigators to lead her to the prison islands, but none will go. Tokoyo must buy her own ship and find her way through strange waters. Along the way, she confronts a ghost ship whose haunting passengers greet Tokoyo menacingly.

a. Tokoyo faces many challenges.
b. The samurai is banished.
c. Tokoyo is a Japanese girl.
d. A ghost ship haunts the waters through which Tokoyo travels.

Page 8

main idea

Name

Go Ahead

Read the following paragraphs and underline the topic sentence in each.

1. That rat! I'll never trust Kevin again, thinks JoJo. JoJo is upset because Kevin has not shown up at the theater. The movie's about to begin. She has waited 15 minutes for that turkey. A couple of small fry are giving her weird looks. This is strange. Kevin has never done anything like this before.

2. Daryl knew just how to get his mom's permission. He rushed into the house after school. No one else had come home yet. He put his book bag away, straightened out the kitchen, and began to practice the piano. For 15 minutes he practiced—and hard too! He was working on the Chopin nocturne when his mom came through the door with a smile on her face.

3. Behind by a goal with a minute left to play, the Kicks' leading forward, Teo Lew, stole the ball from an opposing Bulldog. Immediately the Kicks surged forward. Teo passed the ball through two defensemen to Rob Jakes, who soon was boxed in by two huge backs. Rob passed it back to Toby Key, who nearly had his jersey ripped off him by an overeager, drooling Dog. The guy was a beast! Toby slicked a liner down left where Teo hopped about shamming a sprain. Teo shirked off the back and kicked a beauty just past the fingertips of the Bulldog goalie. Now this was sweet success.

4. The five-year-old girl at the mall had terror in her eyes. She stared at the clerk arranging clothes on the rack. She hurriedly scanned each aisle up and down. Then she looked through the open door of the changing room. She even peeked under the check-out clerk's counter and dropped her tootsie roll. She had lost her dad three stores ago!

Challenge: Choose one of the paragraphs above. On a separate sheet of paper write two more paragraphs to go with it. Your first paragraph should come before the chosen paragraph and the second should follow it.

Page 9

main idea

Name

Hey, What's the Big Idea?

Accept all reasonable answers.

Explain what the members of each group have in common.

areas in a house	hallway, kitchen, bathroom, den, bedroom, parlor, utility room, attic
things at a circus	face paint, wild animals, vendors, large rings, cages, peanuts, popcorn, acrobats
ways to get someone's attention	whistle, honk, wave, rap, shout, cry, snap fingers, clear throat
items in a baby's room	diaper, rattle, crib, teething ring, Barney figure, voice monitor
means of locomotion	pogo stick, roller blades, bicycle, glider, bus, train, yacht, horse
prime numbers	seven, 3, 5, 11, 13, seventeen, 2, twenty-three
capitals of countries	Bonn, Tel Aviv, Tripoli, Havana, San Jose, Moscow, Seoul, Damascus
shades of red	magenta, scarlet, crimson, rose, cerise, cherry, ruby
plumber's tools	pipe wrench, soldering gun, plunger, pipe dope, snake, Drano
parts of a ship	bow, quarters, brig, hold, stern, deck
food whose names contain the letter "l."	melon, olive, liver, blueberry, celery, lettuce, cauliflower
kinds of horses	Morgan, Percheron, Belgian, Mustang, Quarter, Lippizan, Arabian
words for "talk"	chat, converse, speak, mutter, gab, state
letters that have descenders (go below the line)	p j g q y

Page 10

main idea

Name

Lies My Mother Told Me

Imagine that you are an editor for the *Folklore Newspaper*. Write an appropriate headline for each of the following stories.

Answers will vary.

Headline: ______

1. It was a great shock to me. You know, the story of Rapunzel who was nabbed by an evil witch? Do you remember her long hair? Well, hold your britches. The scoop is that it really wasn't her own hair. No siree! It seems she and the witchy-poo had a wig business going for nigh unto five years. I always wondered how anyone could grow hair as long as that.

Headline: ______

2. Don't tell me you believed that story about the wicked wolf blowing down the houses of two of the three little pigs? That's hogwash. I mean, have you ever tried blowing down even a one-foot pile of sticks? Hard to imagine. Now *Folklore Newspaper* has heard from reliable, but anonymous, sources that the wolf purchased seven powerful electric fans. That is the only reasonable solution short of a tornado. Seriously

Headline: ______

3. Ever hear of Mattie Habler? Probably not. People over time have given her the handle Mother Hubbard. Why? Well, we don't know. We can only imagine it's because Hubbard rhymes with cupboard. After all, Mattie was no one's mother. Shoot! She was a mean-spirited, hateful hag, and she was finally kicked out of Gooseberg when she starved that poor dog. No one heard from her since. And there's no truth to her lookin' in her cupboard for dog biscuits or puppy chow with the poor pooch pawing at her feet. The dog, a long, thin St. Bernard, was kept chained in a minuscule pen out back. No love lost between those two, let me tell ya.

Headline: ______

4. Bob Hornel's kid, Jack, was one mischievous little rascal. Ol' Bob never knew quite what to do with that boy. Seems whenever I'd come over for a game of checkers, the boy would either be confined in his room for some transgression or he'd be sittin' in the kitchen corner. That Jack! He had this wonderful grin and the prettiest twinkle in his eyes. Bob could never stay angry with him for long. One time the nervy kid dipped his thumb into a freshly baked cherry pie (no plums at Christmas for him) right in front of his pa. Then he smiled and said, "I'm a good boy, I am, huh, da?" Old Bob just rolled his eyes and shook his head.

Headline: ______

5. The poor troll in the Norse tale of the billy goats really gets ripped off in that story. Here he is taking a swim in the river and just as he's pulling himself onto the bridge to dry, that pesky little goat comes prancing over. The troll is so surprised that he falls back in, breaking his brand-new flippers. Then just as he's pulling himself up the second time, the second old goat steps on his hands and back into the river he goes! As you can imagine, the sight of the third goat scared the short, bearded fellow so much he just plain gave up. He dove into the water and swam away downstream. I still have the shoes he left on the bridge. And that's the truth.

Page 11

sequencing

Name ____________

The World of Fashion

Place the following dates in order. Unless noted, dates are A.D.

Date List

1960s mini-skirts
2000 B.C. Egyptian male skirts
mid 1700s powdered wigs
1200s surcoat tunic
1815 men's trousers
1100s wimples
1970s bell-bottoms
late 1500s whalebone-framed underskirts
23000 B.C. needle invented
mid 1800s Singer sewing machine
late 1600s women's arms are partly bared!
early 1600s shoes with bow trimmings
late 1800s knickers for sports
1910 hobble skirts
late 1400s hennin and long-toed shoes
100 Roman toga
1930s women in slacks
late 1700s pompadours
1100 tailor unions formed

Date	Fashion Item/Event
23000 BC	Needle invented
2000 BC	Egyptian male skirts
100	Roman toga
1100	tailor unions formed
1100s	wimples
1200s	surcoat tunic
late 1400s	hennin and long-toed shoes
late 1500s	whalebone-framed underskirts
early 1600s	shoes with bow trimmings
late 1600s	women's arms are partly bared!
mid 1700s	powdered wigs
late 1700s	pompadours
1815	men's trousers
Mid 1800s	Singer sewing machine
late 1800s	knickers for sports
1910	hobble skirts
1930s	women in slacks
1960s	mini-skirts
1970s	bell-bottoms

Use your completed time line to finish these sentences. Write **before** or **after**.

1. Tailors unionized before bell-bottoms were popular.
2. The Singer sewing machine came after the tailor unions formed.
3. The surcoat tunic came before the powdered wig.
4. Men wore skirts before women wore trousers.
5. Women wore pompadours after the needle was invented.
6. Whalebone-framed underskirts came after the toga.
7. Bow-trimmed shoes came before the hobble skirt.

sequencing

Name ____________

Got the Time, Bud?

Read each sentence below and determine the order of the events. Write each event on the correct line.

1. Cheri could join her friends after she walked her dog.
   first: She walked her dog
   second: Cheri could join her friends
2. Even before he joined the Marines, where he later rose to the rank of captain, Tom loved to eat pasta.
   first: Tom loved to eat pasta
   second: he joined the Marines
   third: he rose to the rank of captain
3. When the sun rises, the cows will return to the pasture.
   first: the sun rises
   second: the cows will return to the pasture
4. Mary remembered that she brushed her teeth and then told Jodi a scary story.
   first: She brushed her teeth
   second: She told Jodi a scary story
   third: Mary remembered
5. The bird fell from its perch because it was weak from hunger.
   first: it was weak from hunger
   second: the bird fell from its perch
6. "I will marry you after I defeat the green aliens," promised Future Man.
   first: Future Man promised
   second: I defeat the green aliens
   third: I will marry you
7. Before she met with her agent, Gus, Goldy Pawn practiced snapping her bubblegum.
   first: Goldy Pawn practiced snapping her bubblegum.
   second: She met with her agent, Gus
8. When the snow has fallen and later melts, Clyde will learn to ride his three-wheeler.
   first: snow has fallen
   second: later (it) melts
   third: Clyde will learn to ride his three-wheeler

sequencing

Name ____________

Out of a Dream

Read the article. Then number the events in chronological order.

Martin Luther King, Junior, a black minister and civil rights leader, was born on January 15, 1929. His parents were devout Christians who raised him to respect the law but oppose the injustices around them. After his college training, Martin met Miss Coretta Scott, whom he married June 18, 1953. The following year on the first of September, he began his ministry in Montgomery, Alabama.

1955 was a whirlwind year. In November, the Kings' first child, Yolanda Denise, was born. A few days later on December 1, Rosa Parks, a black worker in Montgomery, refused to give up her bus seat to a white man and was arrested. The following day many of Montgomery's black commuters rallied to boycott the city buses in protest. As a concerned pastor and counselor to his community, Martin spoke out against the injustices done to the people.

Because Martin dared to speak out against the racist policies, his house was bombed on January 30, 1956. Many threats and troubles followed. In September of 1958 he was knifed by a deranged black woman in New York. In October of 1960 King and his companions were arrested at an Atlanta restaurant that refused to serve them. They were charged with trespassing.

Violence continued and on May 14, 1961, a white mob firebombed a bus carrying Freedom Riders. By now many church leaders had joined King to condemn racial discrimination. In April of 1963, King was arrested for protesting in Birmingham, Alabama. It was during this imprisonment that King wrote the famous Letter from Birmingham Jail. In their protest even black children were arrested for marching May 2, 1963. The following month the home of Martin's brother, A. D., was firebombed. Then on August 28, 1963, Martin Luther King, Jr., in the great March on Washington, D.C., gave his "I Have a Dream" speech.

King was pleased to be present when President L. B. Johnson signed the 1964 Civil Rights Act on July 2. Other important events in King's crusade for justice include his acceptance of the Nobel Peace Prize on December 10, 1964, the 54 mile Selma March for voting rights which began on March 6, 1965, and President Johnson's signing of the Voting Rights Act on August 6, 1965. This bill gave all Americans the right to vote.

The threat of death was never far off. On August 5, 1966, King was stoned when he marched with Chicago's blacks to protest their slum conditions. But he could not stop speaking. In protest of the Vietnam War, King spoke at the United Nations building on April 15, 1967. One year later King was assassinated in Tennessee.

5 Rosa Parks refused to give up her bus seat
15 he accepted the Nobel Peace Prize
14 President Johnson signs the Civil Rights Act of 1964
1 King is born
13 King gives the "Dream" speech in Washington, D.C.
4 Yolanda Denise is born
11 writes Letter from Birmingham Jail
20 King is killed
16 the Selma March began
3 began ministering in Montgomery
12 Birmingham children arrested
8 he is attacked by a deranged woman in New York
19 he spoke against the war in Vietnam
9 King and others are arrested in an Atlanta restaurant
2 Martin marries Coretta Scott
18 he is stoned while marching in a Chicago suburb
7 King's Montgomery home is bombed
6 Montgomery's blacks boycott the city buses
17 President Johnson signed the Voting Rights Act
10 he is arrested for protesting in Birmingham

sequencing

Name ____________

Now That's Old!

List the events in order from most ancient to most recent. Illustrate four of the events in the boxes.

Dates

525 B.C. Persians rule Egypt
300 B.C. Egyptians first use coins
30 B.C. Cleopatra's army is defeated by Rome
2600 B.C. Great Pyramid is built for Khufu
1085 B.C. Egypt divides and its power wanes
1650 B.C. horse-drawn chariots are used
2650 B.C. Zoser dies; first pyramid is built for him
3100 B.C. Kingdom of Egypt is united
1367 B.C. Akhenaten, who tries changing religion, enthroned
3000 B.C. hieroglyphics first used
332 B.C. Alexander the Great conquers Egypt
1700 B.C. Hyksos invade Egypt
2500 B.C. Ra worship becomes Egypt's official religion
670 B.C. Assyrians defeat Memphis and Thebes
500 B.C. Egyptians start to use camels for travel
1570 B.C. Hyksos are forced from Egypt

3100 B.C. Kingdom of Egypt is...
3000 B.C. hieroglyphics....
2650 B.C. Zoser dies; first...
2600 B.C. Great Pyramid....
2500 B.C. Ra worship....
1700 B.C. Hyksos invade....
1650 B.C. horse-drawn chariots...
1570 B.C. Hyksos are forced....
1367 B.C. Akhenaten, who....
1085 B.C. Egypt divides....
670 B.C. Assyrians defeat....
525 B.C. Persians rule....
500 B.C. Egyptians start....
332 B.C. Alexander the....
300 B.C. Egyptians first use....
30 B.C. Cleopatra's army...

Illustrations will vary.

Page 16

Name ______________________

Ten-Hour Madness

On a certain Friday last October, John was assigned to record the events of his amazing day. Now for your assignment. List the events below in the correct order. Then answer the questions.

The Day's Events

9:05	Police arrive. Must prove residence. File report.	4:15	Begin yesterday's homework. Good thing no school today!
7:40	Arrive at school.	7:10	Brush teeth.
3:45	Show mom ankle wound. She sees face. Run to store to buy mom new blades.	8:15	Ask school secretary to use phone. (No money for pay phone.)
6:30	Dress.	7:11	Comb hair.
8:45	Return home. Keys to locked house on bedroom dresser.	10:05	Clean ankle and apply bandage.
10:35	Rest on bed.	8:20	No answer. Start walking.
7:00	Change clothes. (Spilled oatmeal.)	10:28	Apply medicating lotion to shaving cuts.
8:25	Remember city bus. Find bus token.	9:50	Change clothes. (Spilled oatmeal again.)
8:59	Enter through window. Cut ankle.	7:25	Take city bus.
3:15	Clean glass from sink and kitchen floor.	3:12	Awaken to hear mom return home.
6:15	Wake. Take shower.	8:10	Realize no classes due to staff meeting.
10:00	Turn on TV. Turn off TV. Stupid junk! Who writes this anyway?	6:45	Prepare breakfast.
10:15	Shave. Find four whiskers!	9:25	Prepare second bowl of oatmeal. Eat.
8:30	Catch bus.	8:53	Break window over sink.

6:15	Wake. Take shower	8:59	Enter through window....
6:30	Dress.	9:05	Police arrive. Must....
6:45	Prepare breakfast	9:25	Prepare second bowl...
7:00	Change clothes. (Spilled oatmeal)	9:50	Change Clothes. (Spilled...)
7:10	Brush teeth.	10:00	Turn on TV. Turn off....
7:11	Comb hair.	10:05	Clean ankle and apply...
7:25	Take city bus.	10:15	Shave. Find four....
7:40	Arrive at school.	10:28	Apply medicating...
8:10	Realize no classes....	10:35	Rest on bed.
8:15	Ask school secretary...	3:12	Awaken to hear mom...
8:20	No answer. Start walking.	3:15	Clean glass from....
8:25	Remember city bus....	3:45	Show mom ankle....
8:30	Catch bus.	4:15	Begin yesterday's....
8:45	Return home. Keys....		
8:53	Break window over...		

1. How is your life like John's? Name three ways. Answers will vary.
2. How would you describe John? ______________________
3. If you were John's parent, how would you react to his injury and other problems this Friday? ______________________

Page 17

Name ______________________

Back to Nature

Oops! Orville's notes for his camping trip are topsy-turvy. Put them in order.

- Air out the sleeping bag the next day.
- Arrive at campground; check in with park ranger.
- Garnish with the condiments of your choice.
- Decide on a hiking trail suitable for you.
- Roll up the sleeping bag again when you finish camping.
- Soak your blistering feet (if you ignored Step C).
- Open a package of hotdogs.
- When you return to site, decide where tent will be set.
- Open the sleeping bag to check it for damage.
- Place the hotdog on a bun.
- Hike at a leisurely pace to enjoy nature with eyes and ears.
- Check a closet, drawer, or shelf to find your sleeping bag.
- Stuff the delicious food into your mouth.
- Clear the camp floor of debris and set up your tent.
- Roll up the sleeping bag, or discard and find a better one.
- Drive around the campground to find a site you like.
- Lay the sleeping bag out on tent floor. Sleep tight!
- Wear shoes and socks that give feet comfort and support.
- Roast or boil a hotdog.
- Return to camp station to register.
- First, check with park rangers for maps of hiking trails.

I. Sleeping Bag Agenda
   A. Check a closet, drawer, or shelf to find your sleeping bag.
   B. Open the sleeping bag to check it for damage.
   C. Roll up the sleeping bag, or discard and find a better one.
   D. Lay the sleeping bag out on tent floor. Sleep tight.
   E. Air out the sleeping bag the next day.
   F. Roll up the sleeping bag again when you finish camping.

II. Here's the Camp.
   A. Arrive at campground; check in with park ranger.
   B. Drive around the campground to find a site you like.
   C. Return to camp station to register.
   D. When you return to site, decide where tent will be set.
   E. Clear the camp floor of debris and set up your tent.

III. Hotdog Time!
   A. Open a package of hotdogs.
   B. Roast or boil a hotdog.
   C. Place the hotdog on a bun.
   D. Garnish with the condiments of your choice.
   E. Stuff the delicious food into your mouth.

IV. Hiking
   A. First, check with park rangers for maps of hiking trails.
   B. Decide on a hiking trail suitable for you.
   C. Wear shoes and socks that give feet comfort and support.
   D. Hike at a leisurely pace to enjoy nature with eyes....
   E. Soak your blistering feet (if you ignored Step C).

Page 18

Name ______________________

Crusade Confusion

Number the sentences in order to make paragraph for each sentence group.

2 They went on pilgrimages to Jerusalem and other places in the "Holy Land" if they could.
1 About the year A.D. 1000 many people in Europe were Christian.
3 They believed that by making these journeys, they would be forgiven by God.

4 These Turks would not allow pilgrims the same rights.
1 Already in the 600s, the Holy Land was ruled by Arabs who were of the Islamic faith.
3 In 1071 a less amiable people, the Seljuk Turks, took possession of the land around Jerusalem.
2 They permitted Christian pilgrims to worship in their land.

2 Many Europeans listened to his plea for a holy war.
4 Their success produced a new kingdom called the Outremer.
3 They met in the capital city Constantinople from which they sent armies to "recover" the land.
1 In 1095 the Roman pope decried the Turkish lords and called for war.

3 Finally, in 1291 Europe's overlords were driven out entirely.
2 However, the Muslim Turks and their Egyptian allies were able to recapture most of the Holy Land.
1 The Christian knights won many early battles in the roughly 200 years of crusades.

4 Each party often wished to get rich and expand its own lands.
1 The crusades were not merely wars fought so pilgrims could worship freely.
3 Although battles were fought by people who shared a common faith, crusaders also had different heritages and interests.
2 One might better think of them as the real estate programs of conflicting cultures.

Page 19

Name ______________________

Keep Your Eyes Open

The story below has numerous errors. Use the symbols in the key and replace/add the correct words, marks, and letters. Answers may vary.

Key

≡	capitalize	¶	new paragraph
∀ ∀	place quotations	~~word~~	delete
⊙	place period	/	make lowercase
∧	add word	⁀	close up space
∧	add comma	∨	insert apostrophe
letetrs	reverse letters	!	add exclamation mark

long ago on the iland of cyprus their lived pygmalion, a stone sculptor he was a gifted you man who's talents wer admired through out the land yet he was unhappy and owe shall lern why he despised wimen. when a female glance his weigh, he mutter and cursed His lips curled his brows joined, and his eyes squinted yet pygmalions prized sculptor was that of a maiden, a beutiful girl, a masterpeace. as time went on pygmalion become Increasingly obsessd with this sculpture each tap of his hammer each scrape of his chesel each rub of his polising cloth was an appeal for effection Pygmalion was smitten by his Creasion

How awkward this woman-hater was in love but the object of his love was stone cold pygmalion brought her boukeys of flowers he ordered bot tles of wine he scrounged for sweets and meets. He kissed her lips and helded her hand from the markets he purchased robes with whom to adorn his lady nightly he tucked her into bed as won might a cherisht treazure this poor Pilgrim came to the temple of venus to sacrifice and pray bitter tears of anquish showered down the crazed artists cheeks he prayd could not venus, the godess of love, grant me a loving wive like that evoked by my artistreg? pygmalion had little Hope that the goddess would here him when he returned home, pygmalian went to the stone as wuz his costume oh, she looked more reel, more lovely, then possible he kissed her the warmth of his lipps softened the stone which returnd his kiss he grasped her Tightly in her arms and to his amazement she embraced him just as tightle She was alive

he named her galatea and there love was blessed buy heven

proofreading

Name ____________________

The Never-Ending Story

The story below has numerous errors. Use the symbols in the key and replace/add the correct words, letters, and marks.

Key

Symbol	Meaning	Symbol	Meaning
≡	capitalize	¶	new paragraph
∨ ∨	place quotations	~~word~~	delete
⊙	place period	/	make lowercase
∧	add word	⁀‿	close up space
∧	add comma	∨	insert apostrophe
∽	reverse letters	!	add exclamation mark

in the land of tartary their once live a prince who's name was Shah Riyar, now, as a youth he had been deceive by his beautiful wife, who he beheaded in a furry. his anger was so great that he hated all women and trusted the faithfullness of none

however, a prince must have a bride. shah riyar order his vizier, or chief councilor, to search the land four young mai dens daily. each maiden he married he would behead at sun rise the following day. This way he could be sure that she would not decieve him. as you might expect, after three years the vizier have great dificulty finding new maiden's for his master. Those family's witch still had young girls hide their children Knowing the shahs mad mind

the vizier panicked if he failed to find a young woman for his master his own lives would soon be over. now this loyal councilor had two daughters what he loved dearly. The older named Sheherazade was as intelligent, And wise as her father. She new her fathers life was in jeopardy There fore she said father, please send me to shah riyar that your life may be saved. it may be that allah will be graecious and my lifes will be spared

though he could not bare the though of loosing sheherazade, the reluctant vizier finally agreed to take her to the shah. when the prince saw the beautiful girl, fell in love. Yet, as with the others, he promised himself she too would die before the night blossomed in to day. For, he thought, she is so lovely she mussed be duplicitous. when the Day's light began to fall sheherazade asked, The prince May I see my sister before i die To this he gave his permission. When Dunyazad, the younger sister, arrived, she beg sheherazade for a story. This, thought the child, may postpone the death of my sibling. shah riyar ready gave his permission. he loved stories and stay to here the tale. sheherazade, a marvelous spinner of tales, continued her narrative all night long. when the suns rising brightened the eastern, she parched a exciting part of the story here she stoped for sunrise was the time of Execution however her story had stir interest the shah he decided to spare her life/ til the story was fully tolled After a second nights telling she paused at yet another exciting passage and was gave another day's reprieve from execution And so it continue for a 1,001 nights until finally Shah riyar awaken from his madness and announced an end to his evil ways the prince and His wife lived happily for many years.

The stories sheherazade told are recorded in the *Tales from the 1001 Arabian nights.*

Page 20

proofreading

Name ____________________

Whoomp, There It Is!

Improve each sentence or paragraph by rewriting it in standard English.

Answers may vary.

1. Please raise your hand up, Charles.
   Please raise your hand, Charles.
2. As usual, I make breakfast every day.
   I make breakfast every day.
3. Carefully to climb the rocky bluff, Patsy trained for weeks.
   To climb the rocky bluff carefully, Patsy trained for weeks.
4. Hopefully my hard work will get me to rise in the business world.
   I hope my hard work will enable me to rise in the business world.
5. Licking both paws I prepared to feed the fastidious cat.
   I prepared to feed the fastidious cat who was licking both paws.
6. The proud artist stood near her statue of a white sturgeon grinning like a monkey.
   Grinning like a monkey, the proud artist stood near her statue of a white sturgeon.
7. The little boy saw his dentist looking very scared and sucking his thumb. Every year the child had his annual check-up.
   The little boy, looking very scared and sucking his thumb, saw his dentist. Every year the child had his check-up.
8. In my opinion, I feel that you are too noisy. You always are gossiping all the time and you tend to annoyingly talk with food in your mouth.
   I feel that you are too noisy. You gossip all the time and annoy me when you talk with food in your mouth.
9. To well know my dad is to fully enjoy his gift. My dad he is a super cook. His barbecued chicken is loved by us all filling the air with a delicious aroma. His baked potatoes is very excellent too.
   To know my dad well is to love his gift fully. He is a super cook. We all love his barbecued chicken which fills the air with a delicious aroma. His baked potatoes are excellent too.
10. Marching in our band the stray dog joined our ranks. It's funny how it was able to rhythmically beat its tail to our percussion's cadence. It sure liked Penny too. It was following behind her for three blocks.
    While our band marched, a stray dog joined our ranks. It is funny how the dog could beat its tail rhythmically to our percussion's cadence. It liked Penny especially. It followed her for three blocks.

Page 21

proofreading

Name ____________________

Merci

Place punctuation marks where they belong in the story below. Draw three lines under letters that should be capitalized.

that daniel is such a chump burbled betsy boisterously as the two girls strolled down the hallway

what do you mean questioned mandy meekly as she prepared herself for an attack on her main man

oh you know gushed betsy hes always talking french with the language teacher miss defleur as if he understood the language

but he does squeaked the defensive mandy hes been to marseilles and lyons

oh mandy chided betsy condescendingly those are places in ohio hes never even been to cleveland

what are you saying gasped mandy are you telling me my daniel the love of my life would lie to me he calls me his mandy candy

yuck girl and you take that from him get a life better still ask him to say something in french when you see him next oh here he comes

hi danny said Mandy

hi mandy candy my sweet thing greeted her velvet-toned daniel

say uh danny tell me how much you like me in french betsy wants to hear you Mandy said

oh said daniel with sudden caution okay um uh mon petite amie je mange un beau coup

mandy squealed see i told you he could do it daniel youre the best

wow you sure know your stuff chuckled betsy as she sauntered away laughing her head off

uh thanks i guess muttered a red-faced dan with his face hidden in his hands

Page 22

expressive language

Name ____________________

Slinging Slang

Fill the crossword with slang terms. Entries of more than one word are followed by ___ wd. Refer to the choices at the bottom of the page only if you must.

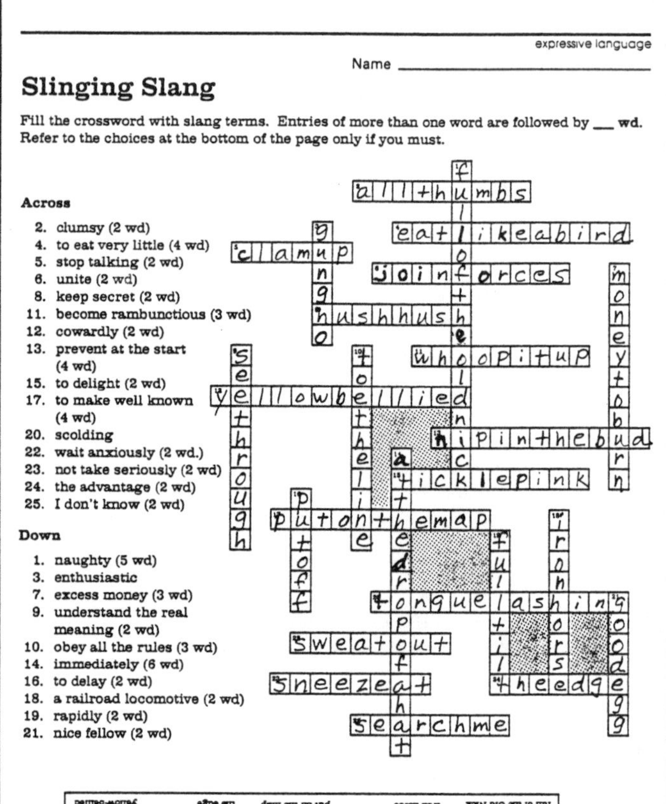

Across

2. clumsy (2 wd)
4. to eat very little (4 wd)
5. stop talking (2 wd)
6. unite (2 wd)
8. keep secret (2 wd)
11. become rambunctious (3 wd)
12. cowardly (2 wd)
13. prevent at the start (4 wd)
15. to delight (2 wd)
17. to make well known (4 wd)
20. scolding
22. wait anxiously (2 wd.)
23. not take seriously (2 wd)
24. the advantage (2 wd)
25. I don't know (2 wd)

Down

1. naughty (5 wd)
3. enthusiastic
7. excess money (3 wd)
9. understand the real meaning (2 wd)
10. obey all the rules (3 wd)
14. immediately (6 wd)
16. to delay (2 wd)
18. a railroad locomotive (2 wd)
19. rapidly (2 wd)
21. nice fellow (2 wd)

Word List

all thumbs, at the drop of a hat, clam up, eat like a bird, full of the Old Nick, full tilt, good egg, gung-ho, hush-hush, iron horse, join forces, money to burn, nip in the bud, put off, put on the map, search me, see through, sneeze at, sweat out, the edge, tickle pink, toe the line, tongue-lashing, whoop it up, yellow-bellied

Page 23

Use with page 25. | expressive language

Name

The Way We Talk

Use words from the list on page 25 to complete each idiomatic expression.

Now, I'm not one to get my dander up, but last Friday my brother Harold really took the cake. It happened out in the barn when Dad was away. Oh, I was ready to spit bullets! There was Harry, just a-layin' there in the hay mow as cool as a cucumber.

"What'cha think you're up to?" I asked, madder than a wet hen. Boy, I thought, did that ever stop him dead in his tracks. Of course, with all that hay there, Harry was as snug as a bug in a rug.

I guess I had his number, though, 'cuz he got up slow, like there was no tomorrow and mumbled, like distant thunder, somethin' about knockin' my block off. Harry can be as phony as baloney.

Yeah, I knew the score. Dad always said to put my thinking cap on when a problem done come. Lazy Harold had to learn to lift a finger and do some work. I decided to make him shake in his boots for a spell.

I said, "Harry, you look like the cat that swallowed the canary! Now, you just look me in the eye and tell me you've been workin' your fingers to the bone. Did you clean out them stalls like Dad done told you just as plain as day?"

Harold hated cat-and-mouse games, so he looked down his nose at me and said, "Just take a gander at the stalls!" I sorta sauntered off like a general inspectin' his troops.

But, sugar in Shiloh! At first blush I saw I had my goose cooked cuz there were the stalls as clean as Ma's good china b'fore Thanksgiving dinner. My twirlin' mind was at sixes and sevens. This was impossible. Meanwhile Harry was on cloud nine, smirkin' like he done catched me with my pants down.

I cried, "How did you do this, Harry? You couldn't finish this job in a month of

Page 24

Use with page 24. | expressive language

Name

The Way We Talk (Continued)

Sundays. This is somethin' else. I figger you must a-worked to set the world on fire! I guess you can really put your shoulder to the wheel when you've got a row to hoe."

Ol' Harry just burst out laughing, cackling like an old hen. Then to add insult to injury, I heard other voices hootin' and hollerin'. I looked up to see a passel of Harry's friends pointin' at me like they'd just seen their first picture show or somethin'.

They put me in my place, and I, blushin' like a new bride, slowly slunk out of the barn with my tail between my legs. The gang, just chock full of beans, danced and pranced off to the ballfield, Harry with them. It kinda put my nose out of joint.

Harry turned to me thinking, I'm sure, that here was a game two could play. He called, "Hey, Sara! Better put your hand to the plow. Dad'll have your hide if you don't finish milkin' soon!"

"Get off my back," I grumbled.

Word List

back	canary	eye	insult	passel	show
baloney	cap	fingers	joint	place	spit
beans	china	fire	lift	plain	tail
block	cloud	game	month	row	tomorrow
blush	cooked	gander	mouse	score	took
bride	cucumber	general	nose	sevens	tracks
bug	dander	hand	number	shake	up
cackling	distant	hide	pants	shoulder	wet

Page 25

expressive language

Name

I've Heard That Before!

What did Pa and Ma say when they woke us up before sunrise? Find out by completing the expressions and filling in the numbered spaces at the bottom of the page.

1. Absence m a k e s the heart grow fonder.
2. You c a n ' t take it with you.
3. Little strokes fell great o a k s.
4. Seeing is b e l i e v i n g.
5. To err is h u m a n, to forgive divine.
6. Jack of all trades, m a s t e r of none.
7. The s q u e a k y wheel gets the grease.
8. Cold hand, w a r m heart.
9. For the want of a nail, a s h o e was lost.
10. Brevity is the soul of w i t.
11. All work and no play makes Jack a d u l l boy.
12. Turn the other c h e e k.
13. Still w a t e r s run deep.
14. Home is where you h a n g your hat.
15. There is no place l i k e home.
16. Bad n e w s travels fast.
17. L a u g h before breakfast, cry before dinner.
18. It's always darkest before the d a w n.
19. Monkey s e e, monkey do.
20. East, west, h o m e ' s best.
21. Easier s a i d than done.
22. There is method in his m a d n e s s.
23. The p e n is mightier than the sword.
24. A m i s s is as good as a mile.

Make hay while the sun shines.

Page 26

expressive language

Name

A Good Time Was Had by All

Write the words in order for each cliché below. Then write a letter from the list at the bottom to match each expression with its correct meaning.

F	1. That's the cookie the crumbles way.	That's the way the cookie crumbles.
J	2. A ton like me hit bricks of it.	It hit me like a ton of bricks.
M	3. Apples do them like how you?	How do you like them apples?
E	4. She wrong up bed of the side out of the got.	She got up out of the wrong side of the bed.
H	5. A need indeed is a friend in friend.	A friend in need is a friend indeed.
S	6. Clock can't the back you turn.	You can't turn back the clock.
B	7. Apron tied he's to the strings.	He's tied to the apron strings.
L	8. Throw the bathwater baby out don't the with.	Don't throw the baby out with the bathwater.
C	9. Back give you the he'd shirt his off.	He'd give you the shirt off his back.
N	10. It's as nose as the face on your plain.	It's as plain as the nose on your face.
R	11. Packed were sardines like in we.	We were packed in like sardines.
G	12. Hard habits die old.	Old habits die hard.
D	13. Nothing is the sun there under new.	There is nothing new under the sun.
K	14. It's off my no nose skin.	It's no skin off my nose.
Q	15. The name game of that's the.	That's the name of the game.
T	16. Low you're the pole on the totem man.	You're the low man on the totem pole.
A	17. You clear I hear and loud.	I hear you loud and clear.
O	18. Don't bag the let out of the cat.	Don't let the cat out of the bag.
I	19. Wash come out in the it'll all.	It'll all come out in the wash.
P	20. It's worth it not the powder up to blow.	It's not worth the powder to blow it up.

Meanings

A. I understand.
B. He is dependent on his mother.
C. He is extremely generous.
D. Everything has happened before.
E. She is having a bad day.
F. What happens happens.
G. People don't change easily.
H. True friends help you.
I. We will find out soon.
J. It gave me a shock.
K. It's no concern of mine.
L. Do not discard the essential with the waste.
M. What do you think of that?
N. It is self-evident.
O. Keep it a secret.
P. It is of little value.
Q. That's what it's all about.
R. We were crowded.
S. You cannot return to a past state of affairs.
T. You are the last in line.

Page 27

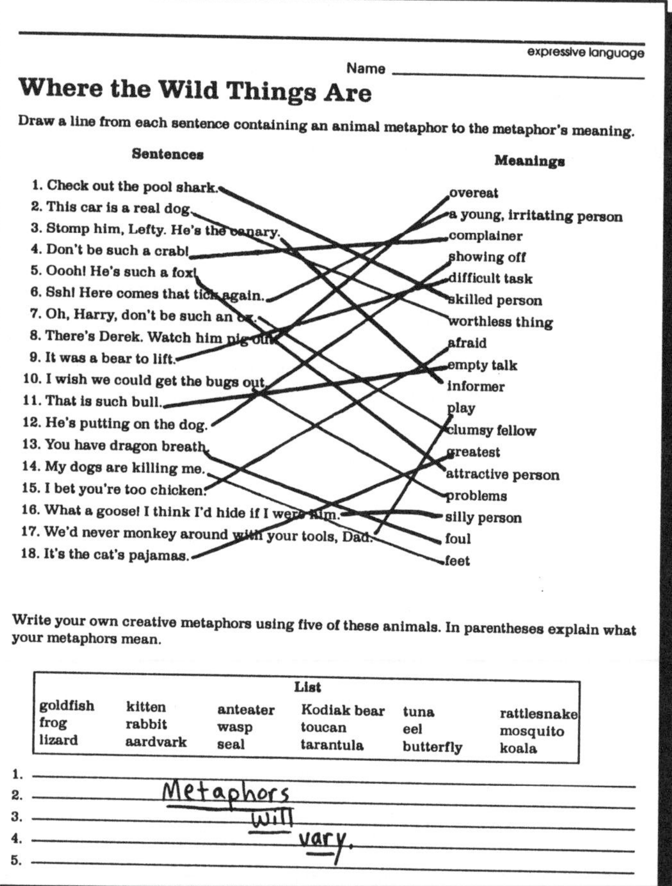

expressive language

Name ____________________

Where the Wild Things Are

Draw a line from each sentence containing an animal metaphor to the metaphor's meaning.

Sentences	Meanings
1. Check out the pool shark.	overeat
2. This car is a real dog.	a young, irritating person
3. Stomp him, Lefty. He's the canary.	complainer
4. Don't be such a crab!	showing off
5. Oooh! He's such a fox!	difficult task
6. Ssh! Here comes that tick again.	skilled person
7. Oh, Harry, don't be such an ox.	worthless thing
8. There's Derek. Watch him pig out.	afraid
9. It was a bear to lift.	empty talk
10. I wish we could get the bugs out.	informer
11. That is such bull.	play
12. He's putting on the dog.	clumsy fellow
13. You have dragon breath.	greatest
14. My dogs are killing me.	attractive person
15. I bet you're too chicken.	problems
16. What a goose! I think I'd hide if I were him.	silly person
17. We'd never monkey around with your tools, Dad.	foul
18. It's the cat's pajamas.	feet

Write your own creative metaphors using five of these animals. In parentheses explain what your metaphors mean.

List

goldfish	kitten	anteater	Kodiak bear	tuna	rattlesnake
frog	rabbit	wasp	toucan	eel	mosquito
lizard	aardvark	seal	tarantula	butterfly	koala

1. ____________________
2. Metaphors
3. will
4. vary.
5. ____________________

Page 28

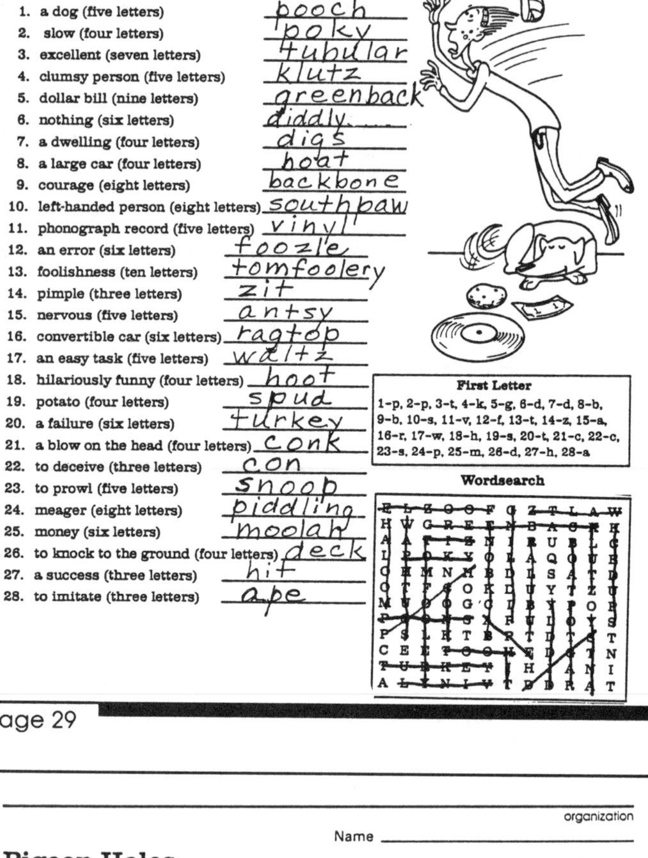

expressive language

Name ____________________

Slick Slang

Draw a line through each slang term in the wordsearch below and write it next to its meaning. The first letter of each slang term is given in the First Letter box.

Meaning	Slang Term
1. a dog (five letters)	pooch
2. slow (four letters)	poky
3. excellent (seven letters)	tubular
4. clumsy person (five letters)	klutz
5. dollar bill (nine letters)	greenback
6. nothing (six letters)	diddly
7. a dwelling (four letters)	digs
8. a large car (four letters)	boat
9. courage (eight letters)	backbone
10. left-handed person (eight letters)	southpaw
11. phonograph record (five letters)	vinyl
12. an error (six letters)	foozle
13. foolishness (ten letters)	tomfoolery
14. pimple (three letters)	zit
15. nervous (five letters)	antsy
16. convertible car (six letters)	ragtop
17. an easy task (five letters)	waltz
18. hilariously funny (four letters)	hoot
19. potato (four letters)	spud
20. a failure (six letters)	turkey
21. a blow on the head (four letters)	conk
22. to deceive (three letters)	con
23. to prowl (five letters)	snoop
24. meager (eight letters)	piddling
25. money (six letters)	moolah
26. to knock to the ground (four letters)	deck
27. a success (three letters)	hit
28. to imitate (three letters)	ape

First Letter

1-p, 2-p, 3-t, 4-k, 5-g, 6-d, 7-d, 8-b, 9-b, 10-s, 11-v, 12-f, 13-t, 14-z, 15-a, 16-r, 17-w, 18-h, 19-s, 20-t, 21-c, 22-c, 23-s, 24-p, 25-m, 26-d, 27-h, 28-a

Wordsearch

E	L	Z	O	O	F	G	Z	T	L	A	W
H	W	G	R	E	E	N	B	A	C	K	H
A	A	T	I	Z	N	I	R	U	B	L	G
L	P	O	K	Y	O	L	A	Q	O	U	E
O	H	M	N	H	B	D	L	S	A	T	D
O	T	F	S	O	K	D	U	Y	T	Z	U
M	U	O	O	G	C	I	B	Y	P	O	R
P	O	O	N	S	X	F	U	L	O	Y	S
P	S	L	H	T	B	P	T	D	T	S	T
C	E	E	T	O	O	H	E	D	G	T	N
T	U	R	K	E	Y	I	H	H	A	N	I
A	L	Y	N	I	V	T	D	B	R	A	T

Page 29

organization

Name ____________________

Come and Go

In each paragraph, one sentence does not belong. Cross it out. Then choose a closing sentence for each paragraph from the list at the page bottom and write it on the line.

1. I really did not wish to climb that tall oak tree. Sam handed me the saw, though, and gave me a push. Up I climbed, higher and higher. I was afraid to look down for fear that my head would start spinning and I would fall. ~~Seven geese flew above us this afternoon.~~
   Add: When I reached the branch that Sam wanted cut, I....
2. Last summer Mattie made plans to mow lawns for her neighbors. She hauled out the weed whacker her parents had recently purchased, a rake, and a basket for grass clippings. ~~In the corner of the garage were a brush and roller.~~ After canvassing her block, she had a list of seven weekly customers. Not bad, Mattie thought.
   Add: The exercise and money would be great bonuses.
3. Dancing would never come easily for Donald, who sat miserably waiting for today's lesson to begin. ~~Last week he played outdoors with his friends.~~ When Donald had informed his mother that he was too embarrassed to take group lessons, he had thought that would be the end of it. Instead, Mom had signed him up for private lessons . . . with Judy Minelli. Nothing could be worse. Judy was intelligent, athletic, and so beautiful that Don stuttered like a fool whenever she asked him a question.
   Add: He began to wish that he had not protested about the group lessons.
4. "Bread, milk, and sugar. Bread, milk, and sugar," Jana said under her breath as she sauntered down the aisle of the small grocery. Her mom had sent her to get a few staples to get them through the weekend. ~~Dad was in the city getting the muffler fixed.~~ So here she was at Martel's Market. Jana glanced at the cereal boxes, wishing her mom had purchased Sweet Treateos instead of that horrid Multi-Bland Granolix last week. Then it happened. Jana backed into a tower of towelettes. It was her worst nightmare.
   Add: Down came 163 packages of super-absorbent Cushy Rolls.
5. Terry groaned as he rolled over on his stomach. He was studying for two tests while lying on his unmade bed. Science was going to be a breeze because he had read up on the stuff. ~~Joel had called to tell him about a new movie.~~ Math, on the other hand, was going to be tough. Who ever heard of "n" to the fourth power?
   Add: Tonight might just be one of those sleepless stretches with....
6. Grandma called to say she was coming over in 15 minutes. Pa was takin' Ma to the hospital 'cuz the baby was coming. Well, the water just broke. And both Pa and Ma were giggling like a couple of eight-year-olds. Yeah, it's about time the little nipper showed his face. Or hers. ~~It was downright stormy outside again.~~ Beth was hoping for a sister.
   Add: Her two brothers were two too many to suit her!

Final Sentence List

The exercise and money would be great bonuses. Down came 163 packages of super-absorbent Cushy Rolls. He began to wish that he had not protested about the group lessons. Her two brothers were two too many to suit her! Tonight might just be one of those sleepless stretches with which Terry was becoming too familiar. When I reached the branch that Sam wanted cut, I stopped to catch my breath.

Page 30

organization

Name ____________________

Pigeon Holes

The words below can be divided into five categories. Write them where they belong. Then add a category and list of your own.

Word List

sow bug	meal preparation	Oprah Winfrey	Tim Allen
levitating body	comets and meteors	Barbara Walters	black holes
Ted Danson	jellyfish	red giants	Connie Chung
bull caribou	lawn mowing	redwing blackbird	witch's cauldron
Milky Way	invisible cloak	bed making	dish washing
garbage removal	quasars	walking on fire	marine mollusk
poltergeist			

Astronomy Topics	Supernatural Occurrences	TV Personalities
quasars	levitating body	Ted Danson
comets & meteors	poltergeist	Oprah Winfrey
red giants	invisible cloak	Barbara Walters
black holes	witch's cauldron	Tim Allen
Milky Way	walking on fire	Connie Chung

Unusual Pets	Home Chores	Answers
sow bug	garbage removal	will vary.
bull caribou	meal preparation	
jellyfish	lawn mowing	
redwing blackbird	bed making	
marine mollusk	dish washing	

Challenge: Now write a short story or article in which you include at least one item from each category above.

Page 31

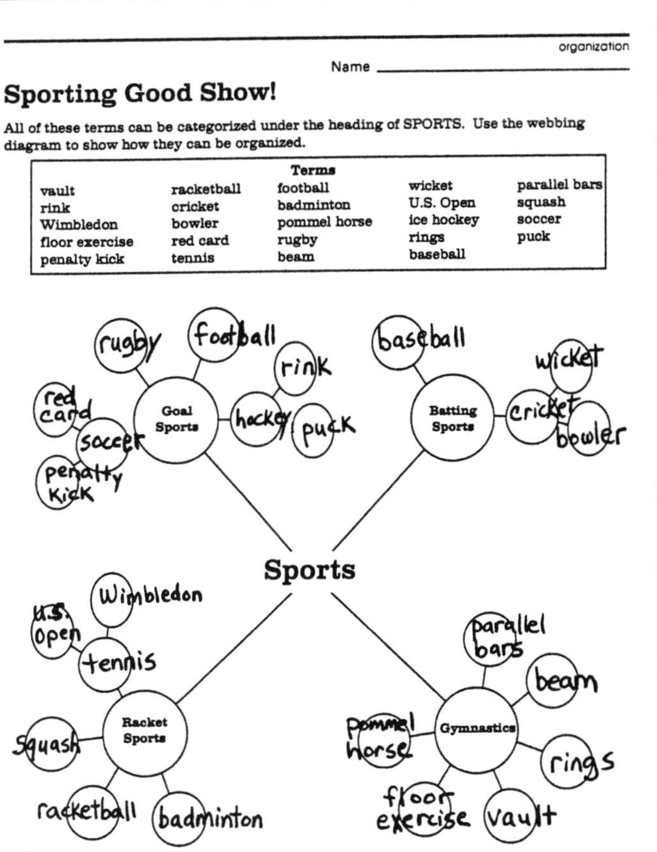

organization

Name ________________

Sporting Good Show!

All of these terms can be categorized under the heading of SPORTS. Use the webbing diagram to show how they can be organized.

Terms

vault	racketball	football	wicket	parallel bars
rink	cricket	badminton	U.S. Open	squash
Wimbledon	bowler	pommel horse	ice hockey	soccer
floor exercise	red card	rugby	rings	puck
penalty kick	tennis	beam	baseball	

Page 32

reference

Name ________________

Shootin' Blanks

Jan Nozdestov studies hard for his school examinations. Help him recall these answers for his history test. Use reference books to answer these questions.

1. In what year did Buddhism come to Japan? AD 552
2. What did the philosopher Diderot compile? the Encyclopedie
3. What does *renaissance* mean? rebirth
4. When was the Battle of Britain fought? late 1940, WWII
5. What weapons were primarily used in this battle? airplanes
6. What is the Kaaba? the square building which houses the black meteorite stone of significance to Islamic people
7. What is Richard Trevithick's claim to fame? invented first steam locomotive
8. What country did Peter the Great rule? Russia
9. What was named after him? St. Petersburg
10. For how many years was the Hundred Years war fought? 116–117 years
11. Who fought against each other in this war? England and France
12. How did the Tokugawa family influence history? They did not allow the Japanese people to leave Japan or foreign ministers to enter.
13. Name five European countries that had colonies in South America in the 17th century. Spain, Portugal, France, England, The Netherlands
14. What two families fought the War of the Roses? Lancaster and York
15. Where do the Masai live? East Africa
16. Who was the first person to reach the South Pole? Roald Amundson
17. In what year was the Red Cross Society founded? 1863 or 1864
18. Why was Liberia formed? as a country for freed American slaves
19. When did the Concorde begin transatlantic service? 1976
20. How did the "Red Flag Law" affect the development of automobiles? It ended the development of autos in England for 30 years.

Page 33

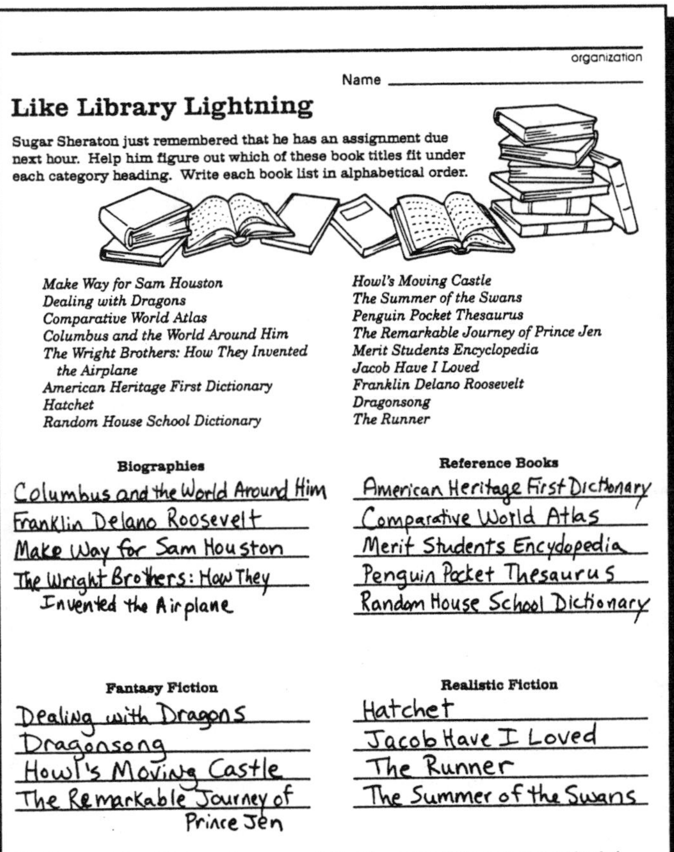

organization

Name ________________

Like Library Lightning

Sugar Sheraton just remembered that he has an assignment due next hour. Help him figure out which of these book titles fit under each category heading. Write each book list in alphabetical order.

Make Way for Sam Houston
Dealing with Dragons
Comparative World Atlas
Columbus and the World Around Him
The Wright Brothers: How They Invented the Airplane
American Heritage First Dictionary
Hatchet
Random House School Dictionary
Howl's Moving Castle
The Summer of the Swans
Penguin Pocket Thesaurus
The Remarkable Journey of Prince Jen
Merit Students Encyclopedia
Jacob Have I Loved
Franklin Delano Roosevelt
Dragonsong
The Runner

Biographies
Columbus and the World Around Him
Franklin Delano Roosevelt
Make Way for Sam Houston
The Wright Brothers: How They Invented the Airplane

Reference Books
American Heritage First Dictionary
Comparative World Atlas
Merit Students Encyclopedia
Penguin Pocket Thesaurus
Random House School Dictionary

Fantasy Fiction
Dealing with Dragons
Dragonsong
Howl's Moving Castle
The Remarkable Journey of Prince Jen

Realistic Fiction
Hatchet
Jacob Have I Loved
The Runner
The Summer of the Swans

Challenge: What? You have time to spare? Find the names of as many of these books' authors as you are able.

Page 34

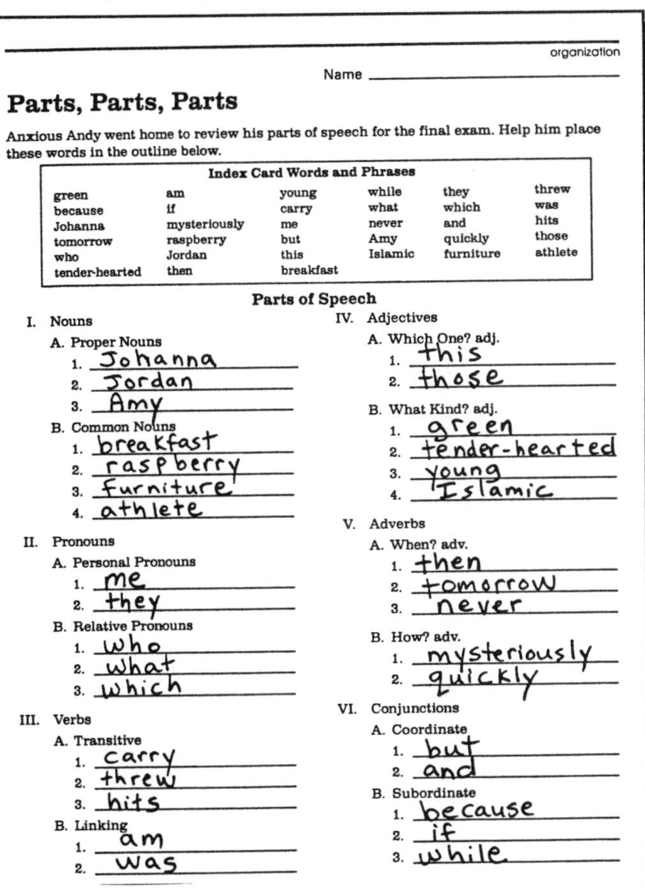

organization

Name ________________

Parts, Parts, Parts

Anxious Andy went home to review his parts of speech for the final exam. Help him place these words in the outline below.

Index Card Words and Phrases

green	am	young	while	they	threw
because	if	carry	what	which	was
Johanna	mysteriously	me	never	and	hits
tomorrow	raspberry	but	Amy	quickly	those
who	Jordan	this	Islamic	furniture	athlete
tender-hearted	then	breakfast			

Parts of Speech

I. Nouns
  A. Proper Nouns
    1. Johanna
    2. Jordan
    3. Amy
  B. Common Nouns
    1. breakfast
    2. raspberry
    3. furniture
    4. athlete

II. Pronouns
  A. Personal Pronouns
    1. me
    2. they
  B. Relative Pronouns
    1. who
    2. what
    3. which

III. Verbs
  A. Transitive
    1. carry
    2. threw
    3. hits
  B. Linking
    1. am
    2. was

IV. Adjectives
  A. Which One? adj.
    1. this
    2. those
  B. What Kind? adj.
    1. green
    2. tender-hearted
    3. young
    4. Islamic

V. Adverbs
  A. When? adv.
    1. then
    2. tomorrow
    3. never
  B. How? adv.
    1. mysteriously
    2. quickly

VI. Conjunctions
  A. Coordinate
    1. but
    2. and
  B. Subordinate
    1. because
    2. if
    3. while

Page 35

organization

Name ______________________

Break Down and Rebuild

A book may be divided into parts by locations or another division of choice. Gary Paulsen's *Hatchet* could be broken down into three sections like the diagram below shows. Take a book you have read and divide it in a similar manner on another sheet of paper.

Example: *Hatchet*

Challenge: Imagine a part of your book from the point of view of an object from it. For example, in *Hatchet* you could imagine the moose's, the plane's, or the hatchet's view. Tell a segment of your tale from the perspective of your choice object.

Page 36

reference

Name ______________________

Fraternal or Identical?

Heteronyms are words that have the same spellings but different meanings and pronunciations. The word *tear* is an example. When you *tear* the skin off an onion, your eyes might *tear*. Use a dictionary to write the phonetic spelling of each bold-faced word.

1. Please set the platter on the **buffet**. — bo͞o fā
   The waves **buffet** the beach like a boxer pounds his adversary. — buf' ət
2. Yehudi slid the **bow** across the strings. — bō
   Please set the rope in the ship's **bow**. — bou
3. The planets rotate on their **axes**. — aks' ēz
   "I have no **axes** to grind," cried Jack. — aks' ez
4. When he lost his puppy, Snoopy **moped** for days. — mōpt
   Toby delivers pizza on his **moped**. — mō' ped
5. "Please do not **refuse** my proposal," pleaded Pat. — ri fyüz'
   Sean carried the **refuse** to the incinerator. — ref' yo͞os
6. The cat destroyed the ball of yarn I had **wound**. — wound
   The dagger delivered an awful **wound**. — wo͞ond
7. The **minute** speck was found by our eagle-eyed sergeant. — mī no͞ot'
   "The **minute** I turn my back you disappear!" cried Aunt Polly. — min' it
8. May I **present** the king of comedy, Mudley Doore! — pri zent'
   This year Jan's **present** was a box of Cheerios. — prez' ənt
9. The large and dirty **sow** chased us across the pen. — sow
   In the yard we watch Mother **sow** grass seed. — sō
10. "We are **putting** this town on the map!" crowed the arrogant clerk. — po͞ot' ing
    Now **putting** on the green is Wom Tatson, the pro. — put' ting
11. "Your good looks **entrance** me," bubbled Cinderella's suitor. — in trans'
    "Just see me to the **entrance**," Cindi retorted. — en' trans
12. Yes, there is Brown Toast in the **lead** by a length! — lēd
    "Carrying all those **lead** pencils sure was hard work!" bragged the five-year-old. — led

Page 37

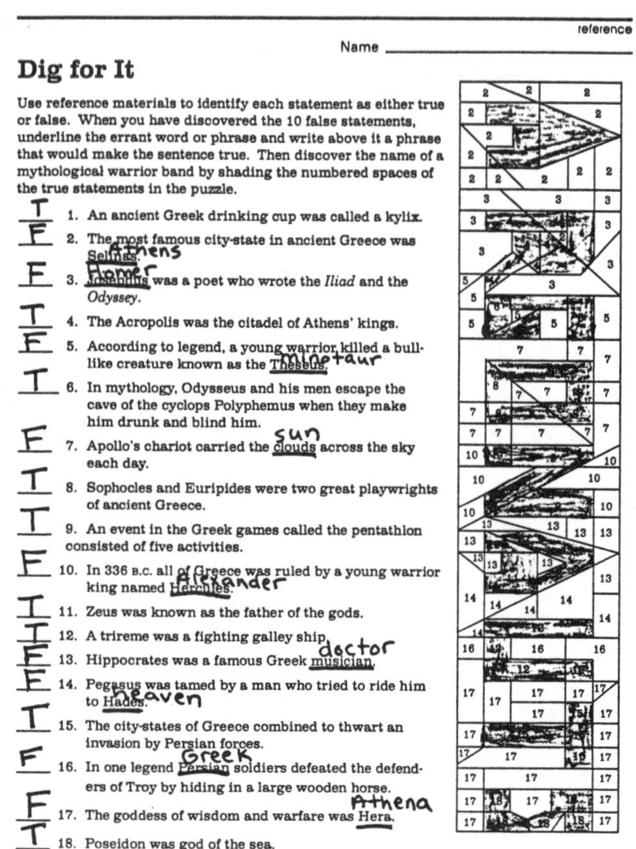

reference

Name ______________________

Dig for It

Use reference materials to identify each statement as either true or false. When you have discovered the 10 false statements, underline the errant word or phrase and write above it a phrase that would make the sentence true. Then discover the name of a mythological warrior band by shading the numbered spaces of the true statements in the puzzle.

T 1. An ancient Greek drinking cup was called a kylix.
F 2. The most famous city-state in ancient Greece was Selinus. (Athens)
F 3. Josephus was a poet who wrote the *Iliad* and the *Odyssey*. (Homer)
T 4. The Acropolis was the citadel of Athens' kings.
F 5. According to legend, a young warrior killed a bull-like creature known as the Theseus. (Minotaur)
T 6. In mythology, Odysseus and his men escape the cave of the cyclops Polyphemus when they make him drunk and blind him.
F 7. Apollo's chariot carried the clouds across the sky each day. (sun)
T 8. Sophocles and Euripides were two great playwrights of ancient Greece.
T 9. An event in the Greek games called the pentathlon consisted of five activities.
F 10. In 336 B.C. all of Greece was ruled by a young warrior king named Hercules. (Alexander)
T 11. Zeus was known as the father of the gods.
T 12. A trireme was a fighting galley ship.
F 13. Hippocrates was a famous Greek musician. (doctor)
F 14. Pegasus was tamed by a man who tried to ride him to Hades. (heaven)
T 15. The city-states of Greece combined to thwart an invasion by Persian forces.
F 16. In one legend Persian soldiers defeated the defenders of Troy by hiding in a large wooden horse. (Greek)
F 17. The goddess of wisdom and warfare was Hera. (Athena)
T 18. Poseidon was god of the sea.

Page 38

reference

Name ______________________

Yea or Nay

Look up the bold-faced words in a dictionary to answer **yes** or **no** to these questions. Write the dictionary page number for each bold-faced word above that word.

Page Numbers will Vary.

1. no — Would an **impeccable** driver **double-park**?
2. no — Is a London **bobby unkempt** in his appearance?
3. yes — Could lack of sleep be an **impediment** to your success on a written test?
4. no — Is the **omega** related to **fennel**?
5. yes — Should a court judge be **impartial** during a trial?
6. no — Is an **unabridged** dictionary shorter than one that is **abridged**?
7. no — Would you expect to see a **spectral** sight on a hot, crowded beach?
8. yes — Might an **adder** crawl through underbrush?
9. no — Would a **lord** pay tribute to his **vassal**?
10. yes — Might you associate a **pommel** with a horse?
11. yes — Would a **suffragette** fight for voting rights?
12. yes — Is the CN Tower in Toronto an **imposing** structure?
13. no — Do many pilots release **okra** during flight?
14. yes — Is a **cosseted** cat likely to get its way?
15. no — Should you expect to see a **vestibule** inside a garage?
16. no — Are **requiems** frequently heard at weddings?
17. yes — Is a summertime **bog** a likely place to find a mosquito?
18. yes — Do raindrops fall **profusely** in a rainstorm?
19. no — Is a freshly oiled roller skate at the top of a playground slide likely to remain **immobile**?
20. yes — Might you expect to hear a **clamor** when a baby awakens?

Page 39

reference

Name

Look-See

Use a dictionary and other reference materials to answer these questions.

1. Is the word **jess** a noun, verb, or adjective? noun
2. Would you use a **sari** to wash, to wear, or to cut? wear
3. How is a **pannier** like a pail? both hold things
4. What does **NOW** stand for? National Organization for Women
5. Where does **Desdemona** appear? Shakespeare's Othello
6. What kind of animal is a **harrier**? a hound dog
7. **Southampton** is a coastal town in both Long Island and . . . England
8. If you were **peckish**, would you be angry, sad, or irritable? irritable
9. Did **Octavia's** husband treat her well? no, he had her killed.
10. Who is Paul John **Flory**? an American chemist
11. From what language does **au courant** come? French
12. What is the **AAF**? Army Air Forces
13. Is **chalcedony** a mineral, an animal, or a vegetable? mineral
14. Does a **roc** fly? yes
15. What word is also spelled both **sluff** and **slue**? slough
16. What is the mineral **turquoise** made of? aluminum + copper
17. In what state will you find **Walden Pond**? Massachusetts
18. What does **Rx** mean in medicine? prescription
19. What is another word for **yelp**? possibilities: cry, bark, squeal
20. In what alphabet would one find the letter **resh**? Hebrew
21. Who is Yehudi **Menuhin**? an American violinist
22. In which two countries is **Patagonia** found? Argentina, Chile
23. With what is **Cosa Nostra** associated? the mafia
24. In which school subject is the word **forzando** most likely to be heard? music
25. Is **Onega** a mountain, a lake, a city, or a river? lake

Page 40

research

Name

An American Who's Who

Research a famous North American figure and record your findings below. You may choose a name from the following list if you wish.

Canada: Samuel de Champlain, Henry Hudson, Martin Frobisher, Louis Joliet, Jacques Marquette, Alexander Mackenzie, Thomas Douglas Selkirk, John A. Macdonald, Louis Riel, Wilfrid Laurier

U.S.A.: John Smith, William Penn, James Oglethorpe, Thomas Jefferson, Meriwether Lewis, Susan B. Anthony, Robert Fulton, Molly Pitcher, Samuel Morse, Thomas Edison, Martin Luther King, Jr., Roberto Clemente

Mexico: Hernando Cortez, Montezuma, Carlos Fuentes, Maximilian, Frida Kahlo, Antonio López de Santa Anna, Francisco "Pancho" Villa, Emiliano Zapata

Full Name: Answers will vary.	Date of Birth Date of Death
Where This Person Lived and Worked	Greatest Achievements
Source(s) of Information	
Other Details from This Person's Life	Illustration

Challenge: Make a time line of this person's life, including 6 to 10 items.

Page 41

research

Name

Look It Up

Use a dictionary to answer these questions. Answers will vary.

1. Turn to page 47. Name the first city that appears on or after this page. ______
2. Which country is found nearest page 127 in your dictionary? ______
3. Name the first language listed in your dictionary. ______
4. What is the name of the last famous person found in your dictionary? ______

Use an atlas to find the name of the country where each of the following places is found. Include the map page number where you find the city.

Answers will vary.

City	Country	Page #
Berat	Albania	
Cape Town	South Africa	
Guayaquil	Ecuador	
Henon	China	
Ipoh	Malaysia	
Keelung	Taiwan	
Göteborg	Sweden	
Valencia	Spain	
Odessa	Ukraine	
Madras	India	
Walvis Bay	Namibia	
Tortuga	Haiti	
Sorocaba	Brazil	
Resht	Iran	
Omdurman	Sudan	

Find cities that start with each of these letters:

W ______
O ______
R ______
L ______
D ______

Answers will vary.

Page 42

research

Name

The Date's Right!

In each statement below, the date is right, but one word is wrong. Underline that word and write a replacement to correct the sentence.

1. On December 7, 1989, the Lithuanian parliament abolished the monopoly of power the Republican Party had held since 1940. Communist
2. On February 27, 1844, the Dominican Republic gains independence from Cuba. Haiti
3. On March 9, 1943, Bobby Fischer, U.S. soccer player, is born. chess
4. On April 23, 1910, Mount Etna, on the island of Iceland, erupts. Sicily
5. On May 19, 1536, Jane Boleyn, second wife of Henry VIII of England, is beheaded. Anne
6. On November 10, 1775, the Continental Congress established a marine corps to fight in the Civil War. Revolutionary
7. On July 11, 1804, Alexander Hamilton was fatally wounded in a pistol duel with Aaron Spelling. Burr
8. On August 18, 1976, Gerald Ford was nominated as the Democrat Party's presidential candidate. Republican
9. On August 30, 1918, Tito was shot by Dora Kaplan in Moscow. Lenin
10. In 1962, U.S. Air Force Major R.M. White made the first shuttle flight into space. rocket
11. Mickey Mouse first appeared in a short cartoon by Walt Disney in 1934. Donald Duck
12. On December 1, 1913, Mary Martin, a U.S. marine, is born. actress

In the following spaces, write the sentence numbers in order from earliest to latest event.

5 6 7 2 4 12 9 11 3 10 8 1

Page 43

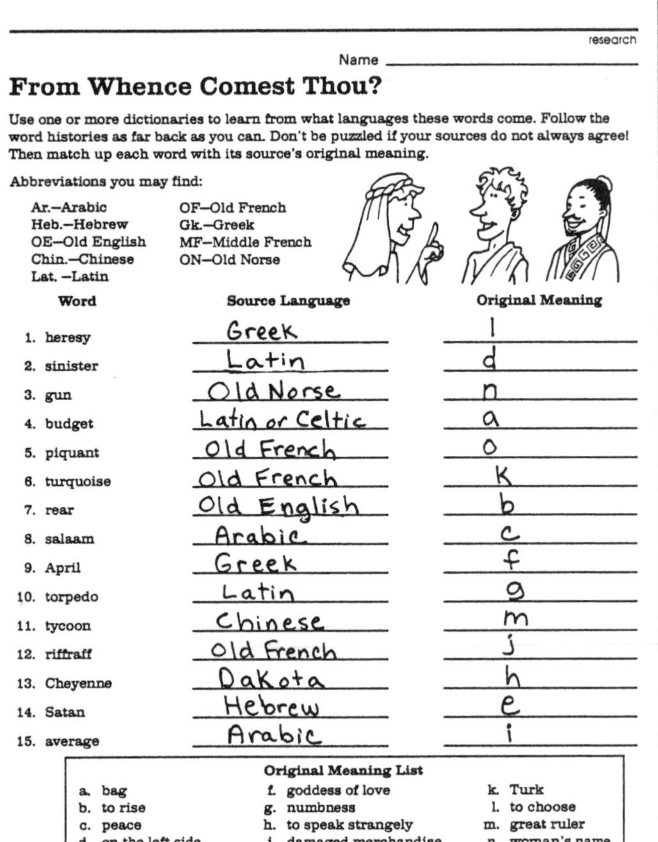

research

Name ______________

From Whence Comest Thou?

Use one or more dictionaries to learn from what languages these words come. Follow the word histories as far back as you can. Don't be puzzled if your sources do not always agree! Then match up each word with its source's original meaning.

Abbreviations you may find:

- Ar.–Arabic
- Heb.–Hebrew
- OE–Old English
- Chin.–Chinese
- Lat. –Latin
- OF–Old French
- Gk.–Greek
- MF–Middle French
- ON–Old Norse

	Word	Source Language	Original Meaning
1.	heresy	Greek	l
2.	sinister	Latin	d
3.	gun	Old Norse	n
4.	budget	Latin or Celtic	a
5.	piquant	Old French	o
6.	turquoise	Old French	k
7.	rear	Old English	b
8.	salaam	Arabic	c
9.	April	Greek	f
10.	torpedo	Latin	g
11.	tycoon	Chinese	m
12.	riffraff	Old French	j
13.	Cheyenne	Dakota	h
14.	Satan	Hebrew	e
15.	average	Arabic	i

Original Meaning List

- a. bag
- b. to rise
- c. peace
- d. on the left side
- e. adversary
- f. goddess of love
- g. numbness
- h. to speak strangely
- i. damaged merchandise
- j. to carry off
- k. Turk
- l. to choose
- m. great ruler
- n. woman's name
- o. to prick

Page 44

reference

Name ______________

Hey, Look Me Over

Choose any book of fiction from a local library and read it. As you read, complete this page.

Answers will vary.

Title: ______________ Time: ______________

Author: ______________ Place: ______________

One Central Character: ______________

Name six attributes of this character:
1. ______________
2. ______________
3. ______________
4. ______________
5. ______________
6. ______________

How are you like this character?
1. ______________
2. ______________
3. ______________

How are you different?
1. ______________
2. ______________

Book Outline: List six main events in this story.
1. ______________
2. ______________
3. ______________
4. ______________
5. ______________
6. ______________

Answer one:
What would you change in the story? Why?
What do you like most about this story? Why?
Which types of readers would like this book most? Why?

Challenge: Build a model environment that will match the story's setting. Label the important items.

Page 45

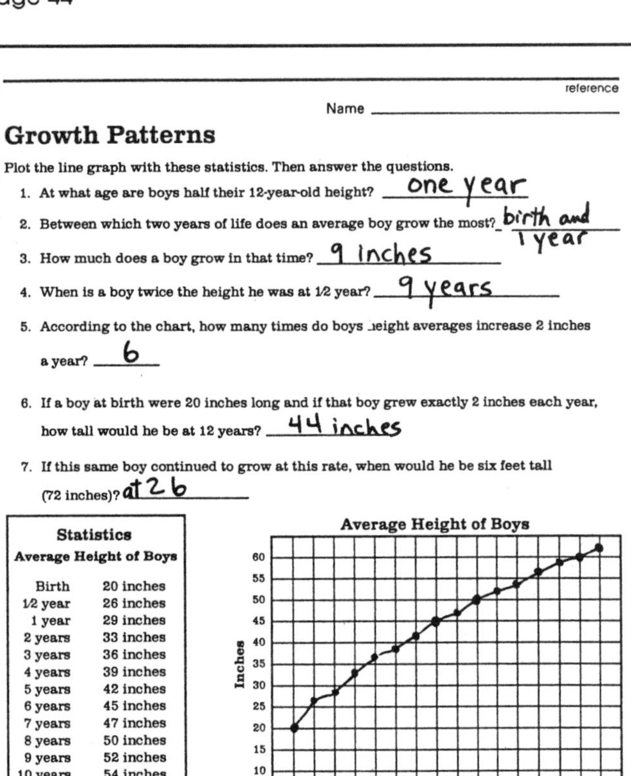

reference

Name ______________

Growth Patterns

Plot the line graph with these statistics. Then answer the questions.

1. At what age are boys half their 12-year-old height? one year
2. Between which two years of life does an average boy grow the most? birth and 1 year
3. How much does a boy grow in that time? 9 inches
4. When is a boy twice the height he was at 1/2 year? 9 years
5. According to the chart, how many times do boys height averages increase 2 inches a year? 6
6. If a boy at birth were 20 inches long and if that boy grew exactly 2 inches each year, how tall would he be at 12 years? 44 inches
7. If this same boy continued to grow at this rate, when would he be six feet tall (72 inches)? at 26

Statistics
Average Height of Boys

Birth	20 inches
1/2 year	26 inches
1 year	29 inches
2 years	33 inches
3 years	36 inches
4 years	39 inches
5 years	42 inches
6 years	45 inches
7 years	47 inches
8 years	50 inches
9 years	52 inches
10 years	54 inches
11 years	56 inches
12 years	58 inches
13 years	60 inches
14 years	62 inches

Page 46

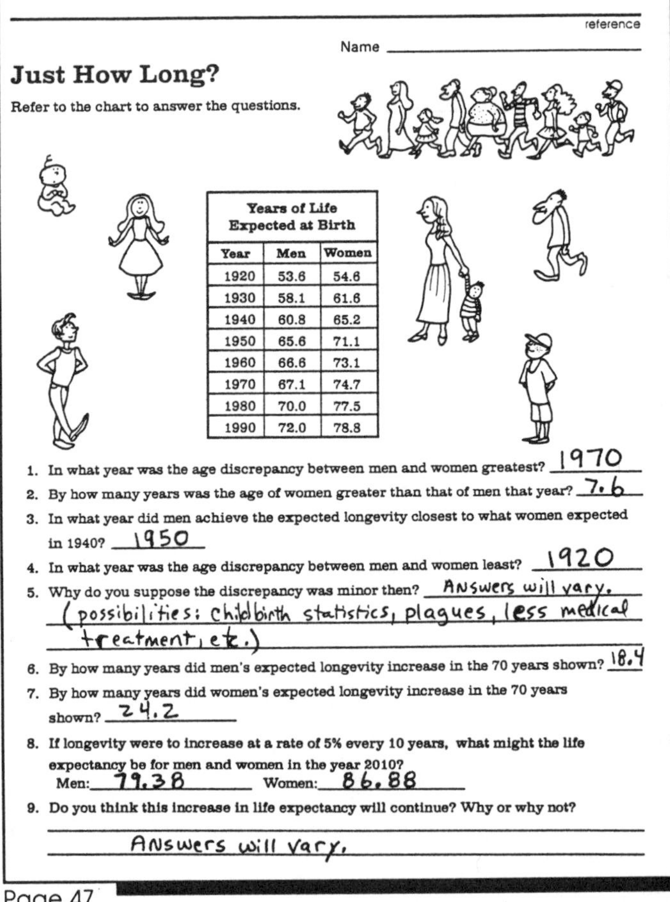

reference

Name ______________

Just How Long?

Refer to the chart to answer the questions.

Years of Life Expected at Birth

Year	Men	Women
1920	53.6	54.6
1930	58.1	61.6
1940	60.8	65.2
1950	65.6	71.1
1960	66.6	73.1
1970	67.1	74.7
1980	70.0	77.5
1990	72.0	78.8

1. In what year was the age discrepancy between men and women greatest? 1970
2. By how many years was the age of women greater than that of men that year? 7.6
3. In what year did men achieve the expected longevity closest to what women expected in 1940? 1950
4. In what year was the age discrepancy between men and women least? 1920
5. Why do you suppose the discrepancy was minor then? Answers will vary. (possibilities: childbirth statistics, plagues, less medical treatment, etc.)
6. By how many years did men's expected longevity increase in the 70 years shown? 18.4
7. By how many years did women's expected longevity increase in the 70 years shown? 24.2
8. If longevity were to increase at a rate of 5% every 10 years, what might the life expectancy be for men and women in the year 2010? Men: 79.38 Women: 86.88
9. Do you think this increase in life expectancy will continue? Why or why not? Answers will vary.

Page 47

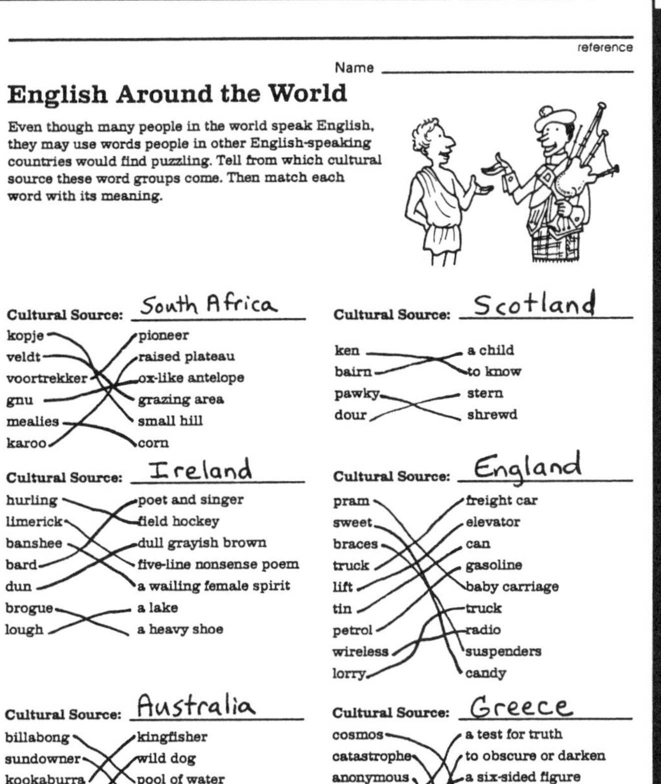

reference

Name ______________________

English Around the World

Even though many people in the world speak English, they may use words people in other English-speaking countries would find puzzling. Tell from which cultural source these word groups come. Then match each word with its meaning.

Cultural Source: South Africa

kopje	pioneer
veldt	raised plateau
voortrekker	ox-like antelope
gnu	grazing area
mealies	small hill
karoo	corn

Cultural Source: Scotland

ken	a child
bairn	to know
pawky	stern
dour	shrewd

Cultural Source: Ireland

hurling	poet and singer
limerick	field hockey
banshee	dull grayish brown
bard	five-line nonsense poem
dun	a wailing female spirit
brogue	a lake
lough	a heavy shoe

Cultural Source: England

pram	freight car
sweet	elevator
braces	can
truck	gasoline
lift	baby carriage
tin	truck
petrol	radio
wireless	suspenders
lorry	candy

Cultural Source: Australia

billabong	kingfisher
sundowner	wild dog
kookaburra	pool of water
fossick	a tramp
dingo	to search

Cultural Source: Greece

cosmos	a test for truth
catastrophe	to obscure or darken
anonymous	a six-sided figure
criterion	universe
hexagon	peculiarity
eclipse	great misfortune
idiosyncrasy	bearing no name

Page 48

reference

Name ______________________

Flying South

Pilot Penelope Phlite just looked at her flight plans for the next few weeks. The problem is, she has the latitude and longitude markings but no names. Please refer to an atlas and fill in the countries to which she will be flying. She will visit some countries more than once.

	Country	Latitude	Longitude
1.	Bolivia	17.26 S	66.10 W
2.	Chile	36.50 S	73.03 W
3.	Brazil	3.06 S	60.00 W
4.	Uruguay	34.55 S	56.10 W
5.	Argentina	33.00 S	60.40 W
6.	Peru	12.05 S	77.08 W
7.	Ecuador	2.13 S	79.54 W
8.	Venezuela	7.46 N	72.15 W
9.	Brazil	8.06 S	34.53 W
10.	Guyana	6.46 N	58.10 W
11.	Argentina	26.47 S	65.15 W
12.	Colombia	3.24 N	76.30 W
13.	Venezuela	10.35 N	66.56 W
14.	Bolivia	17.45 S	63.14 W
15.	Paraguay	25.15 S	57.40 W
16.	Brazil	8.44 S	59.14 W
17.	Bolivia	16.30 S	68.10 W
18.	Suriname	5.52 N	55.14 W
19.	Peru	8.06 N	79.00 W
20.	Brazil	1.27 S	48.29 W
21.	Ecuador	0.14 S	78.30 W
22.	Peru	13.32 S	71.57 W
23.	Brazil	23.33 S	46.39 W

Over which continent is Penelope flying? South America

Page 49

reference

Name ______________________

Lost for Time

Find the dates that correspond with these birthdays, holidays, and historical events.

July 16, 1918 1. Czar Nicholas II, Russian monarch, and his family are executed by order of the Bolsheviks.

April 20, 1893 2. Joan Miró, the famous Spanish surrealist painter, is born.

Dec. 24, 1809 3. Kit Carson is born.

Oct. 11, 1884 4. Eleanor Roosevelt, diplomat, columnist, and First Lady, is born.

March 3, 1847 5. Alexander Graham Bell, inventor of the telephone, is born.

Sept. 7, 1901 6. The Boxer Rebellion ends with the signing of the Boxer Protocol.

July 30 or 31, 1975 7. Jimmy Hoffa, former teamster leader, is reported missing.

May of 1541 8. Hernando de Soto sights the Mississippi River during this month and year.

November 11 9. This is Canada's Remembrance Day.

Jan. 10, 1738 10. Ethan Allen, leader of the Green Mountain Boys, is born.

June 15, 1836 11. Arkansas became a state.

April 18, 1949 12. Ireland declared itself a republic.

1860 13. The year Hamilton E. Smith patented one of the first mechanical washing machines.

1859 14. This year Edwin Drake, a prospector, drills the first successful oil well in the United States.

April 23 15. This is England's St. George's Day.

Dec. 25, 1991 16. The Soviet Union was dissolved.

Oct. 25, 1983 17. The United States invades Grenada.

Challenge: Make a time line showing what you believe to be the ten most important dates of the 20th century.

Page 50

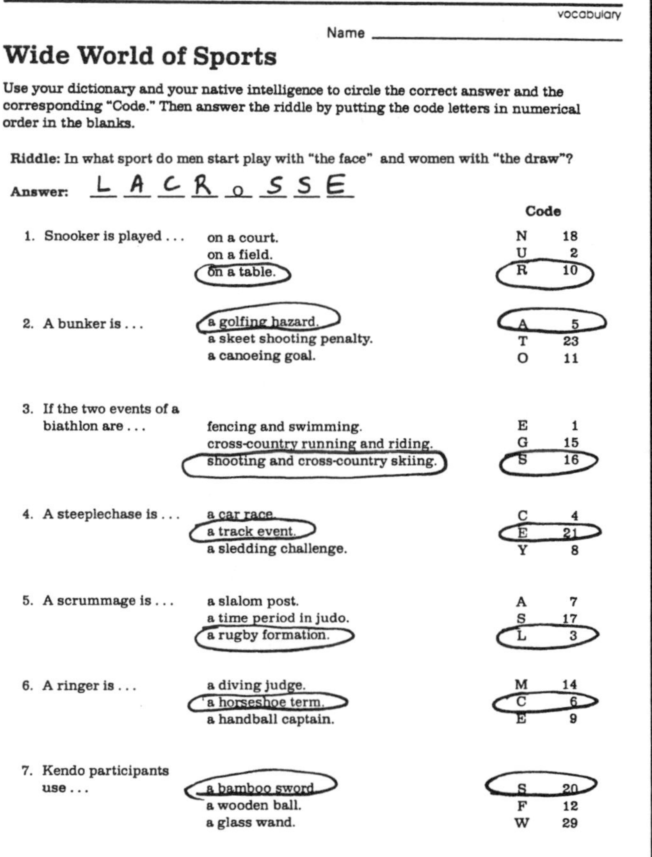

vocabulary

Name ______________________

Wide World of Sports

Use your dictionary and your native intelligence to circle the correct answer and the corresponding "Code." Then answer the riddle by putting the code letters in numerical order in the blanks.

Riddle: In what sport do men start play with "the face" and women with "the draw"?

Answer: L A C R o S S E

		Code	
1. Snooker is played . . .	on a court.	N	18
	on a field.	U	2
	on a table.	R	10
2. A bunker is . . .	a golfing hazard.	A	5
	a skeet shooting penalty.	T	23
	a canoeing goal.	O	11
3. If the two events of a biathlon are . . .	fencing and swimming.	E	1
	cross-country running and riding.	G	15
	shooting and cross-country skiing.	S	16
4. A steeplechase is . . .	a car race.	C	4
	a track event.	E	21
	a sledding challenge.	Y	8
5. A scrummage is . . .	a slalom post.	A	7
	a time period in judo.	S	17
	a rugby formation.	L	3
6. A ringer is . . .	a diving judge.	M	14
	a horseshoe term.	C	6
	a handball captain.	E	9
7. Kendo participants use . . .	a bamboo sword.	S	20
	a wooden ball.	F	12
	a glass wand.	W	29

Page 51

vocabulary

Name ______________________

What's That You Say?

Unscramble the languages below. The corresponding world regions serve as clues.

	Language	Scrambled	World Region
1.	Quechua	EQUHACU	South America
2.	Slovak	KVLOSA	Central Europe
3.	Bengali	LEGAINB	Southern Asia
4.	Danish	SNIDAH	Northern Europe
5.	Ukranian	INNAKRAU	Eastern Europe
6.	English	LESGHIN	North America
7.	Spanish	NHIPASS	Southern Europe
8.	Czech	HECCZ	Central Europe
9.	Farsi	AFIRS	Southwestern Asia
10.	Manchu	NUACMH	Northeastern Asia
11.	Xhosa	HASXO	Southern Africa
12.	Swahili	WIISHAL	Eastern Africa
13.	Basque	ABQESU	Western Europe
14.	Teluga	AGETUL	Southern Asia
15.	Uzbek	BZEKU	Central Asia
16.	Mandarin	RNAADNMI	Eastern Asia
17.	Arabic	CIBAAR	Northern Africa
18.	Hindi	IDIHN	Southern Asia
19.	Korean	AKRNOE	Eastern Asia
20.	Javanese	NEAVSEAJ	Southeastern Asia
21.	Portuguese	STUEOPEURG	South America
22.	Welsh	ELWHS	Northern Europe
23.	Mayan	NMAAY	Central America

Challenge: Find foreign words in a dictionary that come from five of these languages. Then explain what each word means.

Page 52

vocabulary

Name ______________________

Back and Forth: A Game

For this game, you need a host and two teams. First cut out the cards below and place them in a cup. The host will pick a word from the cup but will not announce the word. The team to the left of the host begins. A team may guess the word or ask a "yes/no" question. If a question is answered with a "yes," that team continues play. If a question is answered with a "no," the opposing team takes its turn. A team receives a point for each word correctly guessed. The host chooses a new word after each round and the team receiving the last point goes first. **Both teams have access to the master list below.**

Here are the types of questions a team may ask: Does the word have three syllables? Does the word come before "ominous" alphabetically? Does the word name a verb? Does the word have more than five letters?

Master List

assess	clientele	floe	obscure	repress	sleuth
avert	colleague	fume	ominous	restive	stow
boa constrictor	connoisseur	gondola	peer	ricochet	swell
botanist	cranny	mandolin	pensive	sear	talon
cask	exhilarate	meager	plaque	shiftless	trustee
chaos	flawless	monotonous	prig	skeptical	urchin

assess	cranny	obscure	sear
avert	exhilarate	ominous	shiftless
boa constrictor	flawless	peer	skeptical
botanist	floe	pensive	sleuth
cask	fume	plaque	stow
chaos	gondola	prig	swell
clientele	mandolin	repress	talon
colleague	meager	restive	trustee
connoisseur	monotonous	ricochet	urchin

Page 53

vocabulary

Name ______________________

A Wealth of Words

Fill in the blanks and use the clues to complete the riddle at the bottom.

Word Bank

meager	monotonous	sear	cranny	floe
ominous	exhilarate	ricochet	connoisseur	sleuth
pensive	repress	gondola	mandolin	clientele
flawless	swell	cask	botanist	urchin

			Clues
1.	This noun refers to one's customers.	clientele	(8th letter)
2.	This is a four-syllable verb.	exhilarate	(4th letter)
3.	This word means a barrel for holding liquids.	cask	(4th letter)
4.	This is a name for a detective.	sleuth	(1st letter)
5.	A three-syllable four-stringed instrument is a . . .	mandolin	(4th letter)
6.	This adjective indicates thoughtfulness.	pensive	(1st letter)
7.	This adjective suggests dullness.	monotonous	(6th letter)
8.	This verb means to scorch or burn.	sear	(1st letter)
9.	A plant scientist is a . . .	botanist	(5th letter)
10.	A verb that means "bounces off" is . . .	ricochet	(3rd letter)
11.	This is a large, flat mass of ice.	floe	(3rd letter)
12.	This word names a mischievous child.	urchin	(6th letter)
13.	This adjective means threatening.	ominous	(3rd letter)
14.	A two-syllable word for perfect is . . .	flawless	(2nd letter)
15.	To expand, as in one's injury, is to . . .	swell	(3rd letter)
16.	This word means scant.	meager	(5th letter)
17.	An expert, as of fine wine, is a . . .	connoisseur	(6th letter)
18.	This noun names a small opening.	cranny	(1st letter)
19.	A long, narrow boat is a . . .	gondola	(2nd letter)
20.	This verb means to hold back.	repress	(3rd letter)

Riddle: Pat Donahue ate 91 of these in one minute and eight seconds.

p i c k l e d   o n i o n s
6 17 10 3 1 15 5   7 9 2 11 12 4

Page 54

vocabulary

Name ______________________

A Hex-A-Mammalian Puzzle

Animals can be named by reading the clues below. Write your answers in a clockwise (CW) or counter-clockwise (CCW) direction around each hexagon. You may consult an encyclopedia if necessary.

A. This tusked sea-loving animal has a thick hide. (CW) walrus
B. This pouched animal will play dead (short form). (CW) possum
C. This animal is an acrobatic member of the Primate order. (CW) monkey
D. This animal is a wild dog of Asia and Africa. (CW) jackal
E. This tropical cat of the Americas is spotted and begins with same letter as animal D. (CCW) jaguar
F. This tropical rodent of the Americas is a bit larger than a rabbit and has three hind toes. (CW) agouti
G. This beaver-like rodent with rear webbed feet is also called the *coypu*. Its 3rd letter is T. (CCW) nutria
H. This large American cat is also called the puma or mountain lion. (CCW) cougar
I. This spotted yellowish or reddish wild cat is known as leopard cat and tiger cat. (CW) ocelot
J. This animal is also called the North American prairie wolf. Its 3rd letter is Y. (CW) coyote
K. This small hunter of the weasel family crawls through the tunnel of other creatures to catch its meal. (CW) ferret
L. This is a small member of the weasel family whose 1st and last letter are the same. (CW) ermine
M. This animal is a South American antelope. It has three vowels. (CW) impala
N. This large, burrowing, American rodent has large cheek pouches. (CW) gopher
O. Animals K and L are this type of animal. (CCW) weasel

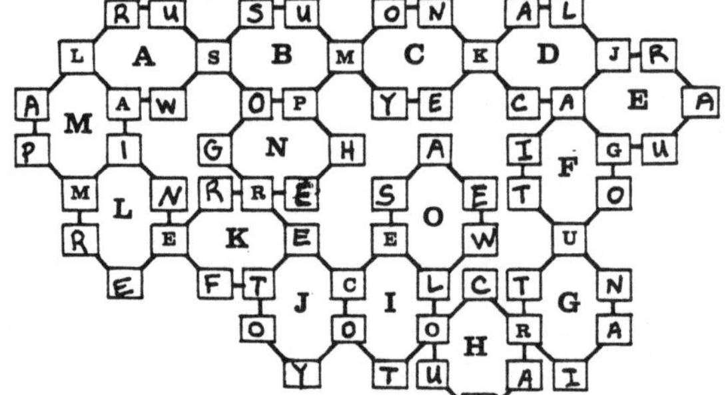

Challenge: Use reference material to find out three additional facts about any one of these creatures.

Page 55

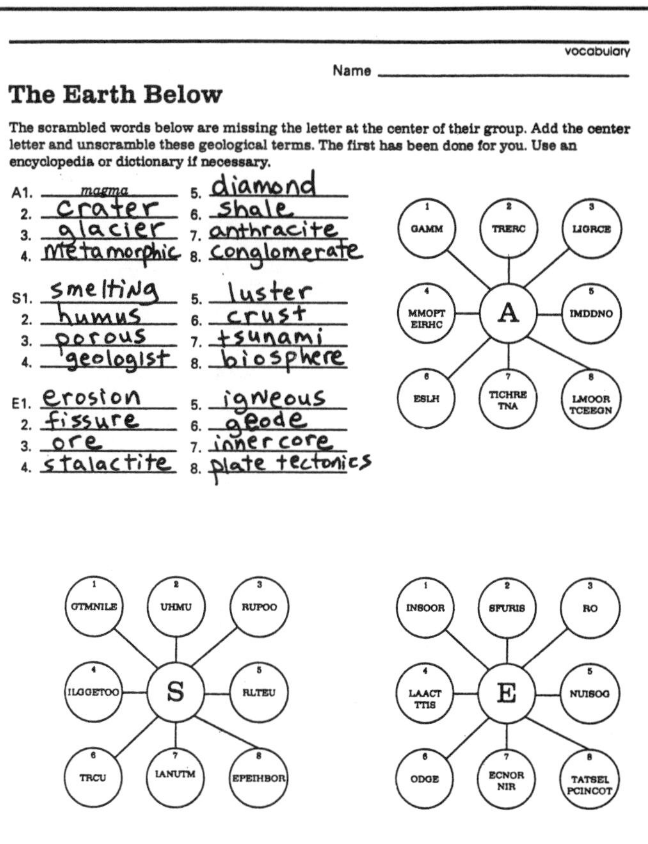
vocabulary

Name ______________________

The Earth Below

The scrambled words below are missing the letter at the center of their group. Add the center letter and unscramble these geological terms. The first has been done for you. Use an encyclopedia or dictionary if necessary.

A1. *magma* 5. diamond
2. crater 6. shale
3. glacier 7. anthracite
4. metamorphic 8. conglomerate

S1. smelting 5. luster
2. humus 6. crust
3. porous 7. tsunami
4. geologist 8. biosphere

E1. erosion 5. igneous
2. fissure 6. geode
3. ore 7. inner core
4. stalactite 8. plate tectonics

Page 56

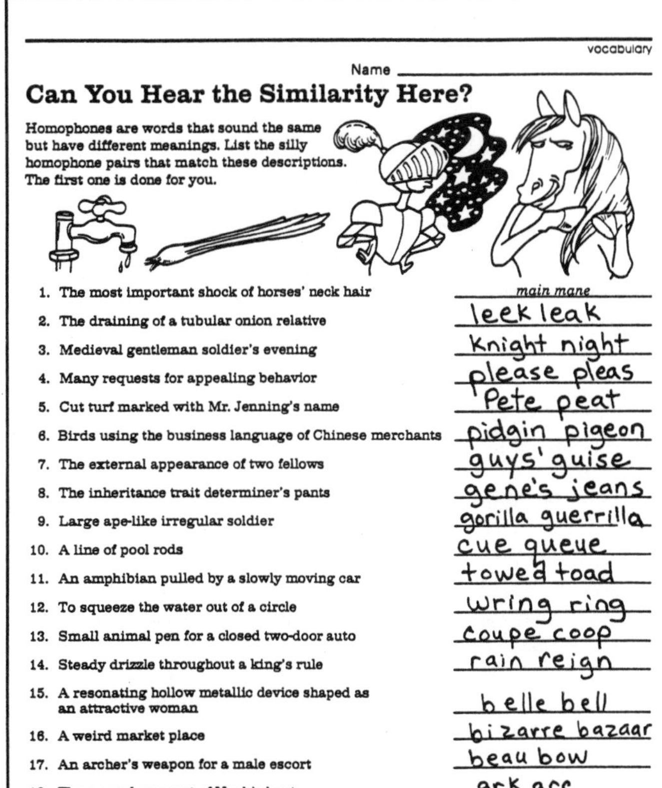
vocabulary

Name ______________________

Can You Hear the Similarity Here?

Homophones are words that sound the same but have different meanings. List the silly homophone pairs that match these descriptions. The first one is done for you.

1. The most important shock of horses' neck hair — *main mane*
2. The draining of a tubular onion relative — leek leak
3. Medieval gentleman soldier's evening — knight night
4. Many requests for appealing behavior — please pleas
5. Cut turf marked with Mr. Jenning's name — Pete peat
6. Birds using the business language of Chinese merchants — pidgin pigeon
7. The external appearance of two fellows — guys' guise
8. The inheritance trait determiner's pants — gene's jeans
9. Large ape-like irregular soldier — gorilla guerrilla
10. A line of pool rods — cue queue
11. An amphibian pulled by a slowly moving car — towed toad
12. To squeeze the water out of a circle — wring ring
13. Small animal pen for a closed two-door auto — coupe coop
14. Steady drizzle throughout a king's rule — rain reign
15. A resonating hollow metallic device shaped as an attractive woman — belle bell
16. A weird market place — bizarre bazaar
17. An archer's weapon for a male escort — beau bow
18. The curved segment of Noah's boat — ark arc
19. An inheritor's atmosphere — heir air
20. A long bladed pole made of a natural mineral — ore oar

Page 57

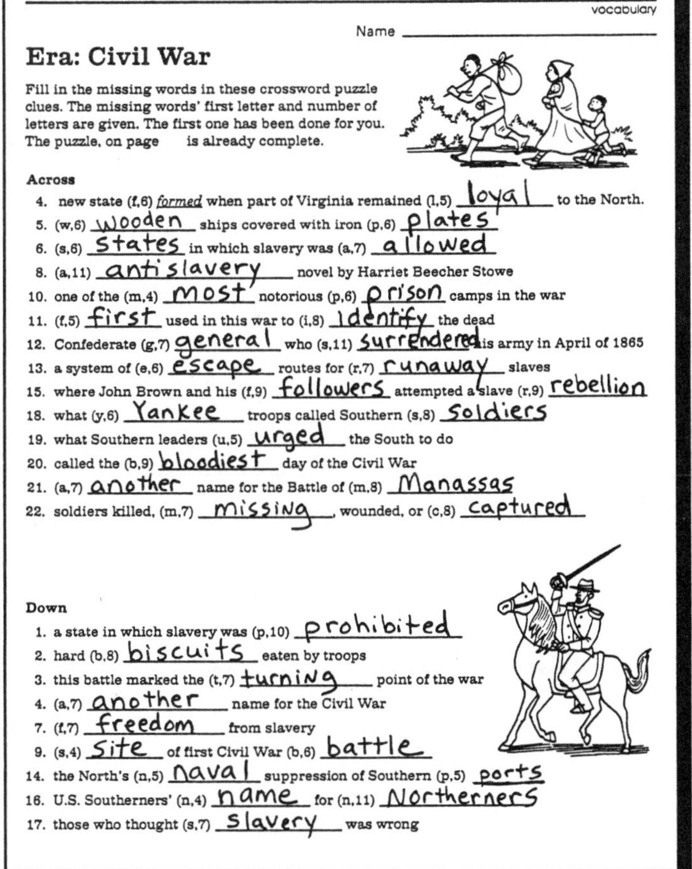
vocabulary

Name ______________________

Era: Civil War

Fill in the missing words in these crossword puzzle clues. The missing words' first letter and number of letters are given. The first one has been done for you. The puzzle, on page is already complete.

Across

4. new state (f,6) *formed* when part of Virginia remained (l,5) loyal to the North.
5. (w,6) wooden ships covered with iron (p,6) plates
6. (s,6) states in which slavery was (a,7) allowed
8. (a,11) antislavery novel by Harriet Beecher Stowe
10. one of the (m,4) most notorious (p,6) prison camps in the war
11. (f,5) first used in this war to (i,8) identify the dead
12. Confederate (g,7) general who (s,11) surrendered his army in April of 1865
13. a system of (e,6) escape routes for (r,7) runaway slaves
15. where John Brown and his (f,9) followers attempted a slave (r,9) rebellion
18. what (y,6) Yankee troops called Southern (s,8) soldiers
19. what Southern leaders (u,5) urged the South to do
20. called the (b,9) bloodiest day of the Civil War
21. (a,7) another name for the Battle of (m,8) Manassas
22. soldiers killed, (m,7) missing, wounded, or (c,8) captured

Down

1. a state in which slavery was (p,10) prohibited
2. hard (b,8) biscuits eaten by troops
3. this battle marked the (t,7) turning point of the war
4. (a,7) another name for the Civil War
7. (f,7) freedom from slavery
9. (s,4) site of first Civil War (b,6) battle
14. the North's (n,5) naval suppression of Southern (p,5) ports
16. U.S. Southerners' (n,4) name for (n,11) Northerners
17. those who thought (s,7) slavery was wrong

Page 58

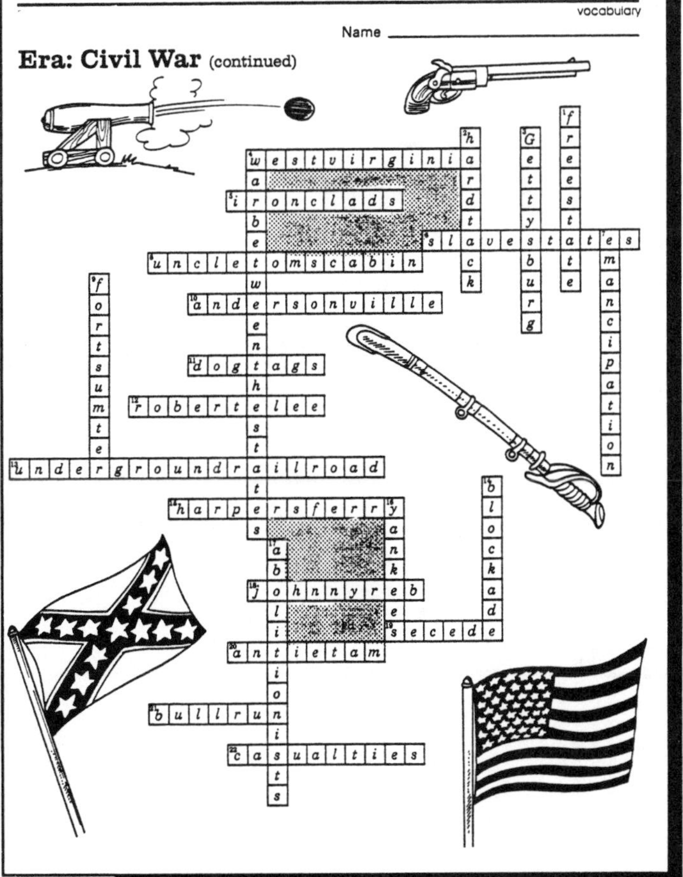
vocabulary

Name ______________________

Era: Civil War (continued)

Page 59

vocabulary

Name ____________

Harassing Homophones

Underline the incorrect homophones below. Then on each line at the bottom, write both the incorrect homophone and its matching replacement.

Four two daze Chester could knot Finnish his lickerish Styx. A peace would ketch on his pallet. Than heed cry allowed, whaling that know won paid attention two hymn annie moor and that he kneaded hour love. Chester wood stick out his tung, titan his fist, and grown, "Ewe awl ken jump inn a creak! Eye hope a harry gristly bytes yore knows off."

Of coarse weed never here him. Wee would bee aweigh inn sum gneiss plaice he'd no nothing about.

four for	two to	harry hairy
daze days	hym him	gristly grizzly
Knot not	annie any	bytes bites
Finnish finish	moor more	yore your
lickerish licorice	Kneaded Needed	Knows Nose
Styx stix	hour our	coarse course
peace piece	wood would	weed we'd
ketch catch	tung tongue	here hear
pallet palate	titan tighten	Wee we
than then	grown groan	bee be
heed he'd	Eye You	aweigh away
allowed aloud	awl all	inn in
whaling wailing	Ken can	sum some
Know No	inn in	gneiss Nice
won one	creak creek	plaice place
	Eye I	No know

Page 60

vocabulary

Name ____________

Take It Away

Remove one letter from each word on the left to make a new word that fits the definition. Write the letter you removed in the small blank to spell a proverb (written vertically). Write the new word.

Word	Removed Letter	Definitions	New Word
APART	A	to separate	part
BEEF	F	buzzing creature	bee
OPEN	O	animal yard	pen
CANOE	O	walking stick	cane
LEND	L	extremity	end
COAT	A	rough bed	cot
RATION	N	proportional relation	ratio
TEND	D	X	ten
SHOD	H	turf	sod
RAIN	I	hastened	ran
START	S	sour	tart
MANGER	M	fury	anger
LOOP	O	cut	lop
BAND	N	naughty	bad
HOPE	E	leap	hop
YEARN	Y	deserve	earn
STAIRS	A	mixes	stirs
SURE	R	bring legal action against	sue
PEAR	E	on average	par
POSSE	S	model	pose
BOATS	O	baseball clubs	bats
STOOP	O	halt	stop
MEANT	N	carnivore's food	meat
SPOIL	P	earth	soil
BEAST	A	finest	best
DREAD	R	deceased	dead
MAT	T	mommy	ma
PINE	E	sharp peg	pin
BARD	D	rod	bar

Page 61

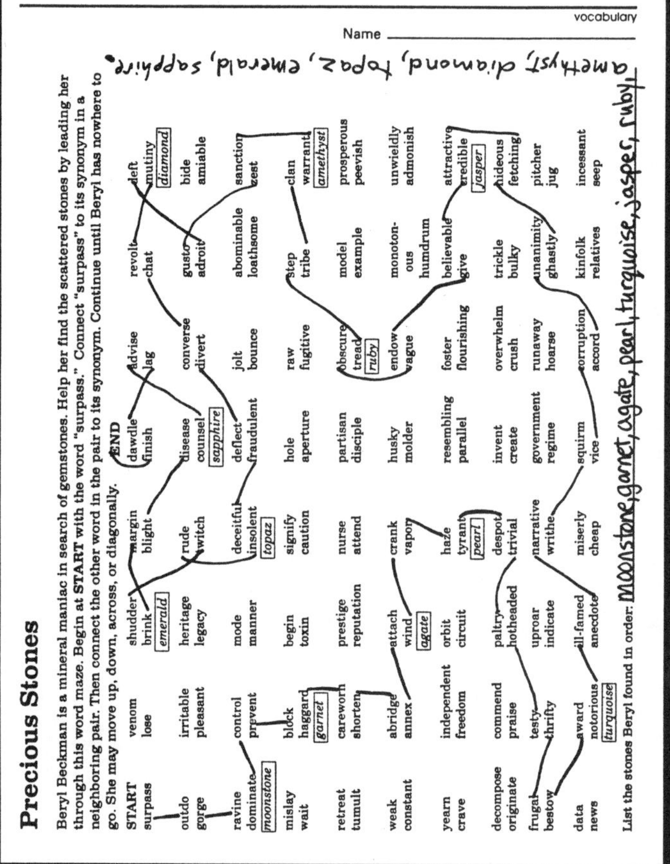

Page 62

vocabulary

Salute to the Past

Name ____________

Fill in the blanks to complete each word. Use the small letters and answers to design your own coded saying. Have a friend complete it.

1. DEINONYCHUS (o w e t) — the "terrible claw," 9-foot-long dinosaur
2. TYRANNOSAURUS REX (p e l i i i r) — notoriously vicious predator with small arms
3. STRUTHIOMIMUS (c p o y) — the ostrich dinosaur
4. DINOSAUR (o l f i) — means "terrible lizard"
5. EXTINCTION (r l x o) — the death of a species of animal or plant
6. BRACHIOSAURUS (m x w i) — this largest of the sauropods stood as tall as a 4-story building
7. TRICERATOPS (p o v i b) — a three-horned, grass-eating creature
8. DIPLODOCUS (h g h q) — a long-necked 80-foot-long beast
9. HADROSAUR (h f i) — one of the duck-billed dinosaurs
10. STEGOSAUR (v a i) — creature with double rows of bone plates on its back
11. COMPSOGNATHUS (y c a t) — a small and speedy meat-eater
12. IGUANODON (a l h) — a plant eater whose weapon was a large thumb spike
13. ARCHAOPTERYX (f t v b e) — debatably a dinosaur with feathers
14. PTERODACTYL (b i x g) — a flying reptile, but not a dinosaur
15. DRAGONFLY (h f a k) — four-winged insect that lives(ed) now and in the age of dinosaurs
16. CHASMOSAURUS (x f y q q) — a horned dinosaur with an enormous neck frill
17. BRONTOSAURUS (m w p c) — also called apatosaurus, about 70 feet long

Page 63

vocabulary

Name ____________________

Telescopic Triumph

Use references and your knowledge of astronomy terms to fill in the boxes below.

Puzzle A

1. a road map of the sky (2 words)
2. a cloud of gas and dust in space
3. an autumnal constellation that is also called the Goat
4. the oval-shaped phase of the moon
5. energy produced when several small particles become one big particle; stars produce energy this way (2 words)
6. a collection of dense matter with such strong gravity that not even light can escape it (2 words)
7. the brightness of a celestial body
8. two dates of the year, about March 21 and September 21
9. a pattern of stars in the night sky
10. this planet was bombarded with comet fragments in July of 1994
11. a star's nuclear explosion that is so powerful and bright it can outshine a galaxy of 100 billion stars
12. a system in which two stars orbit a common center of gravity between them (2 words)
13. large groups of stars often in the shape of spirals
14. the point in the sky directly overhead
15. the summer constellation also known as the Northern Cross

Puzzle B

16. the nearest spiral galaxy to the Milky Way
17. a large orange-colored star 50 times bigger than Sol—it can be found in Taurus the Bull
18. the distance light travels in one year (2 words)
19. rocky bits of asteroids that blaze through the Earth's atmosphere and hit the Earth
20. the space telescope orbiting Earth 400 miles above us
21. stars categorized as the smallest in size

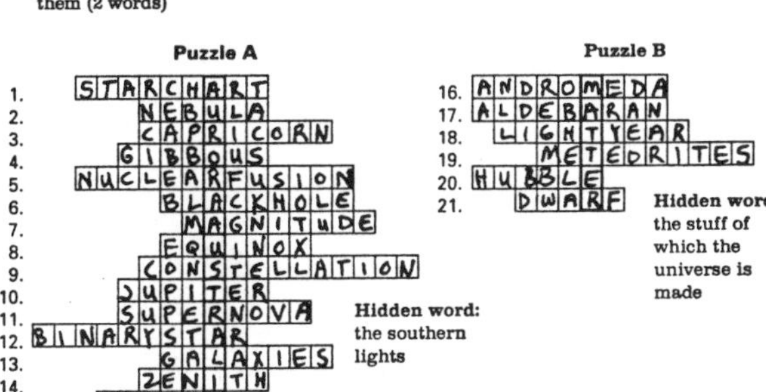

Page 64

vocabulary

Name ____________________

Double Agents

Our poor Word Chief! She has discovered that enemy agents have infiltrated her bureau. But which words are double agents (have two meanings)? Chief has two clues on each double agent. Circle the double crossing word after reading the clues to its double meaning.

Your Clues		The Bureau's Agents			
1. squeeze tightly	improvise	ad lib	**(jam)**	squish	press
2. urge	newspaper folks	writers	prompt	reporters	**(press)**
3. a ridge of earth	home for money	hill	purse	**(bank)**	pocket
4. deduct pay	wharf	**(dock)**	buoy	pier	harbor
5. sheep flock	bend	enclose	fence	**(fold)**	quill
6. burial site	serious	head	**(grave)**	primary	tomb
7. spool	sway	**(reel)**	dizzy	lean	roller
8. high point	child's toy	yo-yo	crux	zenith	**(top)**
9. steal	a weapon	knife	ransack	**(rifle)**	sword
10. you stop with it	a fern	**(brake)**	reins	thicket	grip
11. special market	equitable	carnival	frank	**(fair)**	gentle
12. playing card	military aviator	jack	captain	flyboy	**(ace)**
13. keep watch	trails a boat	trace	**(wake)**	follow	vigil
14. push	rummage	bonnet	sack	**(poke)**	shove
15. to heat and spice	ruminate	line	gingham	ponder	**(mull)**
16. an animal's skin	thrash	fur	wallop	pounce	**(hide)**
17. mother animal	a wall of sorts	**(dam)**	mare	ewe	sheet
18. part of the sea	long, deep bark	yelp	**(bay)**	coast	howl
19. chief	architectural structure	column	**(arch)**	master	supra
20. toll road	fish	highway	sole	**(pike)**	eel
21. record	scratch	stroke	**(score)**	check	cut
22. the play's actors	throw	toss	hurl	characters	**(cast)**
23. kindness	body organ	kidney	gentleness	**(heart)**	arm
24. set against	thin	**(lean)**	place	bother	narrow
25. tolerate	a stream	allow	**(brook)**	endure	river

Page 65

vocabulary

Name ____________________

A Blank Look

Fill in the blanks with words from the list. You will not use every word.

1. Trinidad and Tobago seem like exotic lands to many Northerners.
2. On this auspicious occasion we wish to celebrate with a display of fireworks.
3. The soft belly of a porcupine is most vulnerable to attack.
4. Because of Tom's loathing of broccoli, he starved at supper time.
5. I exhort you to drive on your own side of the divided highway.
6. The unchallenged worker went about her tasks in a most lackadaisical manner.
7. We had our dinner on the veranda overlooking the grounds.
8. Following her punishment, Tony sequestered herself in her room.
9. Jan is fanatical about her bicycle training.
10. The hypochondriac sniffled with a slight cold, scratched with soon-to-arrive hives, and hobbled with a sprained knee.
11. The nestling chirped softly while waiting for its parent.
12. The overlord and his steadfast retinue stalked solemnly into the hall with vengeance in their hearts.
13. The weather signs were foreboding as we prepared for yet another family picnic.
14. The mother sent her kids boondoggling outside just to have silence in the house.
15. When Marty and her brother Jules quarrel, their peace-loving sibling Daniel struggles to remain Neutral.
16. The water from the tap was so brackish we spit it out.
17. Because the caller was interminable in his storytelling, the deejay at WOOF hung up her phone.
18. We added mustard, barbecue sauce, green pepper, and onion to doctor our insipid -tasting hamburgers.
19. My great-uncle Morton is so cantankerous, people run at the sight of him.
20. A fully-loaded baby stroller is a hindrance to a parent looking for bargains at a six-hour sale.

Word List

auspicious	evaded	foreboding	insipid	nestling	sequestered
boondoggling	exhort	gamut	interminable	neutral	veranda
brackish	exotic	hindrance	lackadaisical	proscribe	visionary
cantankerous	fanatical	hypochondriac	loathing	retinue	vulnerable

Page 66

thinking

Name ____________________

Switched at Mirth

Answers may vary.

Change the position of the letters in these words to form other words.

1. evil — live
2. lump — plum
3. lure — rule
4. unite — untie
5. mane — mean/name
6. clam — calm
7. tome — mote
8. stale — steal/tales
9. stake — skate
10. rate — tear/tare
11. teas — seat/east
12. phase — shape
13. nave — vane
14. near — earn
15. item — mite
16. dusty — study
17. cheap — peach
18. save — vase
19. moor — room
20. stare — rates
21. mate — team/tame
22. ate — eat/tea
23. tacit — attic
24. heart — earth
25. throw — worth
26. mete — meet/teem
27. tone — note
28. stoat — toast
29. goat — toga
30. wear — ware
31. post — stop/tops
32. please — asleep
33. staple — pastel
34. leap — plea
35. ripe — pier
36. mates — steam
37. earl — real
38. angle — angel/glean
39. raked — drake
40. vein — vine
41. steal — least
42. bear — bare
43. flesh — shelf
44. blame — amble
45. thorn — north
46. stream — master
47. citric — critic
48. star — rats
49. lance — clean
50. liver — viler

Challenge: List ten words that can be made into new words by rearranging the letters. List the new word next to the original.

Page 67

thinking

Name ____________

Raise Your Hand if You're Sure

Write O if the sentence states an opinion. Write F if the sentence states a fact. Are you sure?

O 1. The pen is mightier than the sword.
F 2. The capital of Colombia is Bogotá.
O 3. Henry is a better name than Tara.
O 4. The best book in the world is *To Kill a Mockingbird*.
O 5. You will never get married.
O 6. This assignment is a cinch to do.
F 7. Stacy's temperature is about 98.6 degrees F.
O 8. Middle school is much easier than kindergarten.
F 9. There are at least four weeks in a month.
O 10. That musician is as gifted as Ludwig von Beethoven.
F 11. In the northern hemisphere, December is generally much colder than June.
O 12. You've got the right one, baby.
O 13. My brother is the best baseball player in town.
O 14. People who own Porsches are popular.
O 15. That book was really exciting!
O 16. Tom's bedroom looks like a hurricane struck it.
O 17. You have the greatest teacher who ever lived.
F 18. I cannot run the mile in less than four minutes.
F 19. Melissa's parents were once teenagers.

1. Which of these sentences did you find the hardest to label? ______ Why? ______
2. Change one opinion into a fact. Sentence # ___ Answers will vary.
3. Change one fact into an opinion. Sentence # ___
4. Write an opinion you have heard in a television advertisement. (Not listed above.)
5. Write a fact you have heard on a television advertisement. (Not listed above.)

Page 68

thinking

Name ____________

Words By Heart

Accept all reasonable answers.

Fill in the blanks with words that complete the associations. The colon (:) stands for "is to."

1. five : ten as three : six
2. word : book as note : song or music or score
3. yes : no as large : small
4. fish : scales as bird : feathers
5. water : drink as bread : eat
6. high : up as low : down
7. hat : head as glove : hand
8. snow : toboggan as ice : skate
9. fly : kite as sail : boat
10. Jack : Jill as Hansel : Gretel
11. Yogi : bear as Rocky : squirrel
12. bulb : light as speaker : stereo
13. Paris : France as Beijing : China
14. strike : bowling as homerun : baseball or softball
15. watch : time as odometer : distance
16. three : triangle as five : pentagon
17. smell : nose as hear : ear
18. cry : weep as chuckle : laugh
19. ab : cd as op : qr
20. tiger : Asia as zebra : Africa
21. Baltic : sea as Atlantic : ocean
22. came : come as saw : see
23. rabbit : hop as shark : swim
24. insect : six as spider : eight
25. go : went as fly : flew
26. 1, 2, 3 : 3, 4, 5 as 2, 4, 6 : 6, 8, 10
27. how : adverb as which : adjective
28. rustle : verb as cattle : noun
29. hour : 24 as minute : 60
30. shiver : cold as sweat or perspire : heat

Page 69

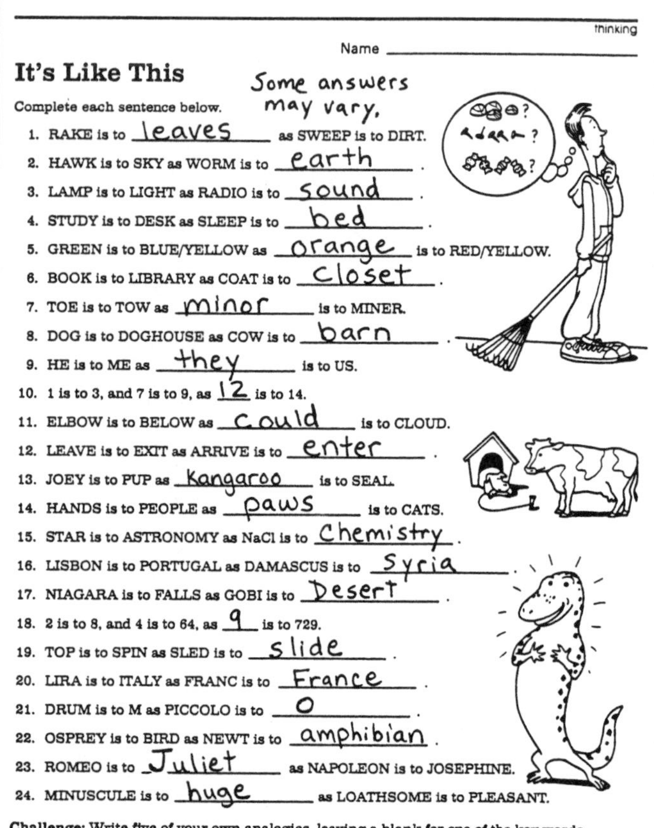

thinking

Name ____________

It's Like This

Some answers may vary.

Complete each sentence below.

1. RAKE is to leaves as SWEEP is to DIRT.
2. HAWK is to SKY as WORM is to earth.
3. LAMP is to LIGHT as RADIO is to sound.
4. STUDY is to DESK as SLEEP is to bed.
5. GREEN is to BLUE/YELLOW as orange is to RED/YELLOW.
6. BOOK is to LIBRARY as COAT is to closet.
7. TOE is to TOW as minor is to MINER.
8. DOG is to DOGHOUSE as COW is to barn.
9. HE is to ME as they is to US.
10. 1 is to 3, and 7 is to 9, as 12 is to 14.
11. ELBOW is to BELOW as could is to CLOUD.
12. LEAVE is to EXIT as ARRIVE is to enter.
13. JOEY is to PUP as kangaroo is to SEAL.
14. HANDS is to PEOPLE as paws is to CATS.
15. STAR is to ASTRONOMY as NaCl is to Chemistry.
16. LISBON is to PORTUGAL as DAMASCUS is to Syria.
17. NIAGARA is to FALLS as GOBI is to Desert.
18. 2 is to 8, and 4 is to 64, as 9 is to 729.
19. TOP is to SPIN as SLED is to slide.
20. LIRA is to ITALY as FRANC is to France.
21. DRUM is to M as PICCOLO is to O.
22. OSPREY is to BIRD as NEWT is to amphibian.
23. ROMEO is to Juliet as NAPOLEON is to JOSEPHINE.
24. MINUSCULE is to huge as LOATHSOME is to PLEASANT.

Challenge: Write five of your own analogies, leaving a blank for one of the key words. Trade analogies with a partner and see if you can complete each other's.

Page 70

thinking

Name ____________

The Mixed-Up World of Sports

Cob Bostas has a terrible time as a sports commentator. He often switches word sounds around into verbal nonsense. Rearrange the letters of the words below and write sensible sentences.

1. Geh Lourig has the grost sland-mams at the age of thwenty-tree.
   Lou Gehrig has the most grand-slams at the age of twenty-three.
2. Heiric Eden won dive findividual mold gedals at the 1980 spolympic skeed cating competition.
   Eric Heiden won five individual gold medals at the 1980 Olympics speed skating competition.
3. Shoeie Willmaker, who fands at stour eet feleven inches tall, is the sost muccessful rorse-jacing hockey.
   Willie Shoemaker, who stands at four feet eleven inches, is the most successful horse-racing jockey.
4. The basest gameball long on record thook thirty-tee pinnings to lay.
   The longest baseball game on record took thirty-three innings to play.
5. Ron ecord the basketest pliallball tayer at feight eet was Uleiman Nali Sashnush lor Fibya in 1962.
   On record the tallest basketball player at eight feet was Suleiman Ali Nashnush for Libya in 1962.
6. The rirst Famerican icycle bace plook tace in Boston on a mee-cile throurse on Tway menty-four, 1878, and cas wompleted in mearly nelve and hone-alf twinutes.
   The first American bicycle race took place in Boston on a three-mile course on May twenty-four, 1878, and was completed in nearly twelve and one-half minutes.
7. On Tarch en and meleven Stavid Deed bolance an bis hicycle on a sarpeted curface for fenty-hour sours mix strinutes twaight.
   On March ten and eleven David Steed balanced on his bicycle on a carpeted surface for twenty-four hours six minutes straight.
8. In 1988 Warles Chalker chayed pleckers against wo hundred and tone sopponents imultaneously and eat bem thall.
   In 1988 Charles Walker played checkers against two hundred and one opponents simultaneously and beat them all.
9. Gesjorie Martring of the Stunited Ates won an Goldympic me oldal in spomen's cringboard dive wompetition at the age of yirteen nears mine thonths.
   Marjorie Gestring of the United States won an Olympic gold medal in women's springboard dive competition at the age of thirteen years nine months.

Page 71

thinking skills

Name

Squaresville, Blockoslavia

In Squaresville all city blocks, as you can tell from the map, are perfectly square. Recently Joni Rundjik put together a trivia quiz about the city. Answer her questions.

1. Which point is five blocks from point A? E
2. Which point is seven blocks from point A? C
3. Which point is five blocks from G and eight blocks from E? C
4. Which point is 12 blocks from C and 11 blocks from J? H
5. Which three points are exactly four blocks from each other? G, I, J
6. Which two points are equal distances from point F—G, B, or C? B and G
7. Starting at point D how might you visit seven different points in 24 blocks?
   D > C > B > A > E > F > H
8. What distance is the shortest circuit to get from J to H to A? Give the number of blocks. 20
9. Which four points create the shortest circuit distance? Give the number of blocks.
   B > A > E > F 18 blocks
10. Which point is four blocks from J, six blocks from F, and seven blocks from C? I
11. Which point is 11 blocks from H, seven blocks from D, and seven blocks from E? B
12. Draw this route starting from point to point, starting from and returning to point I without crossing any lines: 7>4>5>4>11>4>5>4>6>6
    Hint: Move in a counter-clockwise direction.

Page 72

thinking skills

Name

Answer My Question

Each of these groups of words answers one or two questions. Put checks in the boxes of the questions being answered by each word group.

	Where?	When?	How?	What?	Who?
1. suddenly, after the accident		✓	✓		
2. nobody					✓
3. under the ashes	✓				
4. Julius Caesar					✓
5. danced frentically			✓	✓	
6. over the river	✓				
7. at the stroke of 4		✓			
8. on Halloween at the party	✓	✓			
9. the thunderstorm				✓	
10. the young fawn				✓	
11. forever with adoration		✓	✓		
12. our neighbor's sister, traveling				✓	✓
13. awkwardly falling down			✓	✓	
14. in a flash, vanished		✓		✓	
15. every other weekend		✓			
16. the baby mouse				✓	
17. at the mall, stubbornly	✓		✓		
18. a toddler					✓
19. two worlds collided				✓	
20. 9:30 A.M. noisily		✓	✓		
21. Edmonton, Alberta	✓				
22. rowboat out to sea	✓			✓	
23. now at a theater near you	✓	✓			
24. the melancholy troubador					✓
25. here on tiptoes	✓		✓		
26. Goldilocks ran				✓	✓

Page 73

thinking

Name

Capital Questions

Read each sentence below. Mark the phrases that answer the questions *who, what, when, where,* and *why* as follows:

who—underline once
what—underline twice
when —draw an oval around it
where—draw rectangle around it
why—underline with wavy line

1. Senator Bucky Wholsteen, angered when his roast beef sandwich turned cold, climbed the 150-foot satellite receptor pole above the corner of Constitution Avenue and 20th Street last week Saturday.
2. Embarrassed without his effervescent bow tie, Senator Saul Bimon, on the MLK Memorial Library's second floor, hid behind an opened newspaper on November 4, 1995.
3. On Tuesday her Washington page slipped Hennie Pfennig a personal note under the table so fellow representative Tink O'Kwartles would not be made suspicious.
4. During the first course at the President's dinner Congressman Kenny Teddedy, the champion of the space program, suggested that the Pentagon pay for the next five years' space exploration with its excess Star Wars funds because no legislator wished to raise taxes.
5. Since she was exhausted from her afternoon hearing with the health board, lobbyist Smoky Thins skipped the last hour debate being held in Senator Trublood's office.
6. Standing on the podium above the milling crowd of his angry constituents, Representative Mel O. Mahrs, a first-term legislator, waved his hands frantically to ask for quiet at the beginning of the Sweet Tooth Rebellion.
7. Because of the strength of her stalwart aide's study made last July, Claudine Quickhart was able to introduce the popular Caffeine Bill limiting coffee drinkers to three cups per morning session in the House Chamber.
8. After hosting a seminar with East Asian delegates on the lawn outside the Smithsonian Institution Building, St. Paul's own Senator Slick distributed free musical frisbees to close his conference on a high note.

Page 74

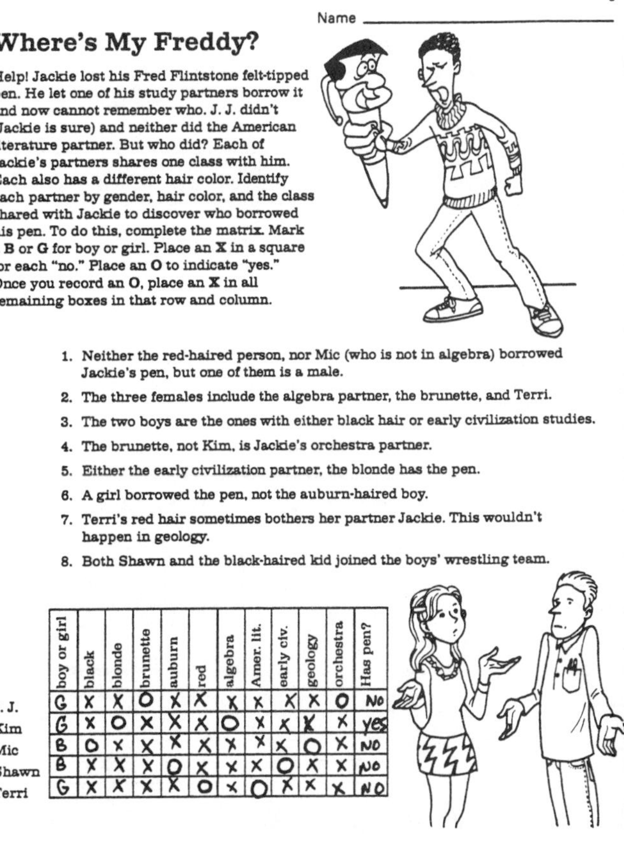

thinking

Name

Where's My Freddy?

Help! Jackie lost his Fred Flintstone felt-tipped pen. He let one of his study partners borrow it and now cannot remember who. J. J. didn't (Jackie is sure) and neither did the American literature partner. But who did? Each of Jackie's partners shares one class with him. Each also has a different hair color. Identify each partner by gender, hair color, and the class shared with Jackie to discover who borrowed his pen. To do this, complete the matrix. Mark a **B** or **G** for boy or girl. Place an **X** in a square for each "no." Place an **O** to indicate "yes." Once you record an **O**, place an **X** in all remaining boxes in that row and column.

1. Neither the red-haired person, nor Mic (who is not in algebra) borrowed Jackie's pen, but one of them is a male.
2. The three females include the algebra partner, the brunette, and Terri.
3. The two boys are the ones with either black hair or early civilization studies.
4. The brunette, not Kim, is Jackie's orchestra partner.
5. Either the early civilization partner, the blonde has the pen.
6. A girl borrowed the pen, not the auburn-haired boy.
7. Terri's red hair sometimes bothers her partner Jackie. This wouldn't happen in geology.
8. Both Shawn and the black-haired kid joined the boys' wrestling team.

	boy or girl	black	blonde	brunette	auburn	red	algebra	Amer. lit.	early civ.	geology	orchestra	Has pen?
J. J.	G	X	X	O	X	X	X	X	X	X	O	NO
Kim	G	X	O	X	X	X	O	X	X	X	X	yes
Mic	B	O	X	X	X	X	X	X	X	O	X	NO
Shawn	B	X	X	X	O	X	X	X	O	X	X	NO
Terri	G	X	X	X	X	O	X	O	X	X	X	NO

Page 75

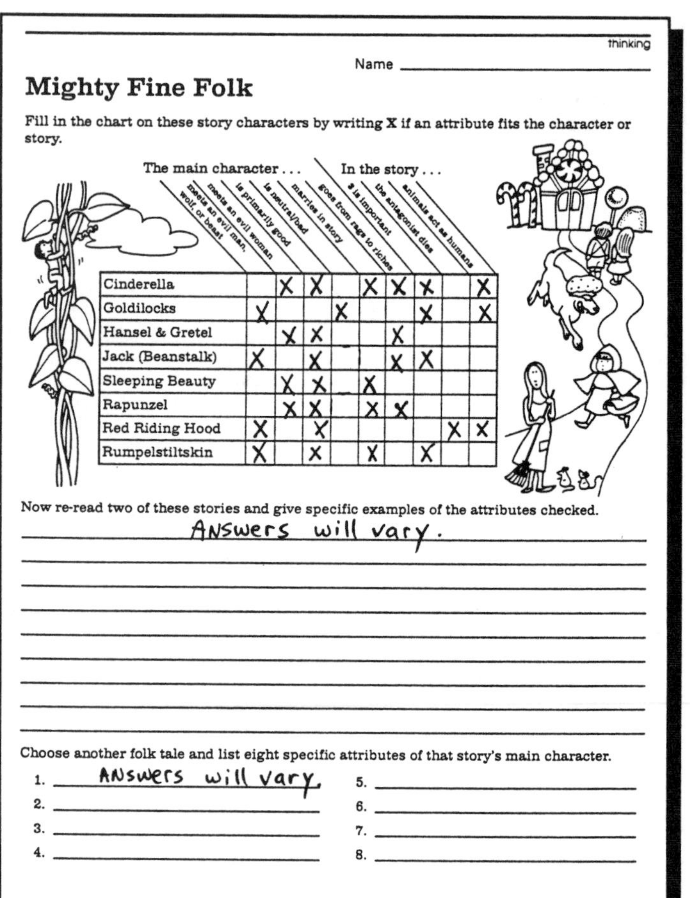

thinking

Name ____________

Mighty Fine Folk

Fill in the chart on these story characters by writing **X** if an attribute fits the character or story.

	The main character ... meets an evil man, wolf, or beast	meets an evil woman	is primarily good	is neutral/bad	marries in story	In the story ... goes from rags to riches	3 is important	the antagonist dies	animals act as humans
Cinderella		X	X		X	X	X		X
Goldilocks	X			X			X		X
Hansel & Gretel		X	X			X			
Jack (Beanstalk)	X		X			X	X		
Sleeping Beauty		X	X		X				
Rapunzel		X	X		X	X			
Red Riding Hood	X		X					X	X
Rumpelstiltskin	X		X		X		X		

Now re-read two of these stories and give specific examples of the attributes checked.

Answers will vary.

Choose another folk tale and list eight specific attributes of that story's main character.

1. Answers will vary.
2. ____________
3. ____________
4. ____________
5. ____________
6. ____________
7. ____________
8. ____________

Page 76

thinking

Brain Power

Name ____________

Use your head, your paper, pencil . . . whatever you need to figure out these problems.

1. Over the next five years Dan, who is 52" tall, will grow at a rate of 2 inches per year. Meanwhile, his younger brother Dave, standing at a mean 48", will grow at a rate of 5 inches per year and Rick, their 36" tall baby brother, 6 inches per year. Call their current height, their height in year 1, and the next year's height, year 2, and so on.
   a. In what year will Rick be four inches shorter than Dan? Year 4
   b. In what year will Dave outgrow Dan? Year 3
   c. What will be the height of each boy in year six?
   Dan: 62" Dave: 73" Rick: 66"

2. Danielle can divide her Gershey Kisses, a famous chocolate treat, evenly among her friends. She is unable to split the candy 5, 8, or 9 ways, but she could evenly divide the candies. She started with a bag of 40 and ate less than 18 herself.
   a. How many friends does she have? 11 friends
   b. How many kisses will each friend receive? 3 kisses

3. A dad and his daughter went fishing. While neither caught fewer than three fish or more than seven, together they caught an odd number of each of three fishes: perch, bluegill, and bass. They told us (truthfully) this:
   They caught more bass than bluegill and perch combined.
   They caught four more bluegill than perch.
   So, how many of each fish did they catch?
   a. number of perch: 1
   b. number of bluegill: 5
   c. number of bass: 7

Page 77

thinking

Name ____________

War of the Networks

Lord Nelson and five other greats from world history were remembered in television specials last week by six television networks including CBS. These famous historical people came from Germany, Mongolia, or four other cultures. Strangely enough, each special ran a different length of time, one as short as 15 minutes.

Using the chart below and the eight clues, learn which historical character representing what culture appeared on which station for what length of time. To use the chart, read each clue. Check a box with an **x** if it is a no. Use an **o** if it is a definite yes. When you enter an **o**, you may place an **x** in all remaining boxes for that category's row and column.

Clues:

1. Joan of Arc, who is not from Egypt, has a longer program than Lord Nelson.
2. Xerxes I, not showing on either CBS or the 45-minute program, is from Persia.
3. Ramses I is not the longest program, but it is 30 minutes longer than Joan's.
4. Rommel, whose program is shorter than Joan's, is not found on HBO. Neither is he from Mongolia.
5. ABC is proud of its Genghis Khan documentary which was 15 minutes shorter than Lord Nelson's but not the shortest program whose historical figure is German.
6. Starting from the very shortest, the programs were FOX, a Mongolian hero, Lord Nelson, and the CBS documentary.
7. The DIS station showed its Egyptian warrior for 90 minutes.
8. The English Nelson program is 15 minutes shorter than the French documentary. Lord Nelson is not on NBC!

TV Specials Chart

	HBO	FOX	NBC	ABC	DIS	CBS	Egypt	England	France	Germany	Mongol	Persia	15	30	45	60	90	120
Joan	X	X	X	X	X	O	X	X	O	X	X	X	X	X	X	O	X	X
Khan	X	X	X	O	X	X	X	X	X	X	O	X	X	O	X	X	X	X
Nelson	O	X	X	X	X	X	X	O	X	X	X	X	X	X	O	X	X	X
Ramses	X	X	X	X	O	X	O	X	X	X	X	X	X	X	X	X	O	X
Rommel	X	O	X	X	X	X	X	X	X	O	X	X	O	X	X	X	X	X
Xerxes	X	X	O	X	X	X	X	X	X	X	X	O	X	X	X	X	X	O

Fill in this chart with the information you discovered.

World History Greats	Culture	Network	Length of Time
Joan of Arc	France	CBS	60
Rommel	Germany	FOX	15
Genghis Khan	Mongol	ABC	30
Xerxes	Persia	NBC	120
Lord Nelson	England	HBO	45
Ramses I	Egypt	DIS	90

Page 78

thinking

Name ____________

Wise Guys Buys

Ted wants to buy his first car, a bright red '67 jeep, which has been advertised in the classifieds for five days. He and his dad checked it out. It was cool. Not a speck of rust showing! Now he must decide where to apply for a loan.

Check out these figures and fill in the chart below to determine the cost of the jeep including finance charges for each institution.

Better Bank and Trust
See Us and Compare
$100 down payment; monthly payments of $25 for 3 years

Honest Folks Loan
Trust Us!
no money down; monthly payments of $65 for 1½ years

Loyalty Loans, Inc.
A flag with every $25 deposit
$99 down payment; monthly payments of $99 for 9 months

Lance's Family Bank
We're like family
$80 down payment; monthly payments of $34.56 for 27 months

Ansel's Banking Corporation
Simple as ABC
$40 down payment; monthly payments of $70 for 14 months

Financial Institution	Monthly Payments		Number of Payments		Down Payment		Total Cost
Better Bank & Trust	$ 25	x	36	+	$ 100	=	$ 1000
Loyalty Loans, Inc.	$ 99	x	9	+	$ 99	=	$ 990
Ansel's Banking Corp.	$ 70	x	14	+	$ 40	=	$ 1020
Honest Folks Loan	$ 65	x	18	+	$ none	=	$ 1170
Lance's Family Bank	$ 34.56	x	27	+	$ 80	=	$ 1013.12

Circle the name of the company that offers the best financial plan. Be ready to explain why you think it is the best plan. Answers will vary.

Page 79

thinking

Name ______

Imagine That!

Answers may vary.

Write responses to each of these situations.

1. You hear a bird flapping its wings and squawking loudly while a cat fiercely cries. What may you conclude? A cat is raiding a bird's nest.
2. You walk into a room to discover glass scattered over the floor and a softball lying on the floor. What may you conclude? People playing softball hit the ball through the window.
3. You see an empty cookie bag held by your brother whose mouth is full. What may you conclude? Your brother ate the cookies.
4. At a campground you hear a whining dog, smell a horrid smell, and watch a young woman leave to buy several cans of tomato juice. What may you conclude? The dog was sprayed by a skunk.
5. At the airport a speaker asks a question, and her listener looks puzzled but makes no reply. The speaker again questions, and the listener still has no response. What may you conclude? The listener speaks another language.
6. You watched a uniformed man run, stop, wait, run, run, and then slide toward another man. What may you conclude? You are at a baseball game.
7. You are surprised by a crack of thunder, and all the lights go off. What may you conclude? Lightning hit an electrical transformer or damaged a power line.
8. A plane smashes into the earth without a sound. No one is hurt. What may you conclude? Someone is playing with paper airplanes.
9. A noisy crowd gathers on the playground. Then, as a teacher approaches, all is quiet. You see two red-faced boys glaring at each other. What may you conclude? The boys have been fighting.
10. All that can be seen down the city block are buzzing insects. No other animals or people are visible. The sun is at its zenith. What may you conclude? The weather is unbearably hot.
11. You wake to a humming sound. Two blades are swishing back and forth as liquid hits the windshield. It is not raining. What may you conclude? The driver is washing the windshield.
12. As you walk into the lunchroom, you see a red-faced boy holding an empty lunch tray. What may you conclude? He spilled his lunch.

Page 80

thinking

Name ______

What Really Happened in the Black Forest

Fill in the blanks in this Hansel and Gretel story to discover the "truth" behind the tale.

Even before Hansel and Gretel made their visit to the forest where they eventually lost their way, the children spent much of their time playing inventive games such as "Escape from the Wicked Witch and "What's on the Roof?"

Now Gretel had the habit of pushing people. One day Hansel's seven-year-old sister pushed him off of a swing which caused him to sprain his finger. Because of her physical and vocal dominance, Gretel developed both strong biceps and a colorful vocabulary.

Hansel had a very vivid imagination. Every tree and rock became a wicked troll or mean-spirited conjurer. He would converse with his kitten as though it were human. Adamantly, he proclaimed that a dove told him its name was Dave. Hansel, an expressive nine-year-old, had no difficulty convincing his sibling that he could speak the languages of birds and beasts.

It is no wonder that the simple-minded Fräulein Trudi, a lonely, crippled almswoman living near the Rhine, became the children's imaginary witch. Her brightly colored hut became a perfect gingerbread house and her grain crib was transformed into a prison cage by the fanciful Hansel and his boisterous sister.

Fortunately, the children's visit was shortened when Gerhardt Buchende, a parish deacon, freed Trudi from her locked cellar. The two soundly-scolded rascals were required to work for Fräulein Trudi for two weeks as punishment. Hence, the children imagined Gerhardt Buchende as a wicked and cruel stepmother.

Did they live happily ever after?

Word List					
beasts	vivid	forest	swing	conjurer	sister
habit	lonely	ever	imaginary	Wicked	freed
became	two	prison	way	imagined	hut
living	sprain	speak	playing	kitten	difficulty
visit	boisterous	soundly	shortened	biceps	dominance
perfect	told	human	cruel	wonder	expressive

Challenge: Write two possible titles for this story. Titles will vary.

3-Word Title ______

5-Word Title ______

Page 81

thinking

Name ______

Good Advice Is Beyond Price

Match each of these sentences with the American proverb given at the bottom.

14 Elevate the part of your face just below your lower lip.

6 Give a guy good food to eat, and he'll warm up to you very fast.

1 Exclamations of expiration are no-nos.

2 If one fails to get the latest information, so much the better.

11 The deprivation of one's treasure brings lamentations; but to he who requisitions the prize belongs the reward.

15 Solid emulsion of milky fat globules should not be diffused over the opposing faces of a portion of baked goods.

4 The pullet who expends all its energy in vociferous cacophony has little opportunity to consume enough to gain in stoutness.

7 One should not be disconcerted by a minuscule soil portion.

3 Fools spend too much of their energy on the mundane.

5 One's blood pump has vision undiscernable to one's central nervous system.

8 A person is doing something? That's cool. But if you add a noggin, you double your power.

10 If you were to eat a McIntosh on Tuesday and again on Wednesday and Thursday, and if you were to continue this pattern for an infinite length of time, most likely you will not be visited by a medical practitioner.

13 How can it be that this ugly human being eating next to you was once a cute little diapered infant?

12 If you hear the canine's yap, you have no reason to concern yourself with its teeth.

9 The dunce is difficult to discern if he is wise enough to keep the vow of silence.

American Proverbs

1. Never say die.
2. No news is good news.
3. Little things worry little minds.
4. A clucking hen never gets fat.
5. The heart has eyes that the brain knows nothing of.
6. The quickest way to a man's heart is through his stomach.
7. A little dirt never hurt anyone.
8. Two heads are better than one.
9. Nothing can hide a fool like a closed mouth.
10. An apple a day keeps the doctor away.
11. Finders keepers, losers weepers.
12. Don't be afraid of a dog that barks.
13. Pretty in the cradle, homely at the table.
14. Keep your chin up.
15. Don't butter your bread on both sides.

Challenge: From neighbors and friends, make a list of ten additional proverbs or maxims.

Page 82

thinking

Name ______

Puzzling Plurals

Answers may vary.

Some nouns are made plural in peculiar ways. Which actual singular/plural pairs would rhyme with the following made-up pairs? If . . .

1. fan became fen? man/men
2. moose became meese? goose/geese
3. blouse became blice? mouse/mice or louse/lice
4. booth became beeth? tooth/teeth
5. fox became foxen? ox/oxen
6. mild became mildren? child/children
7. wish remained wish? fish/fish
8. soot became seet? foot/feet
9. practice became practi? cactus/cacti
10. tedium became tedia? medium/media

Plural rules do not always work. Which of the following noun plurals look right? Circle the correctly spelled plural word for each pair.

11. (bills-of-sale) bill-of-sales
12. (radios) radioes
13. diarys (diaries)
14. tomatos (tomatoes)
15. (chiefs) chieves
16. (corps) corpes
17. loafs (loaves)
18. boxs (boxes)
19. (scarves) scarfs
20. glass's (glasses)
21. ladys (ladies)
22. proves (proofs)
23. (halves) halfs
24. (echoes) echos

Page 83

thinking

Name ________

Yikes! Answers will vary.

What do you think will happen next? For each problem write at least two sentences.

1. You just broke your bed by falling on it too hard. Your mom walks in.
2. You begin running the 100-meter dash and notice that your left shoe is untied.
3. You're beginning to ask a girl out to the ball game and then notice the 6'6" upperclassman behind her.
4. You're holding a crystal bowl filled with punch, and your obnoxious cousin suddenly frightens you.
5. In the middle of an important science test, one of your contact lenses vanishes.
6. You faked being sick so you could stay home. Then you remember that it's the day for the field trip to the best theme park in the state.
7. The jelly sandwich you're eating drips onto the computer keys.
8. Your dad comes in with the mail, which includes your report card.
9. You thought the recipe called for 450 degrees instead of 250 degrees.

Page 84

thinking

Name ________

Think Tank

What do people think about at work? Match these folks to their most likely thoughts.

i 1. botanist
f 2. ice-cream vendor
x 3. coffee taste-tester
v 4. fast-food cook
b 5. newspaper editor
q 6. soldier
j 7. airplane pilot
r 8. deep-sea explorer
d 9. toy-store clerk
k 10. bank teller
e 11. school teacher
u 12. building janitor
a 13. sports announcer
p 14. horse jockey
m 15. beauty pageant contestant
l 16. babysitter
t 17. UPS delivery person
w 18. park ranger
c 19. hospital receptionist
o 20. baseball coach
h 21. hair stylist
g 22. garbage collector
n 23. clock maker
s 24. carpenter

a. Where are the stats on the boxer? I read them ten minutes ago.
b. By 4:00? We've got three more stories to print!
c. Is that the same child who came in yesterday with a broken toe?
d. Do you think that dad will buy it for that whining kid?
e. When will the bell ring?
f. What would you like, Marcy? Last week you chose a fudge bar.
g. Another open bag? This stuff stinks!
h. I really don't know how I can cover his bald spot.
i. Hmmm, let me guess. A double-stemmed bluebell.
j. We are ten minutes out of Cleveland.
k. Let's see, he gets 1 ten and 3 fives.
l. Oh, yeah? Well, I can scowl too!
m. Step, step, step, smile. Step, step, step, smile.
n. Time just keeps on ticking.
o. Three strikes? Can that ump count?
p. Go, Fatal Attraction, go! You can catch her.
q. Attention! . . . At ease.
r. Octopi don't frighten me. It's those spooky squid that shoot by.
s. Oh, no! Dropped the hammer again!
t. If I get bit by another dog, I quit!
u. Who's the kid who put gum on all the door handles?
v. Would you like fries with that?
w. Why is there a fire out of the pit? Where's Smoky when you need him?
x. These beans aren't mountain grown!

Page 85

thinking

Name ________

A Hungry World

People who live in Canada and the United States are among the wealthiest people in the world, and these countries still have hungry people. In other parts of the world the hunger problem is much worse. Read these facts.

More than 15% of the world's population is malnourished.

Some social scientists believe that as many as 67 % of the world population suffers from poor nutrition.

Every year many millions of people die from diseases caused by malnutrition. Of these people, children suffer the most deaths. UNICEF figures show that 15 million children die each year due to famine or illness.

In some countries, 50% of all children are killed by malnutrition before the age of five.

In these countries, the average life expectancy is between 40 and 45 years.

Four chief causes of famine are drought, flooding, plant disease, and war.

In 1993, 29 nations suffered from malnutrition and excessive food shortages because of war. In these countries hunger was used as a weapon by warring parties.

In the United States 12 million children often do not have enough to eat. More than 2,000 babies are born into poverty every day. Each day 107 babies under a year old die as a result of impoverished conditions.

Western industrialized nations donate four billion dollars a year to alleviate world hunger. These same nations spend more than eight billion dollars on sports shoes.

Use facts from the above list to campaign for world hunger awareness in your school and community. Some questions you should answer are these:

1. What specific goal do you have for your campaign?
2. Who is your audience?
3. What medium will you use to spread your message? (Examples: a dramatic presentation, a video message, a song, poem, or story, a visual display such as a painting, sculpture, poster, or banner)

Write a paragraph for your teacher in which you explain what your plans are for this hunger campaign.

Paragraphs will vary.

Page 86

thinking

Name ________

The Absolute Truth Answers will vary.

Respond to these questions. You may need to write some long answers on another piece of paper.

1. What is your greatest fear?
2. What are three of the first words you learned? (guess)
3. What would you most hate to touch?
4. What was the last food you ate?
5. What dream do you remember?
6. Where would you feel the safest?
7. What do you do in your spare time?
8. How would you like to be remembered?
9. What is your favorite three-color combination?
10. How would you help a friend who broke the law?
11. When are you most serious?
12. What would you do if you saw an automobile accident?
13. What foreign country would you like to visit?
14. What one wish do you have to improve your community?
15. What impossible pet animal would you wish to own?
16. What occupation might you enjoy having?
17. What was an unpopular but important thing you once did?
18. Would you read your sister's/brother's diary if you were sure you wouldn't get caught?
19. What would you say if someone accused you of cheating?
20. What would you do if you were required to witness against a friend?
21. How would you react if someone spilled ketchup over your shirt?
22. What would you do if you knew you were dying soon?
23. What is your best memory?
24. Who is the funniest person you know?
25. What is your least favorite question on this page?

Challenge: Write one paragraph answering this question: How would you like to change yourself?

Page 87

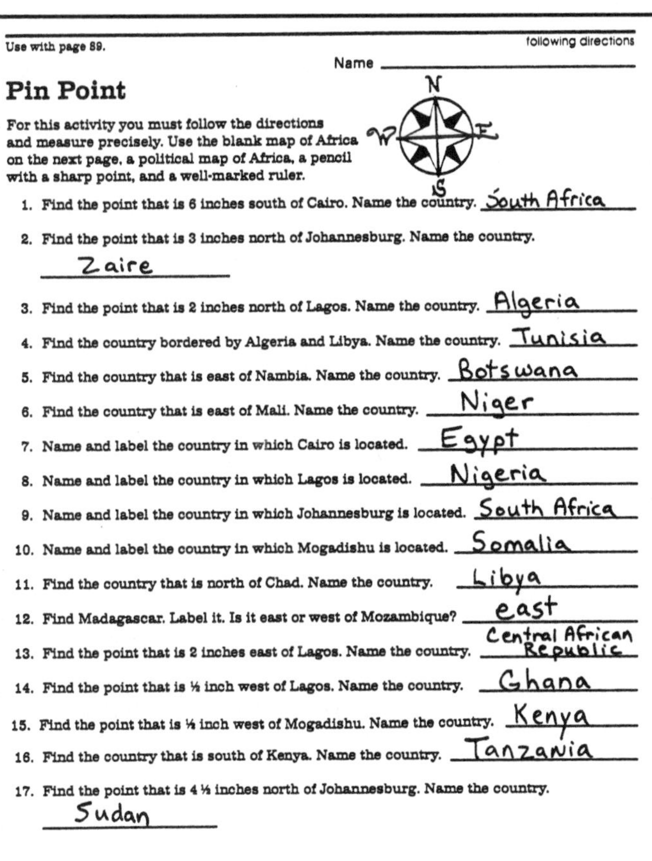

Use with page 89. following directions

Name ____________

Pin Point

For this activity you must follow the directions and measure precisely. Use the blank map of Africa on the next page, a political map of Africa, a pencil with a sharp point, and a well-marked ruler.

1. Find the point that is 6 inches south of Cairo. Name the country. South Africa
2. Find the point that is 3 inches north of Johannesburg. Name the country. Zaire
3. Find the point that is 2 inches north of Lagos. Name the country. Algeria
4. Find the country bordered by Algeria and Libya. Name the country. Tunisia
5. Find the country that is east of Nambia. Name the country. Botswana
6. Find the country that is east of Mali. Name the country. Niger
7. Name and label the country in which Cairo is located. Egypt
8. Name and label the country in which Lagos is located. Nigeria
9. Name and label the country in which Johannesburg is located. South Africa
10. Name and label the country in which Mogadishu is located. Somalia
11. Find the country that is north of Chad. Name the country. Libya
12. Find Madagascar. Label it. Is it east or west of Mozambique? east
13. Find the point that is 2 inches east of Lagos. Name the country. Central African Republic
14. Find the point that is ½ inch west of Lagos. Name the country. Ghana
15. Find the point that is ½ inch west of Mogadishu. Name the country. Kenya
16. Find the country that is south of Kenya. Name the country. Tanzania
17. Find the point that is 4 ½ inches north of Johannesburg. Name the country. Sudan

Page 88

Use with page 88. following directions

Name ____________

Pin Point (Continued)

Cairo
Egypt
Nigeria
Lagos
Mogadishu
Somalia
N
W
E
S
Johannesburg
South Africa
Madagascar

Page 89

following directions

Name ____________

Shadow Boxing

Each number/letter combination labels a square on the grid. Fill in each square listed here. Then give a title to each picture.

Puzzle A

1D, 2B, 2C, 2D, 3A, 3B, 3C, 3D, 3E, 4A, 4B 4C, 4D, 4E, 5A, 5B, 5C, 5D, 5E, 6B, 6C, 6D 6E, 6F, 7C, 7D, 7E, 7F, 7G, 7H, 7I, 7J, 7K 8B, 8C, 8D, 8E, 8F, 8G, 8H, 8I, 8K, 8L, 8M 8N, 8O, 9A, 9B, 9C, 9D, 9E, 9F, 9G, 9H, 9J 9K, 10B, 10C, 10D, 10E, 10F, 10G, 10H, 10I 10K, 10L, 10M, 10N, 11A, 11E, 11F, 11G 11I, 11J, 11K, 11N

Title: ____________

Puzzle B

1A, 1B, 2C, 2D, 2H, 2I, 3E, 3F, 3G, 3H, 3I 3J, 3K, 3L, 3M, 4A, 4B, 4C, 4D, 4E, 4F, 4G 4H, 4I, 4J, 4K, 4L, 4M, 5H, 5I, 5J, 6E, 6F 6I, 6L, 6M, 7G, 7H, 7I, 7J, 7K, 14I, 15I, 16I 17H, 17I, 17J, 18I

Titles will vary

Title: ____________

Page 90

following directions

Name ____________

Lookin' a Bit Dotty

Connect the coordinates in each grouping below. The vertical number comes first.

(1,1),(4,1),(4,4),(4,1),(1,1)
(10,10),(13,10),(13,13),(10,13),(10,10)
(4,4),(6,5),(7,7),(5,6),(4,4)
(10,10),(8,9),(7,7),(9,8)(10,10)
( ),(3,7),(5,6)
(13,4),(11,7),(9,6)
(10,13),(7,11),(8,9)
(1,10),(3,7),(5,8)

(10,1),(13,1),(13,4),(10,4),(10,1)
(1,10),(4,10),(4,13),(1,13),(1,10)
(10,4),(9,6),(7,7),(8,5),(10,4)
(4,10),(5,8),(7,7),(6,9),(4,10)
(10,1),(7,3),(8,5)
(13,10),(11,7),(9,8)
(4,13), (7,11), 6,9)
(4,1),(7,3),(6,5)

Color each quadrilateral so no two polygons of the same color share a common side. Use only these three colors: red, blue, yellow.

Page 91

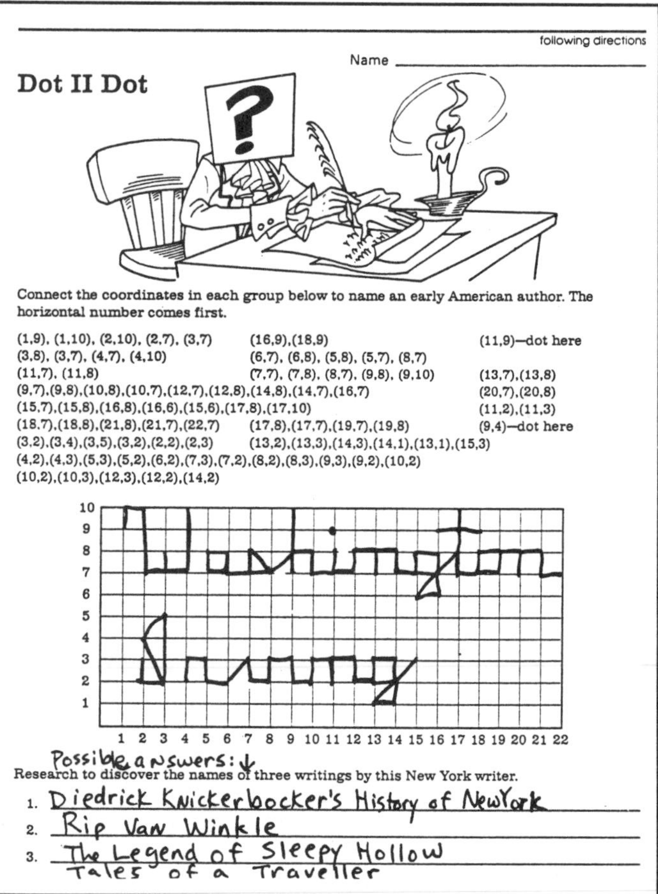

following directions

Name ____________

Dot II Dot

Connect the coordinates in each group below to name an early American author. The horizontal number comes first.

(1,9), (1,10), (2,10), (2,7), (3,7) (16,9),(18,9) (11,9)—dot here
(3,8), (3,7), (4,7), (4,10) (6,7), (6,8), (5,8), (5,7), (8,7)
(11,7), (11,8) (7,7), (7,8), (8,7), (9,8), (9,10) (13,7),(13,8)
(9,7),(9,8),(10,8),(10,7),(12,7),(12,8),(14,8),(14,7),(16,7) (20,7),(20,8)
(15,7),(15,8),(16,8),(16,6),(15,6),(17,8),(17,10) (11,2),(11,3)
(18,7),(18,8),(21,8),(21,7),(22,7) (17,8),(17,7),(19,7),(19,8) (9,4)—dot here
(3,2),(3,4),(3,5),(3,2),(2,2),(2,3) (13,2),(13,3),(14,3),(14,1),(13,1),(15,3)
(4,2),(4,3),(5,3),(5,2),(6,2),(7,3),(7,2),(8,2),(8,3),(9,3),(9,2),(10,2)
(10,2),(10,3),(12,3),(12,2),(14,2)

Possible answers: ↓

Research to discover the names of three writings by this New York writer.

1. Diedrick Knickerbocker's History of New York
2. Rip Van Winkle
3. The Legend of Sleepy Hollow
Tales of a Traveller

Page 92

following directions

Name ____________

Up in the Air

Follow the directions to answer these two questions.

Question #1: Who was the first commander of Skylab? "Pete" Conrad

1. Write SPACE — SPACE
2. Change S to N — NPACE
3. Reverse the first and fourth letters — CPANE
4. Change the 2nd and 5th letters to their alphabetic precedent — COAND
5. Add O's to the beginning and end — OCOANDO
6. Reverse the D and C. — ODOANCO
7. Add T to the beginning — TODOANCO
8. Place a P in the third position — TOPDOANCO
9. Change OA to AR — TOPDARNCO
10. Remove the first O and place the last O before C — TPDARNOC
11. Add E's before and after T — ETEPDARNOC
12. Reverse the first 4 letters and reverse the last 6 letters — PETECONRAD

Question #2: How much did Skylab cost? 2,600,000,000

1. Begin with one gross $ 144
2. Subtract 20 $ 124
3. Divide by 4 $ 31
4. Multiply by 5 $ 155
5. Reverse the order of all digits $ 551
6. Add 452 $ 1003
7. Reverse the 2nd and 4th digits $ 1300
8. Multiply by 2 $ 2600
9. Add 6 zeros to the right $ 2,600,000,000

To learn more about one astronaut's life in space read *How Do You Go to the Bathroom in Space?* by William R. Pogue.

Page 93

following directions

Name ____________

Pathfinder Test #1

1. Write your full name backwards along the bottom of this page.
2. Count by 3's starting with the number 2. Write the 14th number you reach in the square.

(Answers will vary) 44

3. Go directly to direction #8.
4. Write out a nursery rhyme on the back of this page. (Nursery rhyme on back of page.)
5. Draw eight diamonds at the bottom of this page.
6. Underline every second vowel in direction #1.
7. Name three Disney characters to the right of this direction.
8. Do the remaining directions in this order: 10, 18, 14, 11, 9, 7, 5, 12, 6, 15, 4, and 17.
9. Skip the next direction entirely.
10. With your non-writing hand, circle the fifth word in direction #4.
11. Stare at the person directly to your left for three seconds. If there is no one to your left, touch your nose for five seconds.
12. Add these numbers: the month of your birth, your age, the number of people in this room, and 523. Please show your work. (Answers will vary.)
13. Cross out the ninth word in this direction.
14. Fold this sheet into quarters, then unfold it again.
15. Write the name of the last person you spoke to in the triangle under #2.
16. SHAOUKT "I OLOXVEC YOMU, MOARNIGLOLRD!" THRUEED TIAMEUS.
17. Either complete direction #13 or give this sheet to your teacher.
18. Cross out every third letter in direction #16.

◇◇◇◇◇◇◇◇

(backward name here)

Page 94

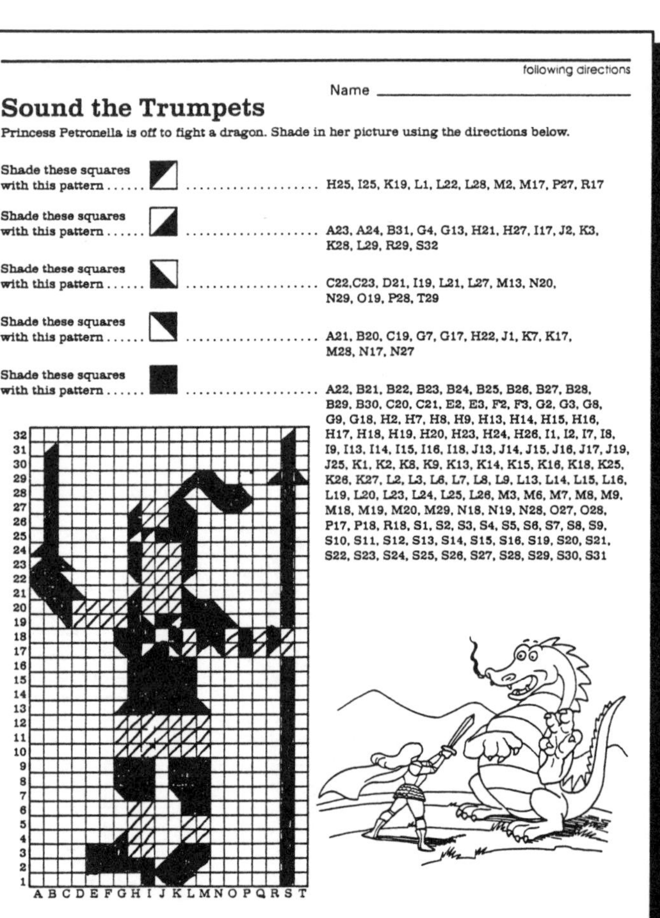

following directions

Name ____________

Sound the Trumpets

Princess Petronella is off to fight a dragon. Shade in her picture using the directions below.

Shade these squares with this pattern H25, I25, K19, L1, L22, L28, M2, M17, P27, R17

Shade these squares with this pattern A23, A24, B31, G4, G13, H21, H27, I17, J2, K3, K28, L29, R29, S32

Shade these squares with this pattern C22,C23, D21, I19, L21, L27, M13, N20, N29, O19, P28, T29

Shade these squares with this pattern A21, B20, C19, G7, G17, H22, J1, K7, K17, M28, N17, N27

Shade these squares with this pattern A22, B21, B22, B23, B24, B25, B26, B27, B28, B29, B30, C20, C21, E2, E3, F2, F3, G2, G3, G8, G9, G18, H2, H7, H8, H9, H13, H14, H15, H16, H17, H18, H19, H20, H23, H24, H26, I1, I2, I7, I8, I9, I13, I14, I15, I16, I18, J13, J14, J15, J16, J17, J19, J25, K1, K2, K8, K9, K13, K14, K15, K16, K18, K25, K26, K27, L2, L3, L6, L7, L8, L9, L13, L14, L15, L16, L19, L20, L23, L24, L25, L26, M3, M6, M7, M8, M9, M18, M19, M20, M29, N18, N19, N28, O27, O28, P17, P18, R18, S1, S2, S3, S4, S5, S6, S7, S8, S9, S10, S11, S12, S13, S14, S15, S16, S19, S20, S21, S22, S23, S24, S25, S26, S27, S28, S29, S30, S31

Page 95

Name ______________

Leading Characters in Greek Mythology

Follow the directions below. Use the letters you find to complete the Greco-Puzzle.

e 1. Write the fifth letter of *tragedy*.
j 2. Use the fourth to the last consonant in *Trojan War*.
p 3. Use the second consonant in *Sophocles*.
u 4. Use the second syllable's vowel in *Mercury*.
l 5. Use the consonant that appears twice in *Apollo*.
a 6. Use the vowel of the third syllable in *Iliad*.
s 7. Look at the third letter of *Zeus* and count back two alphabet letters.
o 8. Use the fourth vowel in *Helen of Troy*.
n 9. For *Kronos* write the letter that lies between the two vowels.
d 10. Look at the seventh letter of *Classical*. Write the letter that follows it in the alphabet.
r 11. Use the fifth letter of *labyrinth*.
t 12. Take the letter that preceeds the second vowel in *Artemis*.
s 13. Use the letter that appears three times in *Ulysses*.
e 14. Use the second vowel in *Menelaus*.
h 15. Take the second letter of the 2nd syllable of *Orpheus*.
m 16. Use the center letter in *Homer*.
c 17. Use the second consonant of the first syllable in *Bacchus*.
a 18. Use the the last letter of *Medea*.

Greco-Puzzle

the killer of the Minotaur	t h e s e u s (12 15 1 13 1 4 7)
the goddess of wisdom, war, and peace	a t h e n a (18 12 15 14 9 6)
the goddess of grain	d e m e t e r (10 1 16 1 12 14 11)
the god of craftsmen	h e p h a e s t u s (15 1 3 15 18 14 7 12 4 13)
a hero renown for strength	h e r a c l e s (15 14 11 6 17 5 1 13)
the Titan who holds up the sky	a t l a s (18 12 5 6 13)
the snake-haired monster	m e d u s a (16 1 10 4 7 18)
the leader of the Argonauts	j a s o n (2 6 7 8 9)

Page 96

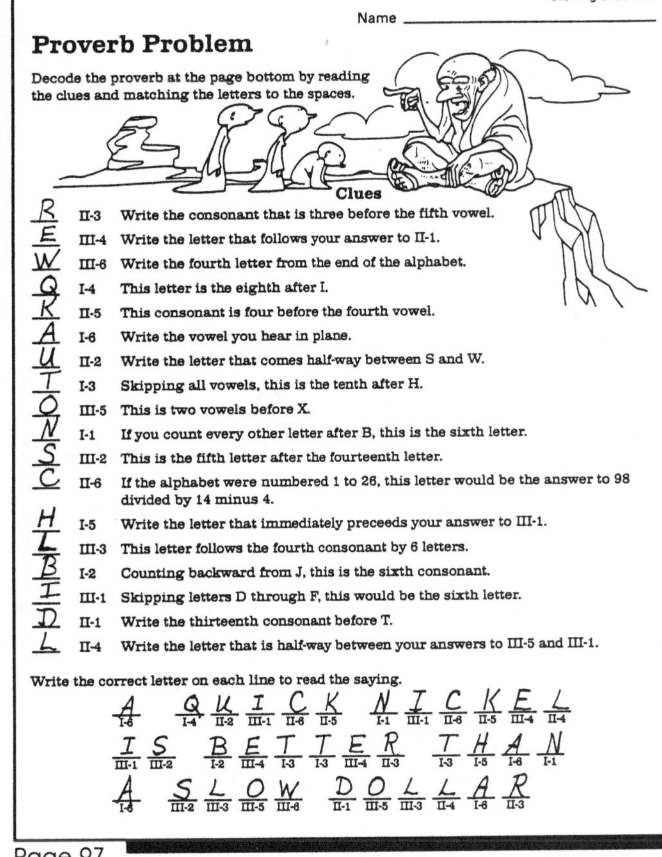

Name ______________

Proverb Problem

Decode the proverb at the page bottom by reading the clues and matching the letters to the spaces.

Clues

R II-3 Write the consonant that is three before the fifth vowel.
E III-4 Write the letter that follows your answer to II-1.
W III-6 Write the fourth letter from the end of the alphabet.
Q I-4 This letter is the eighth after I.
K II-5 This consonant is four before the fourth vowel.
A I-6 Write the vowel you hear in plane.
U II-2 Write the letter that comes half-way between S and W.
T I-3 Skipping all vowels, this is the tenth after H.
O III-5 This is two vowels before X.
N I-1 If you count every other letter after B, this is the sixth letter.
S III-2 This is the fifth letter after the fourteenth letter.
C II-6 If the alphabet were numbered 1 to 26, this letter would be the answer to 98 divided by 14 minus 4.
H I-5 Write the letter that immediately preceeds your answer to III-1.
L III-3 This letter follows the fourth consonant by 6 letters.
B I-2 Counting backward from J, this is the sixth consonant.
I III-1 Skipping letters D through F, this would be the sixth letter.
D II-1 Write the thirteenth consonant before T.
L II-4 Write the letter that is half-way between your answers to III-5 and III-1.

Write the correct letter on each line to read the saying.

A (I-6) Q U I C K (I-4 II-2 III-1 II-6 II-5) N I C K E L (I-1 III-1 II-6 II-5 III-4 II-4)
I S (III-1 III-2) B E T T E R (I-2 III-4 I-3 I-3 III-4 II-3) T H A N (I-3 I-5 I-6 I-1)
A (I-6) S L O W (III-2 III-3 III-5 III-6) D O L L A R (II-1 III-5 III-3 II-4 I-6 II-3)

Page 97

Name ______________

You're the Eyewitness

Number 1–6 to alphabetize the words on each line. Then write each fourth alphabetically ordered word on the corresponding lines below.

A.	6 swiftly	1 softly	3 sturdily	5 sulkily	4 suddenly	2 splendidly
B.	3 backsaw	5 biscuit	4 bandit	2 babushka	6 blow	1 babble
C.	5 clout	3 climb	4 cloth	6 codfish	2 clench	1 class
D.	4 by	1 bus	3 buy	5 bygone	6 byte	2 but
E.	1 skid	4 sound	3 soot	6 speedy	2 sloppy	5 soup
F.	5 echoes	1 eagerly	3 east	4 eats	2 earshot	6 edifies
G.	4 aisle	2 aimlessness	1 agouti	6 Alaska	5 alabaster	3 airway
H.	2 proceed	3 proclaim	5 proffer	6 program	1 prison	4 produce
I.	4 discovers	2 disappoints	6 disinfects	3 discerns	1 directs	5 discusses
J.	3 shear	4 shop	6 sieve	1 semaphore	5 shorten	2 sequel
K.	5 heat	3 hauberk	2 hartebeest	4 head	6 hedgehog	1 ham
L.	4 rushes	1 roosts	2 rows	6 rustles	3 rumbles	5 rusts
M.	6 tourist	2 thirst	5 tissue	1 terrace	4 ticking	3 thyme
N.	1 oatmeal	6 outrigger	4 outrageous	5 outrank	3 occasion	2 obscure
O.	2 squarely	6 stiffly	3 stably	4 stealthily	1 splendidly	5 steeply
P.	5 rakes	4 radishes	1 rabbits	3 radios	2 racks	6 rattraps
Q.	3 sledge	2 slaughter	5 slip	6 slush	1 slack	4 sleep
R.	3 secretly	5 segment	4 security	2 seawater	6 seignior	1 scum

The one-eyed (B) bandit slips through the broken window of the empty (J) shop. Not a (E) sound can be heard but the (M) ticking of a grandfather clock. (O) Stealthily the villain slithers down (G) aisle seven where the fresh (H) produce is displayed. Into a (C) cloth bag go four apples, a bag of (P) radishes, and a (K) head of lettuce. (A) Suddenly an alarm rings out, and (R) security storms in! The thief (L) rushes into the women's bathroom, (F) eats all the produce, and feigns (Q) sleep in the last stall. When security (I) discovers her, they are surprised (D) by the calm on the face of the (N) outrageous chimpanzee.

Page 98

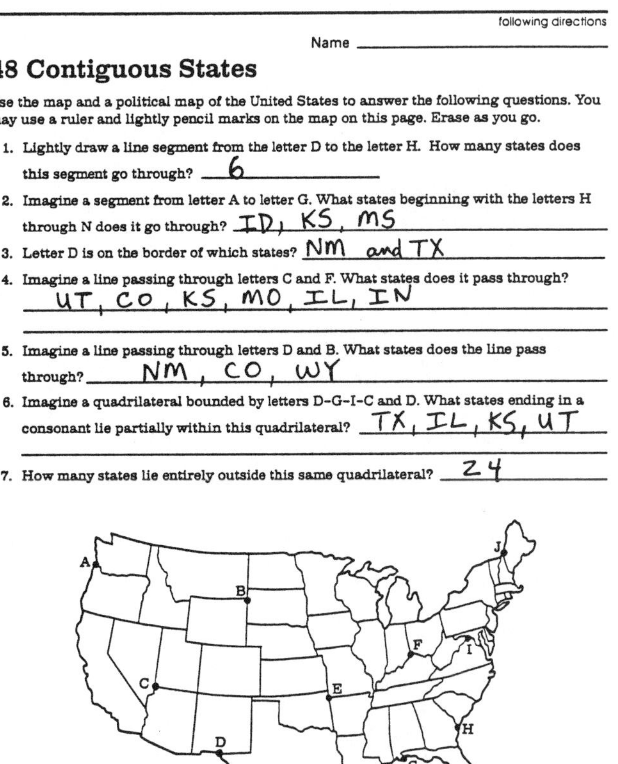

Name ______________

48 Contiguous States

Use the map and a political map of the United States to answer the following questions. You may use a ruler and lightly pencil marks on the map on this page. Erase as you go.

1. Lightly draw a line segment from the letter D to the letter H. How many states does this segment go through? 6
2. Imagine a segment from letter A to letter G. What states beginning with the letters H through N does it go through? ID, KS, MS
3. Letter D is on the border of which states? NM and TX
4. Imagine a line passing through letters C and F. What states does it pass through? UT, CO, KS, MO, IL, IN
5. Imagine a line passing through letters D and B. What states does the line pass through? NM, CO, WY
6. Imagine a quadrilateral bounded by letters D-G-I-C and D. What states ending in a consonant lie partially within this quadrilateral? TX, IL, KS, UT
7. How many states lie entirely outside this same quadrilateral? 24

Page 99

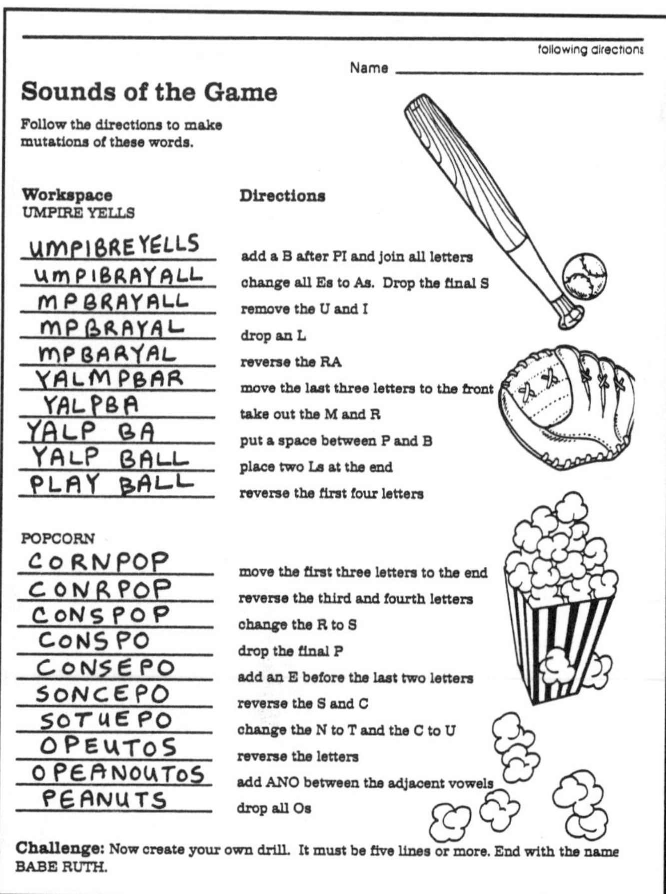

following directions

Name ______________________

Sounds of the Game

Follow the directions to make mutations of these words.

Workspace UMPIRE YELLS	Directions
UMPIBREYELLS	add a B after PI and join all letters
UMPIBRAYALL	change all Es to As. Drop the final S
MPBRAYALL	remove the U and I
MPBRAYAL	drop an L
MPBARYAL	reverse the RA
YALMPBAR	move the last three letters to the front
YALPBA	take out the M and R
YALP BA	put a space between P and B
YALP BALL	place two Ls at the end
PLAY BALL	reverse the first four letters

POPCORN	
CORNPOP	move the first three letters to the end
CONRPOP	reverse the third and fourth letters
CONSPOP	change the R to S
CONSPO	drop the final P
CONSEPO	add an E before the last two letters
SONCEPO	reverse the S and C
SOTUEPO	change the N to T and the C to U
OPEUTOS	reverse the letters
OPEANOUTOS	add ANO between the adjacent vowels
PEANUTS	drop all Os

Challenge: Now create your own drill. It must be five lines or more. End with the name BABE RUTH.

Page 100

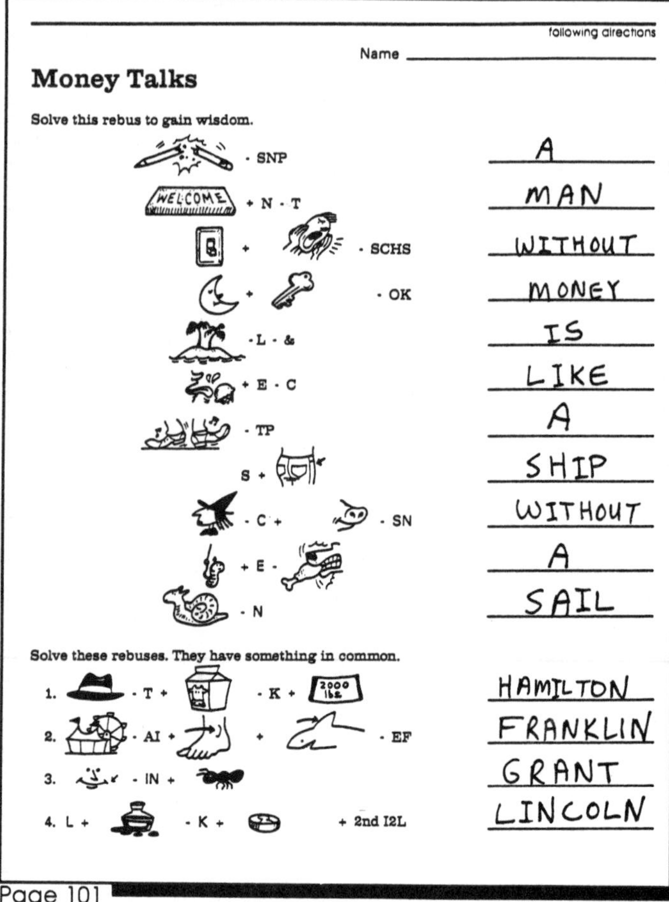

following directions

Name ______________________

Money Talks

Solve this rebus to gain wisdom.

- SNP — A
+ N - T — MAN
+ - SCHS — WITHOUT
+ - OK — MONEY
- L - & — IS
+ E - C — LIKE
- TP — A
S + — SHIP
- C + - SN — WITHOUT
+ E - — A
- N — SAIL

Solve these rebuses. They have something in common.

1. - T + - K + — HAMILTON
2. - AI + + - EF — FRANKLIN
3. - IN + — GRANT
4. L + - K + + 2nd I2L — LINCOLN

Page 101

following directions

Name ______________________

Pathfinder Test #2

Answers will vary.

Read each direction carefully and do exactly what it says.

1. Keep track of how many minutes it takes you to complete this test. Starting Time: ________
2. Starting with the second word, cross out every other word in the following sentence:
   You ~~should~~ never ~~have~~ played ~~hand~~ ball ~~poorly~~ against ~~the~~ Pink ~~Panther's~~ Floyd ~~Randolph~~.
3. Write your full name across the top of the back of this page.
4. Tear off a one-inch square from the bottom right corner of this page. Save it.
5. Name three country capitals that begin with the letter B. Write these along the left edge of this paper. *Answers will vary.*
6. Write your address backwards under your name.
7. Count backward from 10 to 1 aloud; then stand up and say the name of the Vice President of the U.S. or the Prime Minister of Canada or both.
8. Write your initials on the one-inch square and hand it to your teacher saying, "My! This sure is paper!"
9. Add up the number of fingers and toes, ears, and noses you see in the room. ________
10. Circle all of the vowels in #6.
11. Write the palindrome partner of 1,375,731. *1,375,731*
12. Smile serenely at your classmates until someone smiles at you. Write his or her name here. ________
13. On the back of this paper, write a four-line nursery rhyme of your choice, but change the fourth line to something original.
14. Write five prepositions in reverse alphabetical order. ________
15. Circle six words taken from different sentences on this page to form a sentence. Write your sentence here. ________
16. Now circle all numbers on this page containing the digits 2 and 3.
17. Write how many minutes it took to complete this test. ________
18. Place your completed paper on the teacher's desk, return to your seat, and close your eyes for two minutes.

Page 102

Credits

Author: Norm Sneller
Artist: Catherine Yuh
Cover Photo: Frank Pieroni
Project Director/Editor: Rhonda DeWaard
Editors: Lisa Hancock, Linda Triemstra